ROBERT E. HOWARD

The Supreme Moment: A Biography

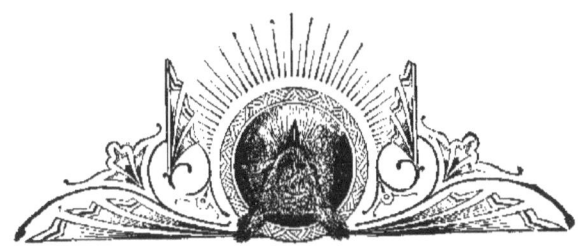

ISBN 978-0-6152-1220-3

Other books by Francis DiPietro include:

Nest: 28 Tales of Pulp Fiction

The Afterlife of Trisha Bumwood

Holland & Bonni

Ethnic Windows & The Outside Within

The Orange Phoenix

The Death Scrolls

Portobello Road

Four Screenplays

Gather the Moon

The Best of Francis DiPietro

The Phoenix & The Scrolls

Eclectic Libbyland

The Taos Sows

The Piltdown Latitudes

Soldier of the Ardennes

Veteran of the Ardennes

The Mandrake SongBook

The Confessioner's Ghost

Swarm of Five

My So-Called Reality

Beat Me Sweetly, Heavy Jesus

Groveling Music: The Soundtrack to My Remarried Life

www.francisdipietro.com / www.francisdipietro.net

ROBERT E. HOWARD
The Supreme Moment: A Biography

Francis DiPietro

ISBN 978-0-6152-1220-3

Robert E. Howard
The Supreme Moment: A Biography
ISBN 978-0-6152-1220-3
© 2008 by Francis DiPietro.
All rights reserved. No part of this book may be used or reproduced by any means, graphic, electronic, or mechanical, including photocopying, recording, taping or by any information storage retrieval system without the written permission of the author except in the case of brief quotations embodied in critical articles and reviews.

Front and back cover artwork and photography by Francis DiPietro; primate images taken at the Rosamond Gifford Zoo.

This book is dedicated to all fans of Robert E. Howard, with special thanks for keeping his work and his life long remembered.

"Do not believe in anything simply because you have heard it. Do not believe in anything simply because it is spoken and rumored by many. Do not believe in anything simply because it is found written in your religious books. Do not believe in anything merely on the authority of your teachers and elders. Do not believe in traditions because they have been handed down for many generations. But after observation and analysis, when you find that anything agrees with reason and is conducive to the good and benefit of one and all, then accept it and live up to it."

—The Buddha

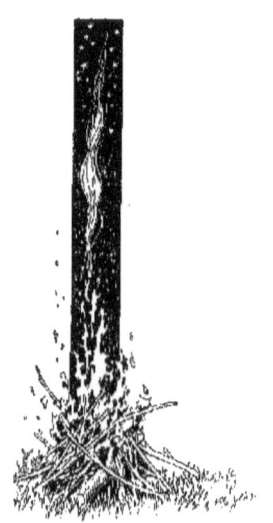

Table of Contents

Introduction 9

Chapter One : A Vague Writhing Shape 15

Chapter Two : Old Names 36

Chapter Three : Wrapped in a Rolling Thunder 51

Chapter Four : Confounded by the Crowd. 63

Chapter Five : Yellowed Leaves 78

Chapter Six : The Stoic 95

Chapter Seven : Interlude - Stories from Brownwood...... 110

Chapter Eight : The Supreme Moment 121

Chapter Nine : Secrets of the Silver Key 135

Chapter Ten : "What else was there in life?" 156

Chapter Eleven : Preparing the Way 182

Chapter Twelve : June 11, 1936 194

Chapter Thirteen : The Afterlife of Robert E. Howard 211

Afterword.. 225

Bibliography.. 229

Period Photos of Interest...235

Addendum...254

Texas cowpunchers in 1901, near the Chisholm Trail
Library of Congress, Prints and Photographs Division, Detroit Publishing Company Collection.

The Burk-Burnett Oilfield, 1919
(Courtesy LOC)

Introduction

Who the hell am I and where do I get off writing a new biography of Robert E. Howard?

Be kind, please, for I am merely a fan, perhaps much like you.

I might have endeavored to write a Howard biography twenty years ago, but of course if I had, there wouldn't be twenty other books under my belt as primer for this moment. So I can at the very least assure you that you are not reading some paid underling of a corporation seeking to profit by strip-mining Howard material. I can assure you that I am quite unpaid or at best wretchedly paid, and have been throughout my literary career. I can assure you that I would sooner not write a word than attempt a Howard biography without my full earnestness, diligence, attention, and heart.

My earlier Howard credentials include a 1995 parody to the REH Conan tale "The Hour of the Dragon," and in 1996 it sold to Yellow Creek Publishing. It was one of the first waves of both traditionally printed and e-books, and was offered on the now-defunct site e-pulp.com. I don't think any Howard fans realized there was a parody of "Hour of the Dragon" out there at all, if sales can be any meter by which to judge. I hate marketing and so I did little to help awareness of the book. Since Howard's work had fallen into the public domain, I used the framework of his tale, essentially paralleling the first third of the book, to create the novel *The Orange Phoenix* featuring brave King Kyle of Tarylia (Conan) getting mixed up with the nasty, resurrected (and rather flamingly gay) wizard Pomothus (Xaltotun). I was asked to write a sequel, which became *The Death Scrolls*, and a sequel to that, which I declined to do. The stories are available today under the book title *The Phoenix & The Scrolls*.

You will quickly note that there is a non-linear style to this book. Recent Howard biographer Mark Finn said of this style in his June 9, 2008 review of an earlier draft of this book in Leo Grin's excellent REH journal *The Cimmerian*, "Pinballs don't get the workout that a reader does going through DiPietro's document." Finn had a severe reaction to it, while REH United Press Association editor Bill "Indy" Cavalier said in his May 1, 2008 review, "Oddly enough, I didn't find this as distracting as it sounds." *The Supreme Moment* was written without an outline, springing from a natural desire to start lending what I hope will be a fresh perspective on the story of this important author, father of *Sword & Sorcery* fiction and creator of Conan and so many other vibrant, energized characters and stories. Previous biographies such as Glenn Lord's *The Last Celt*, and especially L. Sprague de Camp's *Dark Valley Destiny*, and more recently Mark Finn's *Blood & Thunder* had a decidedly linear storytelling fashion, taking the reader almost in a straight line from birth to death. To those familiar with some of the finer details of Howard's story, the linear approach tends to lend you the ability to guess what is coming next, and I find this to be rarely advantageous while reading any book.

In the course of creating this book I have studied every piece of material of which I could avail myself, including the excellent research and essays of current Howard scholars such as Rusty Burke, Don Herron, Patrice Louinet, Leo Grin, Gary Romeo, Frank Coffman, and so many others. However let me be clear that I do not claim to know these people personally, as some folks are bound to accuse me of name-dropping for the sake of insinuating I buy these guys beer every Saturday night. (Much as I would like to do it, I'm just a horrendous crank and an overall schnook.) While writing this book I also kept in mind the vastly important contributions of older Howard scholars such as Glenn Lord and L. Sprague de Camp. I have also spent more hours than I would care to admit going through thousands of files at the Library of Congress in order to locate dozens of relevant photos, such as the 1927 "Pageant of Pulchritude" which Howard attended in Galveston (and REH might even be in the crowd).

When Howard's hometown of Cross Plains was struck by devastating wildfires in late 2005/2006, I attempted to organize a collection, via my web site, to help those affected. I wrote to a local Cross Plains realtor:

Subj: Recent Fires and the Howard Home/Museum
Date: 1/1/2006
To: rlestate@crossplains.com

Dear Jones Real Estate,

   Imagine my surprise when, in my home in central NY, I saw the nightly news report from Cross Plains, covering the destruction of the recent fires. I waited for some mention of the home of Robert E. Howard, but the broadcaster seemed to be unaware of this important historical site.

   I am writing to inquire as to the condition of the Howard home and museum. Has it escaped damage from the recent fires? Also, do you have an address where we might send donations to help in Cross Plains' general recovery from the fires?

   Thanks in advance.

Cordially,
Francis DiPietro

*

Subj: RE: Recent Fires and the Howard Home/ Museum

Date: 1/3/2006 11:49:01 AM Eastern Standard Time
From: rjones@msn.com

Sent from the Internet (Details)

Good Morning Mr. DiPietro!

   I am happy to tell you the Robert E. Howard home did

survive the fires here in Cross Plains.

If you wish to send donations you can send them to the Texas Heritage Bank of Cross Plains. They have a fund set up which goes to the people of Cross Plains who have lost everything in the fires. The address is:

Texas Heritage Bank
P.O. Box 699
Cross Plains, Texas 76443

The people of Cross Plains greatly appreciate your concern.

Thanks again,

Crystal Davis
Jones Real Estate

*

Subj: Fwd: Recent Fires and the Howard Home/Museum

Date: 1/3/2006
To: rjones@msn.com

Dear Ms. Davis,

  Thank-you for the information. As of today, a small check is on the way and I have posted the donation information to my site, thatword.com, as the featured "This Month's Spotlight" near the bottom of the page. This site currently averages a dozen or so hits per day, and hopefully it will help.

Cordially,
Francis DiPietro

   Rusty Burke snapped a striking photograph which shows the fires came so close to the Howard home that they blackened parts of the lawn. But if my site posting encouraged anyone else to donate, I was not informed, and it struck me: even the nightly news report I saw about the Cross Plains fires neglected to mention the national historic landmark of the Howard home. It seemed akin to a report on wildfires sweeping through Cooperstown and not mentioning if they affected the Baseball Hall of Fame. This more than any other reason is why, in the best way that I can, this new Robert E. Howard biography is presented—not as a way to compete on a scholarly level, for I am a writer of fiction and not a biographer, but rather as a way to recount a piece of history, and wherever possible to let history speak for itself so that it may be more completely preserved. Having said that, even scholars might find a few tidbits and perspectives within (perspectives which I have not encountered before) to be of some lasting interest, such as the interpretation of the end of Howard's semi-autobiographical novel *Post Oaks and Sand Roughs*, the Howard dream interpretation about kidnaping, the significant relation Howard had to *The Silver Key*, and of course the story whose title appears on this book cover.

Some have taken the title wholly to mean a reference to death, when in fact the most captivating facet to the term "The Supreme Moment" is Howard's striking, short, brilliant life.

Francis DiPietro
Syracuse, NY
April 20, 2008
revised June 10, 2008

1939 caution against inadvertently starting wildfires. South of Marfa, TX. (It is believed the recent fire which hit Cross Plains started with someone throwing their cigarette out the car window.)
Library of Congress, Prints & Photographs Division, FSA-OWI Collection

And a strange shape comes to your faery mead,
With a fixed black simian frown,
But you will not know and you will not heed
Till your towers come tumbling down.

–REH, letter to August Derleth, May 9, 1936

Chapter One:

A Vague Writhing Shape

I have not heard lutes beckon me, nor the brazen bugles call,
But once in the dim of a haunted lea I heard the silence fall.
I have not heard the regal drum, nor seen the flags unfurled,
But I have watched the dragons come, fire-eyed, across the world.

I have not seen the horsemen fall before the hurtling host,
But I have paced a silent hall where each step waked a ghost.
I have not kissed the tiger-feet of a strange-eyed golden god,
But I have walked a city's street where no man else had trod.

I have not raised the canopies that shelter reveling kings,
But I have fled from crimson eyes and black unearthly wings.
I have not knelt outside the door to kiss a pallid queen,
But I have seen a ghostly shore that no man else has seen.

I have not seen the standards sweep from keep and castle wall,
But I have seen a woman leap from a dragon's crimson stall,
And I have heard strange surges boom that no man heard before,
And seen a strange black city loom on a mystic night-black shore.

And I have felt the sudden blow of a nameless wind's cold breath,
And watched the grisly pilgrims go that walk the roads of Death,
And I have seen black valleys gape, abysses in the gloom,
And I have fought the deathless Ape that guards the Doors of Doom.

I have not seen the face of Pan, nor mocked the Dryad's haste,
But I have trailed a dark-eyed Man across a windy waste.
I have not died as men may die, nor sin as men have sinned,
But I have reached a misty sky upon a granite wind.

--Recompense, REH

There was a light in Cross Plains, though few could truly see it. Beneath the vast web of stars which clung to the wide Texas sky, amid the dirty oil rigs of a sodden boom town, there walked a light within a mind whose scope stretched beyond the curiously narrow borders of this vast unkempt world.

In the beginning, before the land became the loose network of settlements and forts which pocked the earth like bullet holes, there were the Comanche. Ferocity and pride flared within their warriors, who would be considered disgraced if their death did not come in the red blaze of battle. Theirs was the wide sweeping land, unforgiving, and the hills and plateaus which descended toward the rich and limitless sea were inhabited by other indigenous peoples.

Prior to European exploration, several Native American tribes occupied the region between the Red River to the north and the Rio Grande to the south. They did not know their homeland would soon be considered a frontier. To the west were the Apache, east were the Caddo, and south were the Karankawas and Coahuiltecan. Central and northern areas were the domain of the Lipan, Comanche, and Tonkawa.

Starting in 1528 with the shipwreck of Cabeza de Vaca on what was probably Galveston Island, European presence and exploration of the region had begun, as had a severe outbreak of the plague in Europe. In 1540 as Henry VIII married his fifth wife Catherine Howard (interesting name, that) Francisco Vasquez de Coronado led an expedition into the present southwestern United States and across northern Texas. By 1685 Robert Cavelier, Sieur de LaSalle established Fort St. Louis at Matagorda Bay, and thus formed the basis for France's claim to Texas. Two years later, LaSalle was murdered by his own men.

Catherine Howard (Katheryn was the way she spelled it) was a cousin of Anne Boleyn and niece to the Duke of Norfolk. She arrived at court as a lady-in-waiting for the king's fourth wife, Anne of Cleves. Catherine soon captured the fancy of Henry VIII, who called her his "rose without a thorn." A mere girl of barely nineteen, her reign as queen lasted seventeen months. She was beheaded for adulterous treason on February 13, 1542. One of her lovers, Francis Dereham, was dragged to his place of execution, hanged for a short time until near death, then castrated and disemboweled while conscious, had his entrails and genitalia burned before his eyes, then was beheaded and had his body divided into four parts. Believe it or not, this was a common punishment for treason until the 1800s.

It is not known what precise ancestral relation Robert E. Howard may have had to Catherine Howard, but the presence of possibility merited the preceding description. It would be interesting if the pretensions to ancestral royalty which his mother sometimes exhibited were actually more solidly grounded on Howard's paternal side. At any rate, while Catherine's execution was being conducted, European interest in the lands of Texas was just beginning.

Mexicans also considered that land to be their own. In April of 1689 as Louis XIV was declaring war on Great Britain, Mexican explorer Alonso de Leon reached Fort St. Louis, and found it abandoned, during an expedition planned to reestablish Spanish claims in Texas. Spurred by the brief presence of LaSalle and his claiming the area for France, the eighteenth century would see Spain establishing Catholic missions throughout Texas, giving rise to the towns of San Antonio, Nacogdoches and Goliad. In 1719 France declared war on Spain. In Texas bloody skirmishes which erupted like wildfire also served as a warning to all those civilized and genteel persons living in cities far to the east: the area was like an outpost on another planet. The pirate Jean Laffite occupied Galveston Island and used it as a base for his smuggling and privateering operation. People ventured into the lands of Texas and were never heard from again; for in the blaze of the desert sun, graves were luxuries which birds of prey denied.

Yet still they came. The memory of the land retained its unwritten secrets. Settlers of many nationalities came to stake their claims and form their new lives.

Soon Mexico forbade further emigration into Texas by settlers from the United States, giving rise to the 1832 Battle of Velasco, wherein the first casualties between the two were suffered as Andrew Jackson watched from the White House. Although the Mexicans under Domingo de Ugartechea were forced to surrender for lack of ammunition, the victory was short-lived, as even greater dissatisfaction grew between the settlers with the policies of the government in Mexico City. The revolution began on October 2nd 1835 as Texians (or Texicans, the terms used to refer to settlers before the region had achieved statehood) repulsed a detachment of Mexican cavalry at the Battle of Gonzales.

The Goliad Campaign of 1835 ended when George Collingsworth, Ben Milam, and forty-nine other Texans stormed the presidio at Goliad and a small detachment of Mexican defenders. As Halley's Comet returned to the night's sky, later that year Jim Bowie, James Fannin and 90 Texans defeated 450 Mexicans at the Battle of Concepcion, near San Antonio. Texas wanted autonomous rule, and a document known as the Organic Law outlined the organization and functions of a new Provisional Government.

After further victories by Jim Bowie and Ed Burleson, Mexican General Cos surrendered San Antonio, and on March 2nd 1836 the Texas Declaration of Independence was signed by members of the Convention at the village of Washington-on-the-Brazos, in the blacksmith shop of Noah T. Byers, who served as the armorer to Sam Houston's army. While on the other side of the pond the first cricket match was played in London, the delegates and the newly formed government of the Republic of Texas adjourned in haste during the early morning hours of March 17, following news of the approach of Santa Anna and the Mexican army.

Texans under Colonel William B. Travis were overwhelmed by the Mexican army in the Battle of the Alamo on March 6, 1836. There followed Sam Houston's withdrawing from Gonzales on March 10, and the execution of James Fannin and nearly 400 Texians under the order of Santa Anna at the Goliad on March 27.

Photostats of $1, $20, $50, and $100 bills of currency issued by the Republic of Texas, circa 1837.   Courtesy LOC.

The Comanche also challenged the settlers of the new republic, culminating with the Battle of Plum Creek on August 11, 1840. In March 1842 San Antonio was briefly occupied by Mexican Rafael Vasquez and over 500 of his men, and later that year 1400 Mexican troops under Adrain Woll would again control San Antonio.

Retaliation was authorized by Sam Houston in the autumn of 1842, and after three more years of continued fighting, President James Polk signed legislation to annex Texas on December 28, 1845, making it the 28th state in the union. But by February 1861 Texas seceded from the Federal Union following a 171 to 6 vote by the Secession Convention. One of the few opposing voices was Governor Sam Houston. The Battle of Palmetto Ranch in the far south of Texas would be the last land engagement fought in the Civil War. The era of Texas trail drives, cowpunchers and longhorn cattle had begun.

Robert E. Howard's maternal grandfather Colonel George Washington Ervin came into Texas in 1866 as the 14th Amendment passed, prohibiting Civil War rebels from holding government office and repudiating Confederate war debts. Texas was readmitted into the Union on March 30, 1870, but reconstruction was another matter entirely, and would take additional years.

The Agricultural and Mechanical College of Texas opened its doors on October 4, 1876, marking the state's first venture into public higher education. Tuition totaled $10 per semester. That same year the hotly disputed presidential election would see Democrat Tilden with 184 electoral votes and Republican Hayes with 164 electoral votes, with 20 votes being in dispute. The trailer in votes, Rutherford B. Hayes, would become the country's 19th president. Seven years later the University of Texas opened in Austin. Robert E. Howard's paternal grandfather William Benjamin Howard would move to Texas in 1885, and the long-planned completion of the new state capitol would come to fruition in May of 1888.

On January 10, 1901, a vast quantity of oil was discovered at the Spindletop oil field near Beaumont, launching the beginning of the boom which Robert E. Howard would both witness and despise, for it brought out the worst in common men and vaunted corporations alike.

The Texas in which Robert E. Howard grew up was a combination of fading pioneer legend and burgeoning modern industrialism. Like leaves changing colors with the passing of the seasons, some towns dimmed to relics while others became flush with richness. And wherever the oil derricks sprouted there were, played out again and again, the tales of individual rags-to-riches as landowners discovered black treasure without ever leaving their property. Meanwhile the rustic ranchers and cowpunchers drove their herds over ranges which business magnates in the east were beginning to covet. It was as if the foundation of rising and falling cultures had been purposefully laid, like a jewel to tantalize those dreaming of wealth, and a trap to ensnare those who yearned for the vanishing mainstays of the Old West. What new stories and what new men would be borne on the wings of this rising shadow?

For fans of great storytelling, the date of January 22, 1906 should have especially potent significance. Born on that day in tiny Peaster Texas (in Parker County, northwest of Weatherford and about forty-five miles west of Fort Worth,) Robert Ervin Howard was the only child of two very different parents, Dr. Isaac Mordecai Howard and Hester Jane Ervin. Although his record of birth in Parker County reports January 24 (Rusty Burke, *A Short Biography of Robert E. Howard*) both Howard and his father later confirmed January 22. Of his father's side of the family he wrote to his noted correspondent Howard Phillips Lovecraft in October of 1930, "My branch of the Howards came to America with Oglethorpe in 1733 and lived in various parts of Georgia for over a hundred years. In '49, three brothers started for California. [They embarked as part of a group seeking to profit from the gold rush. Cholera hit the party of forty-niners in Arkansas, and their original number of nineteen dwindled to seven. In that same year two of Hester Jane Ervin's brothers would also embark for California.] On the Arkansas River they split up; one went on to California where he lived the rest of his life, one went back to Georgia and one, William Benjamin Howard, went to Mississippi where he became an overseer on the plantations of Squire James Harrison Henry, whose daughter [Eliza] he married [on December 6, 1856.] In 1858, he moved, with the Henrys, to southwestern Arkansas, where he lived until 1885, when he moved to Texas. He was my grandfather." William Benjamin Howard fought in the Civil War and with Louisa Elizabeth (Eliza) Henry had six children. The Ervins, Howard's maternal side of the family, are given a lengthier account by Howard in *The Wandering Years: A History of the Howard Family and its Branches* which appeared in Glenn Lord's *The Last Celt* and was earlier sent by W. Paul Cook for publication in the May 1945 issue of *The Ghost*. We will later highlight the Ervins with a focus on Howard's mother Hester, whose longstanding illness would ultimately claim more than just herself.

"We are constantly confronted with the limitations of the body," Howard wrote to his friend Tevis Clyde Smith in August of 1925. "My body seems a mere encumbrance to me; an imbecilic wagon, hitched to the horse of desire, which is the soul. Without my body, I feel I could spurn the earth and mount to those vast, sapphiric peaks of accomplishment and soluble mystery, which by reason of my lumbering an utterly useless body, I can but catch brief glimpses, across the uninteresting and monotonous expanses of worldly life. Yet, it may be that this beastly body of mine has a purpose. Perhaps abstract desire must take concrete from ere any step can be made toward accomplishment and knowledge.

"My soul, if soul I have, is tugged two ways by the idealist and by the materialist in me. The more I learn, the less I know; the more capable I become of forming opinions, the more loath I am to form one. There is so much of the true and false in all things. Sometimes I believe that the whole is a monstrous joke and human accomplishment and human knowledge, gathered slowly and with incredible labor through the ages, are but shifting, drifting wraiths on the sands of Time, the sands that shall some day devour me. Will it be the changing of bodies, the discarding of this form for perhaps a lighter, more beautiful one, or will it be merely the merging of dust to dust? Who knows?"

At the time Smith may have been the most appropriate party to which to pose this question, but as Howard more established himself in writing and began to appear with increasing regularity in the classic pulp *Weird Tales*, more correspondents became open to him. Prime of these was H.P. Lovecraft. The two shared an appreciation for each other's work, and embarked on a spirited journey of the exchange of ideas through a series of vastly detailed letters, starting in 1930. Lovecraft was Howard's elder by some ten years, and in subtle ways he seemed inclined to use this to an almost sibling advantage, such as in the much-adopted

"Two-Gun Bob" nickname he decided to bestow upon Howard. It has since been taken wholly as a term of affection, but to an intellectual like Lovecraft who despised sports and was all too aware of his own frail body, dubbing a smart man from Texas who could also excel in sports "Two-Gun Bob" seems to have more than just simple camaraderie or even adumbrative meaning behind it. Whereas a Texan might see a compliment within the moniker of "Two-Gun," to a New Englander, a Yankee, a gentleman from Rhode Island, etcetera, calling a southerner "Two-Gun" conjures a somewhat comical, depreciative stereotype, such as in the 1918 film "Two-Gun Gussie," a comedy in which a timid piano player is mistaken for an outlaw.

Lovecraft, living with two aged aunts in Providence (Lilian D. Clark, widowed in 1915, and Annie E. Gamwell, separated from her husband in 1916,) was likely more comfortable with the colorful idea of "Two-Gun Bob" because such a moniker could lessen the true importance of Howard as a literary pioneer and more neatly place him on the outward fringe of the small circle of writers which Lovecraft endeavored to enlighten and connect through correspondence. "Some say that Howard was not part of this intellectual artistic community," Don Herron wrote in *The Dark Barbarian*. "Howard himself disclaimed such pretensions....Yet Howard did create an intellectual artistic counterpart to cosmicism, a quality that lifts his tales above the run-of-the-mill spectres and swashbucklers of his time and ours. Howard's imaginative sweep is not based in cosmic space, but in humanity itself." The dark cerebral horror which Lovecraft could so poignantly illuminate was oftentimes a marked dissimilarity to the vibrant energy of pure storytelling and spells of uncompromising action which Howard could weave with seeming effortlessness. Antiquated and backward opinions on nationality and race which Lovecraft expressed (he hated immigrants and foreigners, feeling that they robbed him of his Anglo-Saxon birthright) could be translated (or rather seeped) into his sometimes overly professorial correspondence with and attitude toward Howard, who originally struck upon the polite course of deferring to the elder Lovecraft's judgments (whom he at first believed to be a professor or at least the holder of some advanced degree) but later quite neatly and expertly corrected many of the confidant errors the Rhode Islander put forth, particularly relating to matters of history. In latter correspondence Howard was more comfortable to drop the air of deference to Lovecraft and tactfully assert his greater knowledge about the history of this and other countries, in the process calling upon great sums of facts, names, dates and places to dispel the lighter assertations of his penpal. Late author Jane Whittington Griffon wrote of their correspondence, "Although he [Howard] finally realized that Lovecraft pretended to profound knowledge on matters he knew little about, such as the Southwest, the friendship lasted until Howard's death."

In one of the latter missives to Lovecraft dated February 11, 1936, Howard wrote, "Your defense of the modern habit of bombing defenseless towns and butchering helpless non-combatants is a striking example of the difference between the European viewpoint and the Western-American viewpoint. My people, in all their many wars, never found it necessary to destroy women, old men and children, even when savages were their opponents. You maintain that such butchery is merciful. I'm glad the Yankee soldiers who sacked my grandfather's farm in Mississippi didn't have such ideas of mercy. They stole everything they could get their hands on, but they didn't consider it would be an act of mercy to cut my grandmother's throat and impale my aunts on the fence pickets. Regardless of their looting, they didn't offer the helpless women-folk any harm. European ideals certainly must be invading the country if Americans are advocating and applauding the wholesale destruction of helpless non-combatants."

Howard went on to rebuke Lovecraft's "intense admiration" for Benito Mussolini and his "sympathies" for the Fascist movement. "Mussolini's no Caesar," wrote Howard, "he's a damned rogue." Howard realized that Lovecraft had come to revere and idealize the concept of a cultured "civilization" as having greater right to liberties, and he was firm to point out that all people should be equal. Noted author and Howard chronicler L. Sprague de Camp wrote, "...he [Lovecraft] and Robert Howard argued and sometimes battled over a wide range of ideas." From the bio *Dark Valley Destiny*: "Lovecraft admired Mussolini and, until shortly before his death, took an indulgent view of Hitler. Howard, an antiauthoritarian, libertarian democrat, had no use for either; and he denounced Mussolini as a racketeer and Hitler as a madman." Gone were the days when Howard would pile praise upon a platter for Lovecraft's ego to devour, and emerging for the final and decisive round (mere months before his suicide) was the unconquerable spirit and sense of true justice and true freedom which was uniquely Howard's. In December, 1935 he told Lovecraft, "You express amazement at my statement that 'civilized' men try to justify their looting, butchering and plundering by claiming that these things are done in the interests of art, progress and culture. That this simple statement of fact should cause surprise, amazes me in return. People claiming to possess superior civilization have always veneered their rapaciousness by such claims."

Howard was studying obscure texts relating to the Picts in a New Orleans library on Canal Street when he was 12, long before he felt the desire to make the ancient peoples a driving force in many of his stories. It is this process of self-education which best served Robert E. Howard and his writing. And while his formal education included college, the feelings he expressed through the thinly veiled character of Steve Costigan (himself) in his semi-autobiographical book *Post Oaks and Sand Roughs* well reflect his long-held beliefs in the importance of individual education and finding one's own way without many of the conventional constrictions and limitations, orders and regimentations imposed by an organized collective society. He said of himself in the book, "Steve had a great many doubts about his bookkeeping ability, even though he had finished the course. He did not believe himself to be much of a bookkeeper. He had cheated considerably in order to graduate, and he had little faith in his ability to get a job and maintain it." He would later confide to Wilfred Blanch Talman (a fellow writer whose poem *The*

Haunted Isle impressed Howard and appeared in the January, 1928 *Weird Tales,)* "After completing the course, it was a bigger mystery to me than when I started on it." Howard also more plainly stated in a short autobiographical piece, "I hated school as I hate the memory of school. It wasn't the work I minded; I had no trouble learning the tripe they dished out in the way of lessons—except arithmetic, and I might have learned that if I'd gone to the trouble of studying it. I wasn't at the head of my classes—except in history—but I wasn't at the foot either. I generally did just enough work to keep from flunking the courses, and I don't regret the loafing I did. But what I hated was the confinement—the clock-like regularity of everything; the regulation of my speech and actions; most of all the idea that someone considered himself or herself in authority over me, with the right to question my actions and interfere with my thoughts. Things I have discovered to be most true I have learned mostly without formal teaching."

In his vision of the wild man, Howard was able to break the ever-tightening chains which he saw employed all around him. A lover of true stories of the Old West and the hard-fought history of Texas, many of his characters retained that pioneer spirit and individualistic drive. It seemed to Howard that life, at its best, was a series of one-person choices which led to interspersed rewards. He may have regarded himself as an island, as he expressed in a February, 1930 letter to his local buddy Tevis Clyde Smith (note: it would not be until late in 1930 that Howard would begin to correspond with fellow author, Lovecraft friend and contributor to *Weird Tales*, August Derleth of Sauk City, Wisconsin, who would later found the publishing firm Arkham House and reprint many of Lovecraft's stories):

"The older I grow the more I sense the senseless unfriendly attitude of the world at large. I reckon it isn't that way everywhere, but it seems so. The average man is such a fool he hasn't enough sense to keep his head out from under the axe. He goes out of his way to make trouble. The people in this town treat me in several manners; contemptuously ignore me, which doesn't bother me any; go out of their way to start trouble with me, which does; and assume a sort of monkey in a cage attitude. Those who deign to notice me at all are forever on the lookout for some peculiarity, some difference that will stamp me as an eccentric. The infernal fools can't seem to understand that a man can make his living some other way besides dressing tools or selling stuff, and still be an ordinary human being with human sensations. The more money I make at my trade the more strangely they see me. I can feel their damned lousy stares on me every minute I'm on the streets; eagerly watching for me to do something that they can garble and chatter and jabber among themselves. It's a price a man pays for being any way different from the mob. Well, damn the mob. Let them stare and whisper behind my back, but let them do it behind my back. Ninety-nine men out of a hundred are brainless fools that were born to be failures. Fools. The cringing, crawling, blind, senseless reptiles. Damn the mob! There's only one way they can break me—and that's what I'm afraid of all the time. That some cursed slack-jawed jackass-eyed damned fool will push me too far some day and I'll lose control of myself. If they'll let me alone, I'll get along alright. It's a cinch I'll let them alone." (note: *"The right to be let alone is indeed the beginning of all freedom." –Supreme Court Justice William Orville Douglas*)

This earlier opinion, expressed when Howard was 24, had yet to evolve into the more tolerant and self-confidant outlooks he discussed with Lovecraft. The two would not become penpals until that August. What remained constant in Howard's mind was the acute loss of individuality once any peoples relinquish their choices to any governing body or narrow principle. The consensus of the mob to which he refers reflects less of any hatred Howard may have harbored toward certain individuals and more accurately portrays his greater loathing of blind, unquestioning, unjustified prejudice or hypocrisy of any sort. To Lovecraft he wrote, "You will probably take all this a direct attack on civilization. It isn't intended as such. I'm only replying to your comment that you were surprised that I should say that civilized men justified their thieveries and butcheries by asserting motives of progress. You don't have to go to war to find hypocrisy. Every corporation that has every come into the Southwest bent solely on looting the region's people and resources has waved a banner of 'progress and civilization'!"

Howard's oft-repeated defense of the true honor of a barbaric spirit and code (and the influence such an ideal had on him) is perhaps best exemplified in a tale regarding his father, Dr. Isaac Mordecai Howard. He relates to Lovecraft in a very long letter from October/November 1932, "I was talking about duels a while ago, and I said the custom was never much in fashion in Texas, which is true. But there was a form of dueling extant here, which was a little too tough for most of the early settlers of the West. It was employed by the Comanches; the contestants had their left hands tied together, and fought with knives in their rights until both were carved to pieces. This never found much favor with white men; it was too bloody and definite. One of the most desperate men in the state refused to fight that way, when challenged by my father, when he, my father that is, was a young man. The other fellow had had the best of a fist-fight, but a fist-fight didn't settle matters in Texas—not in those days. With guns and fists this fellow was a real scrapper, but steel was something different. Though urged by my father, he refused to fight Indian-style; and when my father, enraged, laid the edge of his knife to the fellow's throat and damned him for every scoundrel under the sun, he said nothing, nor did he reach for his gun, standing white and shaking. He didn't like the feel of the edge; not many men do."

Whether or not this tale happened exactly as described (or at all) is not entirely significant when compared to the fact that Howard *represented* it as happening, and the image occupied a portion of his mind. Later chroniclers such as Robert M. Price have contended "the precocious genius did not yet have a personality to share," and "whatever personality Howard may have possessed was derived from the literary and regional lore he absorbed." (*Selected Letters, 1931-1936*) In a deeper sense, however, Howard was creating his own mythology. His solitary life as a writer and his devotion to his ailing mother occupied much of his time, so his personality was forced to evolve through channels which most people disregard. The bent of his narrations in letters tends to exhibit a kind of "method actor" approach, reflecting not only the flavor of many of his stories, but the constant themes running through his mind. And though introverted most of the time, Howard would sometimes explode in great gusts of raucous behavior, all-night drinking, and socializing in small groups. On the rare occasions where he met a fellow quieter and shyer than himself, as was represented in a tale within his semi-autobiographical book "Post Oaks and Sand Roughs," Howard could be downright sociable and understanding. That, more than anything else, is indicative of his personality and its inherent sense of fairness.

In a *Post Oaks* scene of a planned drunken weekend with Steve's buddies Sebastian (Truett Vinson,) Clive (Clyde Smith) and a new and timid German acquaintance Hubert Grotz (Herbert Klatt,) "a stocky, diffident youth of medium height, with a strong German accent. He did not appear worldly or sophisticated at all, and Steve, feeling in the evident rural aspect of the youth a fellowship which the others did not feel…really warmed to the young German, much more so than did the others." To complete the scene he describes how "Grotz had brought along some homemade sausage as a treat," but the rest of the group is interested in drinking "Jamaica ginger weakened with Coca Cola and orange juice…a more hideous concoction can scarcely be imagined." Grotz remains teetotal, and before long Clive and Sebastian are alarming the mild-mannered Grotz with their behavior as they "engaged in combat and tumbled off the bed onto the floor, after which Sebastian crawled under the bed for a reason known only to himself, and Clive raced outdoors to yowl and gibber at the windows. He seemed to be laboring under the impression that he was a werewolf." Howard goes on a calming walk with Clive, which offers Grotz the opportunity to unclench his wariness somewhat. When the two others, who have drunk more than Howard, finally sleep, "Steve and Grotz spent the rest of the night in conversation." The next morning, as the group is breaking up to go their separate ways after what Grotz was under the impression would be a kind of "literary retreat," Clive laments, "I sure was disappointed. I was expecting a sophisticated sort of fellow. And bringing that sausage—that got me down." Steve retorts, "You got it down, too. I noticed you didn't kick when he brought in a tub for you to vomit in, neither."

The real Hubert Grotz, Herbert C. Klatt, would live to be just 21 on his family's farm in Hamilton County, Texas. It was Truett Vinson who introduced Klatt to Howard and Smith, and Vinson who wrote to Smith on April 26, 1926, "H. Klatt is now corresponding with Robert, and he tells me in his last letter that Robert advises him to read Talbot Mundy for some real thrills. Robert tells him that you and I don't agree with him on the subject of T. Mundy, and so I write Klatt and tell him that we don't." (from Glenn Lord's *Herbert Klatt: The 4th Musketeer*) Mundy, a *Weird Tales* regular and liked by Howard, would suffer the indignity of having his own earlier worked called "Howardesque." But Klatt, born on January 5, 1907 in Bosque County, would often find himself too busy working the farm of his father C.F. Klatt to do all the leisure reading he might have liked. He was an avid member of the Lone Scouts (an organization formed by W.D. Boyce to provide an alternate, solitary approach to scouting similar to that of the Boy Scouts) and he wrote for the Lone Scouts journal as well as farm magazines. "I have a collection of about 700 amateur Lone Scout papers," Klatt wrote to Smith. "These and my copies of Lone Scout constitute one of the most valued parts of my library. Linked with some of the pleasant memories of my life, they always will interest me. Somehow there is nothing other like them. They enhold the essence of boyish enthusiasm, ambition and pep." Klatt's work also appeared in amateur journals such as the round-robin paper *The Junto* and Truett Vinson's *The Toreador* (whose slogan was "We are out to slay the bull.") Klatt's writing was described as brilliant by longtime Howard friend Harold Preece.

Among his small group of local friends, Howard's personality was often a stabilizing force. I have four main reasons while I feel this to be true. 1.) The round-robin paper *The Junto* and its local contributors could pretty much count Howard as a steady force amongst them. To quote de Camp, "He was the star of *The Junto*; and their members' fascination with his erudition and soaring imagination held the group together."; 2.) Howard's oft-cited congeniality when he wished it; 3.) As a frequently published writer with an amazing output, local friends such as Tevis Clyde Smith and Truett Vinson could appreciate this part of Howard and no doubt held it in high regard, and; 4.) In their "drunken weekend" in the cabin, Howard describes Vinson as crawling under the bed and Smith as howling like a werewolf, which sounds like juvenile college kids when compared to Howard staying up and talking with Herbert Klatt. Thus, to those who knew him, having Howard in your group (when he wished to be there) was very much like an anchor. And while the events in *Post Oaks* are not proof that things transpired exactly as the book describes, for someone who put so much of himself into everything he wrote, it seems terribly unlikely that they are very far off the mark.

By the spring of 1930, with his stories selling regularly, Howard indulged in the purchase of a horse; a silver mare. Since the death of his beloved dog Patch (a well-known story, well related in the biography *The Last Celt*, is that when the dog was on the way out, Howard went to nearby Brownwood and he did not wish to return until the dog had passed—more on this later) he had missed having an animal. He named the horse Gypsy and kept it in the backyard barn, often riding to visit friends or for excursions into the countryside. In a May/June 1933 letter to Lovecraft which is briefly referred to in *Dark Valley Destiny*, Howard relates, "I have a scar on my wrist; the fellow who put it there was trying to sink his knife into my throat, instead of my hand. A few years ago I was examining my saddle, and found that somebody had cut the stirrup leather nearly through, cutting from each side, and leaving only a shred of leather in the middle. It was well up near the frame, and hidden by the fender. It was merely by chance that I discovered it. It was, moreover, on the right side. No chance of me discovering it as I mounted, by breaking the leather as I swung up. But the first time my horse started bucking, or running, and my full weight was swung onto my right stirrup, the leather would have snapped, leaving me with a broken leg or a broken neck." This nearly solid proof of enemies, coupled with the general regard of the locals as previously described, contributed much to Howard's practice of carrying a pistol, usually discretely in the glove compartment of his 1931 dark green two-door Chevy sedan (which he bought used and for which he paid cash; the sum of three hundred and fifty Depression-era dollars, dumbfounding the salesman). Contrary to this *Dark Valley Destiny* description of Howard's Chevy, scholars Rusty Burke and Rob Roehm have indicated the "Inventory and Appraisement" of Howard's estate to list a "1935 Model, Standard Chevrolet Sedan," and the man who ran the Magnolia Service Station in the days when Howard frequented it, Mr. Cross, stated the car was a "'35 Standard, 4-door Chevy, black." Howard's writer friend E. Hoffmann Price, who visited him twice in Cross Plains, recounts in *A Memory of R.E. Howard* that Howard asked him about having enemies, and as they were driving Howard slowed the car and, "He reached across us, and to the side pocket. He took out a pistol, sized up the terrain, put the weapon back again, and resumed speed."

Earlier, Howard said goodbye to Gypsy when the family purchased a Guernsey cow named Delhi, and the small family barn could not serve as both garage and stable. Plus the one-man upkeep of a horse surely cut into Howard's writing time. He thereafter satisfied his desire for pets by feeding stray cats, and soon, as reported by N.P. Ellis, there were over a dozen felines hanging around the vicinity of the Howard home, and the writer had even trained some of them to sit up while a stream of milk was squirted into their mouths as the cow was being milked.

In October 1930, acting on the advice of his father, Howard went to the Scott and White Clinic at Temple, which is south of Waco. He had concerns regarding his general development as well as some minor health issues such as gas pains and a varicocele. While there he reported his mother's take on their family history to the doctors (that she was five years younger than her husband, which she was not, and that she did not have tuberculosis, which she did) and he discovered that he had a slight tendency to tachycardia, a quickening of the heart prompted by stress. Overall his heart action was normal and he fell well within the bounds of good health, weighing at the time 191 pounds and standing five feet eleven inches tall. The primary physician reported to Howard's father, "We do not think there is anything wrong with Robert. We can find no varicocele of any consequence, his organs are normally developed and he tests out good in every respect. His trouble, in our judgment, is due to his thinking there is something wrong. After he has dispelled this thought from his mind he will be in fine shape."

The amount or intensity of amateur boxing Howard did may have prompted his vascular concerns. He recounted in a September 1932 letter to Lovecraft, "Yet when I look for the peak of my exultation, I find it on a sweltering, breathless midnight when I fought a black-headed tiger of an Oklahoma drifter in an abandoned ice-vault, in a stifling atmosphere laden with tobacco smoke and the reek of sweat and rot-gut whiskey—and blood; with a gang of cursing, blaspheming oil-field roughnecks for an audience. Even now the memory of that battle stirs the sluggish blood in my fat-laden tissues. There was nothing about it calculated to advance art, science or anything else. It was a bloody, merciless, brutal brawl. We fought for fully an hour—until neither of us could fight any longer, and we reeled against each other, gasping incoherent curses through battered lips."

Compare this fight's description with the following passage about vasculitis: "Vasculitis is a clinicopathologic process characterized by inflammation and necrosis of blood vessels. This disorder may range from a major primary vascular problem to a relatively insignificant component of another disease. It may involve any organ system, and arterial involvement may span a large range of vessel size....While the most common pathophysiologic feature of the vasculidities is arterial damage mediated by immune complexes, any mechanism causing an inflammatory injury to the vessel wall can cause Vasculitis." (*Anesthesiology & Vascular Surgery: Perioperative Management of the Vascular Surgical Patient*, edited by Mark P. Yeager and D. David Glass, © 1990 Appleton & Lange)

It is known that Howard had noted further damage to his eyes due to the blows they sustained while he was boxing (letter to R.H. Barlow dated June 14, 1934,) and the varicocele—sometimes called the "bag of worms"—which troubled him in his groin could have been a last-ditch target area in a street-brawl-style boxing match, further lending to Howard's concern. In fiction Howard wrote a Steve Costigan boxing tale where the referee was prejudiced against Costigan and gave special allowances to his opponent (*Sluggers on the Beach*,) and made slight reference to burst blood vessels (*The Sign of the Snake.*) It is not clear which of Howard's amateur boxing matches even had a referee, but if any did it was likely a casual referee at best, more inclined to let any number of illegal blows slide. One or more of these boxing blows may have caused or heightened Howard's concern regarding a potential varicocele. Still, for the most part and based upon what is known for certain, Howard's physical health was quite good despite weight fluctuations between 184 and 209 pounds.

This is not to say that Howard was devoid of quirks and idiosyncrasies. In truth, he was rather full of them. There is the tale told by neighbors of the Howards, the Bonds, regarding a time Robert was walking down the middle of the road in the moonlight, shadowboxing and singing at the top of his lungs, frightening a visitor at the Bond house. From *Dark Valley Destiny:* "Another person remembers that, when walking, Howard would now and then stop, turn back, and take a few steps in order to upend a stick or stone and peer beneath it. In the street he often passed people he knew without a sign of recognition, being completely wrapped up in his own world of imagination."

Part of this behavior is likely explained by Howard's own words in a letter to Auburn, California poet and fantasy writer Clark Ashton Smith (1893-1961). The letter, circa March 1934, offers great illumination into that seemingly odd practice of stopping to overturn sticks and stones: "One of the most nauseating memories of my life is that of laying my hand on a live water moccasin as I climbed a creek bank. I escaped being bitten only because it was as much a surprise to the snake as it was to me, though I doubt if his nervous system suffered as much as mine did. On another occasion I was about to step over a large rock when some instinct that I have never been able to explain caused me to change my mind suddenly and leap as far from it as I could, almost in panic. I jumped, and cleared by some feet a big rattler coiled at the foot of the rock. If I'd stepped down, I'd have stepped full into his coils. Another time I almost put my foot on an eight-rattle diamondback in the darkness. My foot was poised in the air, when the rustling of his scales as he tried to crawl, caused me to look down and discern a vague writhing shape on the road. It was fall weather and he was too sluggish to strike, but even so it was some minutes before my hair would lay down on my scalp again. But the worst scare I ever got from a snake was from a harmless chicken snake, when I was a kid. I saw a chicken with its foot apparently caught under an old discarded stove door, so I bent and lifted the door. The snake had it by the foot, and it instantly released the chicken and struck at my hand—missed it and its head bumped against my bare foot." This theme of serpents ran like a strong vein of ore through many of Howard's stories, the Conan tales especially.

Chapter Two:

Old Names

In devising the Hyborian world, Howard created a wondrous pre-cataclysmic forgotten realm. His excellent essay which lays down the history of this world, "The Hyborian Age," gained instant praise from Lovecraft, whose only objection was with some of the nomenclature. In forwarding this essay to the publisher of a fan magazine, Lovecraft said, "The only flaw in this stuff is R.E.H.'s incurable tendency to devise names too closely resembling actual names of ancient history—names which, for us, have a very different set of associations. In many cases he does this designedly—on the theory that the familiar names descend from the fabulous realms he describes... Howard is without question the most vigorous and spontaneous writer now contributing to the pulps—the nearest approach (although he wouldn't admit it himself) to a sincere artist."

Howard himself does a better job of justifying his place name derivations in a letter to Clark Ashton Smith from the spring of 1934: "I've often wondered if, in the legends and myths of the ancients that have come down to us through the ages, there does not exist a foundation of truth, twisted and distorted beyond recognition. Suppose that at some immeasurably distant time a real civilization existed, whose builders were possessed of infinitely greater knowledge than ourselves. If some cataclysm of nature were to destroy that civilization, remnants of knowledge and stories of its greatness might well evolve into the fantastic fables that have descended to us. We know how distorted a fact can become, even when passed through the mouths of a generation of fairly well educated people; how much more, then, must truths be twisted into myths at the hands of savages and barbarians through the ages. Sometimes it seems to me that there might be a blind spot in our conception of history and pre-history—a whole undiscovered continent of facts, lying beyond our horizon; a vast, forgotten reservoir of knowledge, of which our modern sciences are but seepings, trickles from the greater store."

However even among Howard's closest friends was a critical view toward the nomenclature which Howard felt was indicative of a layering effect—a "forgotten knowledge" of sorts—among the strata of ancient civilizations. Friend E. Hoffman Price recalled later (from Redwood City, CA in May of 1971,) "Bob's history and map of the Hyborian Age was a nightmarish and irritating thing, and his nomenclature was the supreme affront." As a fellow contributor to the legendary pulp magazine *Weird Tales*, Price and Howard corresponded with regularity and even visited. In a letter to Clark Ashton Smith postmarked May 21, 1934 Howard relates, "Since writing you last I had the privilege of meeting E. Hoffman Price, who stopped by a few days on his way to California. A most interesting and delightful character. I hope to see more of him." To Lovecraft Howard would later relate, "One market I tried was Spicy Adventures, a sex magazine to which Ed [Price] is the star contributor." Price first visited Howard April 8-11, 1934, making the 545 mile drive from Pawhuska, OK to Cross Plains, TX en route to CA in his Model A Ford with his new bride. "There were shorter routes to California," said Price, "but this was the only one which passed Bob Howard's door, so I took it." Two years previous in 1932 Howard wired Price regarding an upcoming trip Lovecraft was planning for New Orleans, and suggested that Price, who had just lost his job as the superintendent of an acetylene plant, make the effort to meet the Rhode Islander. Price later recalled, "In the manner of two ex-soldiers re-fighting a war, we discussed Howard, quoting his sayings and whimsies." In roughly October of 1935 Price would visit Howard again, this time while on his way to Mexico City, making the five hundred mile detour from El Paso to Cross Plains simply to tell Howard in person that his faith in Price as a writer and his prediction that the young man had a career for himself in the craft had worked out. Idly the two envisioned joining Lovecraft for "a motor invasion of Mexico, half seriously, half in whimsy."

Said Howard, "I am interested in all nations and all men, some more than others." Howard's much-publicized relationship with teacher and would-be writer Novalyne Price Ellis (whose biographical notes regarding Howard in her book *One Who Walked Alone* formed the primary basis for the film *The Whole Wide World*) is markedly underemphasized in some previous Howard biographical material. One theory is that Howard might have lived longer and not been tempted to suicide if Novalyne had stayed with him in Cross Plains instead of moving away for college. Another suggests that Howard was at least equally (if not moreso) fond of a local Sunday school student, and it is known that Howard confounded his friends in their small literary group The Junto by going so far as to join her Sunday Bible study group. This girl was Ruth Baum, the pretty blond daughter of a prominent Cross Plains Methodist family. From *Dark Valley Destiny*, "Ruth attended Sunday school and belonged to the Epworth League, the young people's auxiliary of the Methodist church. Robert joined both organizations, writing Booth Mooney [a farm youth with literary ambitions who lived near Decatur and was friends with Harold Preece] that he did so in hopes of getting to know the girl better. Soon he was elected vice-president of the Sunday-school class. The members of The Junto were horrified."

Fortunately for his literary group, Howard and Ruth Baum never quite connected. Ruth later attributed it to them both being extremely shy. And without further attempts to court the muse which had smitten him, Howard soon left the church group.

"In my younger days, I thought that to win a rare, fair, bare maiden, you approached her something like the high priests of

Babylon approached their idol. I have changed my mind; if I ever (for the sake of theory) wish to propose to a girl, I will use the old caveman tactics and lead up to the proposal by a fast left to the chin, followed by a wicked right to the solar plexus," Howard wrote to Tevis Clyde Smith in January 1928, his level of seriousness only a modicum unclear.

Far more clear was that Howard and Novalyne *did* make a strong connection. In a May 1978 interview, Novalyne related her first real date with Howard. She persuaded a friend to drive her to the Howard home, where she asked to see Bob. It was Howard's father who had answered the door, and when he announced, rather awkwardly, that Robert had a female caller, the writer emerged stridently and said, "Why, hello, Novalyne! How nice of you to come!"

The two went riding and parking for the bulk of the evening. Howard returned home once at ten o'clock to give his mother medicine. When Novalyne inquired as to why his father could not administer it, Howard replied simply, "Well, I always do it." After that short break in their date they motored away again, drunk with the act of learning more about one another. Soon it was not uncommon for the young couple to see each other several nights in a row. This clearly distressed Howard's mother Hester (who had garnered the nickname Heck from Howard's father,) and Novalyne reports being told by Hester that Robert was away from home when she tried phoning him. During one of his two visits with Howard, E. Hoffmann Price recalled in a 1945 letter to *The Acolyte*, "REH did, I infer, have feminine friends. One phoned during my visit in Cross Plains. Robert's mother told the lady that Robert was not in; actually he was in his office, within easy call." Howard initially denied being away, but when Novalyne clarified that she had heard it from his mother, Howard protected the word of the ailing woman and said, "Oh—ah—yes, I was away. I guess I forgot." After repeatedly sensing hostility from Howard's mother, Novalyne communicated with him by mail, which Howard always retrieved personally from the post office, thus avoiding any maternal censorship.

"Mama, does this mean we're going to lose our boy?" Isaac Howard had asked his wife at the very beginning of the new relationship, but she reassured him that would not be the case. Throughout Howard's early and formative years his mother had been the central figure in his life, for the family of a traveling country physician could not reasonably expect a steady fatherly figure at home. The family was always on the move when Howard was a child. Born in Peaster, Texas, he was soon moved to Dark Valley in the Palo Pinto hills, then to Seminole on the Staked Plains near New Mexico in 1908, Bronte in west Texas in 1909, Poteet (1910), on a ranch near Atascosa County, Oran (1912), a cattle town in the Wichita Falls country (1913), Bagwell in east Texas (1913), then on to the central Texas towns of Cross Cut (1915), Burkett (1918), and finally Cross Plains.

While in Bronte the Howard family would have had ample opportunity to learn of a local man who was known to tens of thousands throughout Texas as the greatest master of wild horses: Samuel Thomas Privett, known as a legend under the name Booger Red. Born on a ranch near Dublin in Erath County on December 29, 1864, he began riding at the age of ten and two years later was known as the Red-Headed Kid Bronc Rider (Elizabeth Doyle, 1938 interview with Mollie Privett, San Angelo, recorded with the Library of Congress, American Life Histories: Manuscripts from the Federal Writers Project).

Booger Red got his name from an accident at the age of thirteen. He and a pal had filled a tree hollow with gunpowder and they set it off without being at a safe distance. The blast killed his friend and left Privett with severe facial scars. From the account, "As he was being carried to the hospital in a farm wagon, a small boy friend hopped on the side of the wagon, looked over at Red and thoughtlessly remarked, 'Gee, but Red is sure a booger now, ain't he?' Thus, the famous 'Booger Red' nickname which went with him to his grave."

His parents would die when he was fifteen and Red would set

himself on the path to be a legendary bronc buster. He married Mollie Webb in Bronte in 1895. "My father performed the wedding ceremony for Booger Red right out on the street in Bronte," said fellow rider Ervin Cumbie in a September, 1938 interview with Annie McAuley (source: LOC). "Booger Red was the best rider or at least the best bronc buster I ever knew. He was the originator of rodeo shows in this part of the west." He and his new wife Mollie would eventually settle in San Angelo. By this time the crowds who came to see him perform were bigger than any tent that could be provided, and Booger Red advertised his appearances ahead of time so that anyone in Texas or anywhere in the country could bring their toughest horses for him to ride. He offered to pay $100 if there was a horse he could not ride, and throughout his career it is said he never once had to pay it. Fellow bronc riding champion Walter R. Morrison said of him, "He was a top rider, but the loop was his main stunt. That man could loop any leg of a running critter from any position. He could just make a rope talk." (Source: LOC)

At least twenty-three first place rodeo prizes went to Booger Red and he appeared at the St. Louis World's Fair with Will Rogers. In 1915 he won the world championship at the San Francisco World's Fair. "His personal best for a single day was in 1915 when he rode 86 bucking horses in San Francisco," documents Charlsie Poe in her book *Booger Red, World Champion Cowboy*. His last appearance was just forty-five miles east of Cross Plains in Fort Worth. There, in 1924 at the Fat Stock Show, he was near the end of his life and had intended just to be a spectator, but when a horse threw its rider and broke free in the arena, Booger Red rose one last time. "He rode the old horse to a finish and many said it was the prettiest riding they ever saw. He was at that time probably the oldest man on record to make such a ride. [...] If he had lived until the picture business became more prominent he would have been as famous in the Movie world as he was in the show life of his day."

Howard mentions rodeos in his correspondence, such as at the annual picnic. In Howard's Texas the local fat stock shows were not only attended by the cattlemen and their families but by the surrounding community and were an important social occasion. Kids who were attending school took holidays to come to the show, but these weren't the kind of events which were likely to interest a refined school teacher. With Novalyne, Howard was able to have some of the vibrant feminine companionship for which he had longed. Unlike Ruth Baum, Novalyne came to Howard and wasn't shy about her interest. Previously most of his contact with a female involved his mother, driving the frail woman to the clinic, errands, or simply to get the air and see the country. Now he could run hand-in-hand with Novalyne along an open road in the moonlight, get dressed up and take her to the movies in Brownwood or Abilene, or simply drive around and have a soda outside the drugstore. They did all these things, and a bit more. Novalyne later said of Howard's ability to kiss, "He was very good at that."

Novalyne had learned from her stepfather to use some pretty colorful language—far moreso than the conventional Howard expected to hear from a young woman. Likewise there were things about Howard which Novalyne wished to change. Still, they were a couple, and they talked of the concept of marriage, and at times each seemed to take their turn in either suggesting or shying away from committing to an engagement. Novalyne had many ambitions career-wise, but Howard idealized the classic housewife, and this was a recurring bone of contention. In Howard's younger days when his mother was in better health, she would act very much like his maid, bringing him food silently on a tray as he worked at his typewriter, plus she remained interested in accompanying Howard almost everywhere he went, whether it was to shop, go for a drive, or to call on friends. The low, constant fever of her tuberculosis had the one benefit of making her appear in the pink of health to the casual observer, and her dress was always fashionable and ladylike. This led Novalyne to suspect that Mrs. Howard was not as sick as she had led her son to believe. Hester in turn, when she saw Novalyne, would speak grudgingly, "glowering at me as if I were some sort of venomous reptile," said Novalyne in a November, 1977 interview.

Still, Novalyne harbored strong feelings for Howard, and she frequently sought his counsel with regard to her own fledgling writing. The oft-published author would have preferred her to incorporate elements of the fantastic into her stories, but Novalyne much preferred realism. Again Howard encountered a tinge of the prejudice the people of his own town held against the strain of author whose writing appeared in strange magazines with artwork of scantily-clad women on the cover. Still, Howard tried to steer Novalyne away from teaching so that she could spend more time writing. He held her boss, school superintendent Nat Williams, in general disregard, and he disliked those students of hers whose abilities she praised. But Novalyne insisted that any writer could benefit from higher education, and told Howard she felt he was mistaken to abandon college. This triggered within Howard a kind of raging exasperation, and he mimicked the speech of a local illiterate as he replied sardonically, "Ah don't know nothin'; Ah ain't got no education like you!"

Their relationship was flagging by early 1935, and Novalyne began to more fully realize that Hester Howard had a firmer hold on her son, made no demands of him, didn't try to change him, and lauded exactly who he was. As the year continued Novalyne resolved with her mind not to marry Howard, even if he should ask. The reasons had crystallized: Howard would expect her to be a housewife, she would be alone during the endless hours he worked, she would always be despised by his mother, and she would have to abandon her ambitions. This conflict wore on Novalyne's health, and she was hospitalized in Brownwood for recovery, with orders that only doctors could visit her bedside. Howard would spend a full month during 1935 away from Cross Plains, by his mother's side in Temple, where she inchingly recovered from gallbladder removal at King's Daughters Hospital. Wanting to reserve whatever cash he had to help defray his mother's medical expenses, Howard stayed at the cheapest rooming house he could find and he lost fifteen pounds that month. He tells Farnsworth Wright in a letter dated May 6, 1935,

"My mother was forced to have her gall bladder removed, a very serious operation, especially for a woman her age and state of health. She has been almost an invalid for years. She was in a hospital at Temple for a month, during which time I stayed with her, and was not able to do any writing at all during that time. But for the professional discount on the operation, my father being a physician, I do not know how we would have been able to meet the expenses." His concern for his mother superceded his thoughts of Novalyne. He wondered how much longer she had to live.

Howard, contrary to some accounts, had already witnessed human death by this time; and not just any pleasant passing, but gruesome death. He recounts in a July 4, 1935 letter to August Derleth, "...the liquor has stirred up old memories and set the ghosts of the dead walking in my mind. Old names that are already meaningless as the wind that blows through the trees at midnight. Steve Baccus; a quiet, harmless man was Steve, who passed with me many a pleasant time of day. One of the more recent dead. Only a few months have passed since the sheriff's bullet cut Steve down, him standing bewildered and empty-handed, hardly knowing that a raid was on. And there was Tinney, a great, dark, awkward, honest man from Alabama, working on a rotten rig to pay his debts, and knowing he risked his life in doing so. I liked Tinney well. On that last night he awoke from a doze and said to the driller: 'I dreamed of my wife standing and staring at me with her eyes as big and black as disks cut out of the black night out there; I'll never get off this job alive.' He went away for a drink and as he came back into the rig there came a crash like Judgment Day and the driller ran out shouting: 'Run, man, run, the bullwheel's given away!' Tinney stood stock-still, with his face white in the gloom, like a man already with his death wound. Then as the driller screamed, he turned, like a man in a daze—three lumbering steps he took and then the madly spinning wheel flew to pieces, a fragment of wood crushed in the back of his head and an iron bolt struck him between his big shoulders and ripped through him like a bullet from a gun. That was not so long ago, but my memory goes further back and I remember Oscar Oliver, the first man of my acquaintance to be killed in an oil field. He stood upright on the crown-block, wielding a sledge-hammer and a high wind blowing. The wind caught him, shoved him off-balance, thrust him off solid footing and sent him spinning down—down like a plummet he fell, a writhing atom of life in the immensity of thin air, with the solid world rushing up to meet him with an awesome and definite thunder—he broke his back across the walking beam, slipped from it and crashed through the heavy planks that composed the roof of the engine-house—smashed shatteringly down upon the engine, rebounded and fell to the concrete floor. There was not a bone in his body bigger than the bones in your finger left not splintered...." Howard may have known Oscar Oliver through Nathan Oliver (or vice versa,) also an oilfield worker, who along with his wife Opal would later rent the living and dining rooms of the Howard home during the peak of the local oil boom. Howard's time spent covering oilfield news to scrap together an early income had not been lacking in danger.

Oilfield worker in Kilgore, TX in 1939.
Library of Congress, Prints & Photographs Division, FSA-OWI Collection

But other forms of death surrounded Howard. Old schoolmates were killed, as well as lawmen, regular townsfolk, and even rodeo participants. He tells Derleth, "They'll probably have a small rodeo here at the annual picnic, with the attendant casualties. Last year it was a cowboy from Oklahoma who called himself Jack O' Diamonds. He was lean and hard and tough but the wild bull he tried to ride was tougher. It threw him and jumped on him and broke his ribs and one stuck through him just under the heart. They raised him up and saw that he had his death-wound, and they told him that when they drew out the broken rib it would be his finish, and they asked him who his people were, and what his real name was. 'Jack of Diamonds,' he said, with the blood bubbling under his lips. 'It was good enough to live by; it's good enough to die by. Pull out the damned rib.' So they pulled it out and the blood gushed out of his mouth and he died."

Rodeo performer bulldogging a calf at the rodeo of the San Angelo Fat Stock Show, 1940. Courtesy LOC, FSA-OWI Collection

Still more stories of death were commonplace to Howard: "Skeezicks Ramsay was more recent. I remember well the last time I saw Skeezicks. I lay on my back with five stitches in my throat and my body so badly bruised from a car wreck that I could scarcely walk." Note: the accident happened on the night of December 29, 1933. Howard and three friends were returning from a football game under rain and fog. The car ran into a steel pole and Howard received a gash that narrowly missed his jugular vein. He was also thrown into the steering wheel with such force that it nearly bent double. "He [Skeezicks] came to drag my smashed-up auto down to town for repairs—he being a mechanic—and I thought enviously how healthy and lusty he looked. A few days later I heard he was dead—thrown from a truck as it ran along the highway, and his brains dashed out on the road. There was Melson Wakefield, a schoolmate—shot his girl-wife with one barrel of his shotgun and those wakened by the shot and running to investigate got there in time to see him put the barrel under his chin and blow his head off. I remember the last time I saw Bob Ensor—coming out into the road out of the hills where he had lived for more than fifty years, he and his wife in single file like Indians, and he tall and lean and dark and silent, whose record as a deputy marshal was without stain. A week later he was dead not so far from where I saw him last—shot down from the brush in an old feud that had smoldered for thirty years. And there was Arch Davidson, the last man killed in a fight in this town—he was warned to keep out of Walt Farrow's place, but he kicked open the door and lurched in, in his bravado—and there he froze suddenly, with the knowledge of death on him, in the glare of Farrow's eyes, in the sixshooter in Farrow's lifted hand. Then the gun crashed and the bullet tore his brains out and [Farrow] hurled him headfirst out into the crowded street, where women shrieked suddenly to see that limp shape lying with the shattered head in a slowly widening pool of crimson." Farrow's place was reported by a local to have been a "hamburger joint," although the mind is tempted to picture a private residence here.

"And there was Clyde Keith, another schoolmate. It was a fight on a lonely road, and he had his man down, feeling for his eyes. 'A fight is a fight,' said the other, 'but I'll not go through life with my eyes out; let go, or I'll do you a mortal hurt.' But the liquor was on Clyde, and he said: 'I'll gouge the eyeballs out of you like rotten grapes.' So the man below reached up with his knife and ripped the life out of him at one slash. And I remember the Englishman, Ellis, and his wife. He was a fine figure of a man, and had held high command in the British army once. He was of good blood and well educated, but the devil was in him. She ran out of the house with him behind her, threatening her with a shotgun and she begged a boy who was passing in an automobile to take her away. But Ellis threw his gun on the boy and bade him mind his own business. Then he turned on his wife and the first charge struck her in the thigh and flank, so she staggered to the steps of the porch and sank down, with her hand on her wound, begging for her life. But he placed the muzzles of the gun between her breasts and blew the life out of her; then he laid down the gun and went into the yard and cut his own throat with his knife. And there he lay long, spurting blood like a stuck hog and groaning and no man would soil the hands of him by touching him, until at last there came a doctor who was from Kansas and who sewed up his wound and saved his rotten life. While he waited for his trial he wrote a most courtly letter complimenting me on a story of mine he had read with the hope he would get to read more. But it was not my hope that he would, for I hoped he would hang before the first snow flew; but he only got ninety-nine years."

Moore County, Texas. Oil field roughnecks shooting at tin hats. While the rotary drill is "making hole" roughnecks have lots of spare time. Courtesy LOC, FSA-OWI Collection

Still more death surrounded Howard; local deaths by various poisons and even stories of desperate women who had committed suicide with guns or slashed their wrists with knives. "While the things he met couldn't put a dent in his athletic body, they were too much for his sensitive spirit," E. Hoffmann Price wrote *The Acolyte* in 1945. "He saw much more than he could understand or interpret, and these things drove him to create worlds of imagination in which there were greater brawls than any Texas oil boom could offer." Under the light of such stories, it becomes easier to understand the mindset of Howard and many of his contemporaries, that suicide could be viewed not just as an option, but as a fundamental right basic to intelligent life; the right to chose one's exit place from this world—moreover, an act which at times could be honorable, when suffering was deemed too great.

Something tapped me on the shoulder
Something whispered, "Come with me,
"Leave the world of men behind you,
"Come where care may never find you
"Come and follow, let me bind you
"Where, in that dark, silent sea,
"Tempest of the world ne'er rages;
"There to dream away the ages,
"Heedless of Time's turning pages,
"Only, come with me."

"Who are you?" I asked the phantom,
"I am rest from Hate and Pride.
"I am friend to king and beggar,
"I am Alpha and Omega,
"I was councilor to Hagar
"But men call me suicide."
I was weary of tide breasting,
Weary of the world's behesting,
And I lusted for the resting
As a lover for his bride.

And my soul tugged at its moorings
And it whispered, "Set me free.

> *"I am weary of this battle,*
> *"Of this world of human cattle,*
> *"All this dreary noise and prattle.*
> *"This you owe to me."*
> *Long I sat and long I pondered,*
> *On the life that I had squandered,*
> *O'er the paths that I had wandered*
> *Never free.*
>
> *In the shadow panorama*
> *Passed life's struggles and its fray.*
> *And my soul tugged with new vigor,*
> *Huger grew the phantom's figure,*
> *As I slowly tugged the trigger,*
> *Saw the world fade swift away.*
> *Through the fogs old Time came striding,*
> *Radiant clouds were 'bout me riding,*
> *As my soul went gliding, gliding,*
> *From the shadow into day.*
>
> –The Tempter, REH

And dark times were ahead in his personal life, with his mother's treatments becoming increasingly severe and painful. Regularly in and out of hospitals, Hester was taken to the Torbett Sanitarium in Marlin in mid-November, 1935, where over a gallon of fluid was drained from her pleura (the thin covering that protects and cushions the lungs; the pleura is made up of two layers of tissue that are separated by what is normally a small amount of fluid.) She stayed there a week, went home for two weeks, and needed to go to Shannon Hospital in San Angelo (105 miles southwest) when her pleura filled again. From there she was moved to a sanitarium in Water Valley to the northwest, where she remained for six weeks.

Chapter Three:

Wrapped in a Rolling Thunder

Howard's writing sales for 1935 were over two thousand dollars, which made him one of the higher paid men in his locality, but by no means rich. Much of his income was now dedicated to his mother's medical care, and when she was in the hospital he would often find a cheap boarding house nearby, check-in with his typewriter in tow, continuing to create stories in the long stretches between visiting hours. It must have been a troublesome existence for a man almost thirty, and during the long trip back from Temple earlier that year, Howard confided to his father that he did not wish to live if his mother passed away. Perhaps the old doctor tempered these words with the fact that Robert's car had broken down twice during that drive back, and he was coming off another extended stay in the vicinity of a hospital. Isaac had surely heard such depressed talk before from family members in his various duties as a country physician. The strain of seeing a loved-one suffer often caused more distress than after that suffering had ended, and fortunately such morbid spells usually passed without sparking further harm.

When Novalyne returned from Brownwood, she did see Howard again, but their new relationship was more aloof. She informed him that she intended to meet his tall, handsome friend Truett Vinson. She reported Howard's scoffing reaction: "He'd never take *you* out! No guy would fall for you; you're just saying that to make me jealous." This reaction only increased Novalyne's determination to have a date with Vinson. She did, and then told Howard about it. He refused to believe her at first, and later became furious and refused to see her again.

Weeks passed. Howard sent her a letter refusing her invitation to visit and intimating that her behavior with Vinson was not a fair way to deal with him. She replied saying that she had been fair in informing him of her intentions and would continue to wish him success and happiness. For Howard the situation smacked of a certain unpleasant familiarity. Novalyne, before dating Howard, had dated his other local friend Tevis Clyde Smith for four years. She had a date with Smith two weeks before his sudden marriage to another woman, Ecla Laxon. And she retained Smith as a friend. Now she was going out with Truett Vinson of nearby Brownwood, and wished to retain Howard as a friend. In truth, Howard was still the only man in Cross Plains with whom she could discuss literature.

As more weeks passed, Howard consented to seeing her again. He recalled her saying that she liked a thin, small mustache on a man, and he took the liberty of growing a comically large, walrus-like mustache, "sporting this outsized hirsute ornament just to annoy her," as it is put in *Dark Valley Destiny*. Despite this act of upper lip insubordination, by February of 1936 they had another date.

Novalyne had not completely abandoned her hope of guiding Howard away from his mother into being more independent (and closer to what she likely felt was "husband-quality" material). This would mean Howard would have to refuse to do so many of the things his mother relied upon him to accomplish, and at a time when she was more ill than ever. The thought of leaving her when she needed him most must have horrified Howard, and more clearly demonstrated to him, moreso than any infidelity, that Novalyne did not truly want to accept the type of person he was. She, the only girl who had taken him so seriously as to have considered marriage, even she did not wish to afford him the luxury of choosing the routine of his days, much less embracing it.

They erupted in quarrel. It would be their last date. Soon after Howard shaved the unwieldy moustache.

That spring Novalyne left for Louisiana State University to study for her master's degree. Howard may have seen her departure as an augury that another woman would soon leave his life. Or secretly he may have thought that if he gave up Novalyne, the gods would grant his mother a reprieve. He tells Lovecraft in February, 1936, "Her condition is very bad, and she requires frequent aspirations, which are painful, weakening and dangerous. It is wonderful with what fortitude she endures her afflictions; in every hospital she has been, the doctors and nurses speak of her cheerfulness, her nerve, and her steadiness in the highest terms. But it is only what can be expected in a woman of the old pioneer stock. This has been a bitter winter, and the harshness of the weather has hurt her. First one woman and then another we hired to help wait on her has been taken sick herself, so the job of nursing my mother has been done largely by my father and myself. She is subject to distressing and continual sweats, and naturally has to have constant attention, so I find little, if any, time to write, which is why this letter is brief, and possibly so disconnected. Some times we have to be up all night with her. There seems to be little we or anyone can do to help her, though God knows I'd make any sacrifice, including my own life, if it could purchase her any relief."

The aspirations to which Howard referred involved a long needle being inserted between the ribs and into the pleural cavity. The pain of both patient and provider, whether it was Isaac or Robert, increased when air is blown into the tube in order to induce temporary lung collapse. The working theory was that a resting lung would be better able to build up resistance to tubercular infection.

During this time Howard adopted several unusual behaviors

which have later been interpreted (by some) as a silent cry for help, but to Novalyne Price they seemed more like Howard's unabashedly bold statement that he was different from the regular townsfolk. He started wearing a long gray frock coat of nineteenth-century fashion that might have actually been a Confederate officer's coat (both his grandfathers, William Benjamin Howard and Colonel Ervin, had fought in the Civil War.) This he coupled with a wide-brimmed Mexican sombrero, or coupled the sombrero with an outfit described by Novalyne as the style of a vaquero, freely wearing these garments around town, in direct violation of his years earlier statement that he disliked having eyes upon him, whispers about him, or people who waited for bizarre behavior from him. Howard himself spoke of the vaqueros in a December 1932 letter to August Derleth. In it he talked of gunmen, and how John Wesley Hardin invented the "six-shooter roll" which Billy the Kid got credit for: "To the best of my knowledge Hardin invented it, and it was practiced by all the vaqueros who hazed doggies up the old Chisholm." Now dressed as a vaquero himself, it seemed as if Howard's actions were meant to mock the stereotypes that the townspeople feared, so that he could, in his own way, finally say to them, "Your worries aren't much compared to what ails me, and all this nonsense you call your daily lives is just a silly, petty mess."

Howard had also long been known amongst friends to have a tendency toward sleepwalking (which may have dissipated as he entered his thirties) and he took to the habit of tying a rope around his foot and attaching the other end to the bedpost. Before the rope tying, Howard had once awoken in the middle of the night and walked straight out of a first floor window while staying at a rooming house in Brownwood. He later describes a vivid dream which caused him to make use of this rope in a letter to Tevis Clyde Smith: "The other night I started eliminating the Yellow Peril with a butcher knife and in the conflict bounded out of bed and on the account of my foot, did a neat nose-dive onto the floor which skinned my face somewhat."

This dream may have formed part of the inspiration for the (understandably) little-known Howard tale *Blow the Chinks Down!*, featuring Steve Costigan actually separated from his bulldog Mike, whom he says is "laid up with distemper." It was first published in the October, 1931 edition of *Action Stories* and later given the more politically correct title of *The House of Peril*. The "Yellow Peril" is thinly veiled in the new title, as the bulk of the story takes place in a large house occupied by the Chinese. Similar to the conditions of a dream, the fight scene in the tale takes place in utter darkness—darkness so complete nothing can be seen. In a chamber in which Steve is put and told to fight for his life, Howard describes the action: "I heard 'em swish past my head in the dark and purty soon I stopped one of them fists with my nose. Whilst I was trying to shake the blood and stars outa my eyes, my raging opponent clamped his teeth in my ear and set back. With a maddened roar, I hooked him in the belly with such heartiness that he let go with a gasp and curled up like a angle-worm. I then climbed atop of him and set to work punching him into a pulp, but he come to hisself under my very fists, as it were, pitched me off and got a scissors hold that nearly caved my ribs in."

Howard's dreams often caused him to rise from bed, and the aforementioned dream of killing a perceived enemy is significant. Robert Smith of the Michigan State University College of Human Medicine conducted two studies which explored a possible biological role in dreaming (these two studies being *The Meaning of Dreams: The Need for a Standardized Dream Report* and *Evaluating Dream Function: Emphasizing the Study of Patients with Organic Disease*.) Smith's work is summarized in the following passage from *Our Dreaming Mind* by Ph.D. Robert L. Van de Castle: "In one study, forty-nine medical inpatients reported dreams occurring within the preceding twelve months to an interviewer. Most of these patients had cardiovascular disease, but some were suffering from Pulmonary disease, infections, or other general medical problems. The state of their health was evaluated six months after they were discharged from the hospital. Dreams were scored for the presence of 'death,' which included references to graveyards, funerals, wills, or conditions such as the heart stopping. Another dream category dealt with separation and included references to disruptions of personal relationships or displacement from the home. Smith found a significant association between death references in the dreams of males and a subsequent deterioration in their medical condition, while women's medical conditions deteriorated when their dreams contained references to separation."

In that quote we have the trifecta of potential Howard problems: 1.) He believed he had a variocele as well as a problem with his heart and had briefly taken digitalis (whose side effects include depression) after a car accident; 2.) He spent his life living with his mother's infectious pulmonary condition; 3.) He was often separated from his home during his mother's illness and he was often separated from his mother due to hospital visiting hours. One or more of these factors may have crept into his dreams. The passage from *Our Dreaming Mind* continues, "In his second study, Smith obtained dreams from forty-eight patients who were undergoing cardiac catheterization. Most of these patients had cardiac problems, but a few had cancer or diabetes. He found that the severity of cardiac dysfunction was related to the number of dream references to death for males and to separation for women. Smith concluded that 'these dreams had a warning function, signaling the presence of severe biological impairment. If a useful intervention occurred as a result of these warnings, the dreams would have an adaptive meaning or function.'"

One of the most striking and haunting examples (outside of another Howard dream which we will later discuss) of the oracular power manifested in certain dreams is the 1917 precognitive dream of psychologist and Episcopal minister Walter Franklin Prince. On the night of November 27, 1917 he dreamed a woman brought to him a small paper with an order written in red ink for the execution of the bearer. The woman who showed it to him was slender, about thirty-five years of age with blond hair, and she indicated her willingness to die with the one proviso that Prince hold her hand. He does so, and after examining the paper once more the lights suddenly went out and Prince can tell by the grip of the woman's hand that she had, right then and there, been put to death. He felt with one of his hands the hair of her head, and he could tell that the head had been severed from the body. The fingers of his other hand became caught in the woman's mouth, which opened and shut several times. Prince was horrified by the idea of the woman's severed head retaining animation. The next morning he told the details of the dream to his wife and later that day to his secretary.

Two days later, in an article which appeared in the local paper, the grisly story of the death of Mrs. Sara Hand was told. At about 11:15 on the night of November 28, Sara Hand had deliberately placed her head on the tracks of the Long Island Railroad Station as a train was approaching. Police found a new butcher knife and cleaver near her body, which she had decided not to use for her self-decreed death. In her handbag they found a note:

> *"Please stop all trains immediately. My head is on the track and will be run over by those steam engines and will prevent me from proving my condition.... My head is alive and can see and talk, and I must get it to prove my case to the law. No one believed me when I said I would never die and when my head was chopped off I would still be alive. Everyone laughed and said I was crazy, so now I have proved this terrible life to all. Please have all trains stopped to save my head from being cut into fragments. I need it to talk to prove my condition and have the doctor arrested for this terrible life he put me in."*

Sara Hand fit the physical description in Dr. Prince's dream. She purchased the butcher knife and cleaver the same night Prince had his dream. She was still unsure of how she would sever her head, hence the lights going out in the dream. And the focus on "hands" in the dream is uncanny, from the woman wanting Prince to hold her hand, to Prince's own hands becoming entangled in the woman's hair and caught within her biting mouth after the head was severed. Dr. Prince being horrified that the head was still alive and biting him in the dream parallel's Sara Hand's belief that her head would remain alive after decapitation.

Having suffered the death of her young daughter a few months prior to her suicide, Sara Hand was thrown into a state of severe mental depression and delusion. The story ran in *The Evening Telegram* in Long Island and it was just the sort of eye-grabber that would likely have been picked-up by other newspapers across the country. Howard would have been almost twelve years old at the time. If Hand's dreams were as equally disturbing as Prince's, the incident is strong support for Dr. Robert Smith's study.

This is not put forth to suggest any unqualified diagnosis has been made, but rather to inform those interested in the subject. Although it is a faint tangent, biological factors within Howard may have manifested in some of his dreams. He knew at some point he would be separated not only from his mother, but also from Novalyne, who was planning to leave the state for the continuance of her college studies.

"I feel that Bob felt that friends had deserted him, his life was torn up completely, and he had an over protectiveness of his mother that few people have," Novalyne said in *Day of the Stranger*, a short follow-up to the success of *One Who Walked Alone*. "But at that time, keep in mind, people expected to take care of their mothers, […] I don't know why it made me so angry and so turned off when he told me that he changed his mother's nightgown three times during one night. That nearly killed me. Because I didn't think it was his place – that was one thing. Here is the son doing what I thought the father should have done. […] He had all those things – the heartache of his mother's illness, the frustration that he felt, and what he considered a lack of friends. He didn't see anything to live for."

While in the midst of the Great Depression Howard had put his savings into two local banks, only to see both of them fail. *Weird Tales* alone owed him hundreds of dollars worth of payment for stories they had previously published, and it got to the point where he was reluctant to send anything more to them, knowing how great their tab was with him. But he branched out and sold nearly every type of genre story, from his excellent westerns, to Oriental adventures, detective stories, his popular and entertaining boxing stories (boxing and football were his favorite sports,) his spicy stories written under the name of Sam Walser, stories of the Crusade, Spanish conquistadors, horror and ghost stories, science fiction, etc. During the winter of 1935-36 he sold five westerns to the highly respected *Argosy* magazine alone.

Later authors as well as some of Howard's contemporaries have wondered exactly what precise combination of factors were in play which could grip Howard into taking his own life, just as his writing career was ever-rising and the promise of his future readers and admirers numbering in the millions was in its infancy of materialization. As the authors of *Dark Valley Destiny* (essentially de Camp) poignantly state, "We who have studied the man and his works shall never entirely know the source of the jets of agony and the crimson pain of which he complained in his poetry." The poem in question here is called *Lines Written in the Realization That I Must Die*, although that title sounds like it may have been selected by the Popular Fiction Publishing Company for its appearance in *Weird Tales* in August 1938. The poem is as follows:

>*The Black Door gapes and the Black Wall rises;*
>*Twilight gasps in the grip of Night.*
>*Paper and dust are the gems man prizes—*
>*Torches toss in my waning sight.*
>
>*Drums of glory are lost in the ages,*
>*Bare feet fail on a broken trail—*
>*Let my name fade from the printed pages;*

Dreams and visions are growing pale.

Twilight gathers and none cane save me.
Well and well, for I would not stay:
Let me speak through the stone that you gave me:
He never could say what he wished to say.

Why should I shrink from the sign of the leaving?
My brain is wrapped in a darkened cloud;
Now in the Night are the Sisters weaving
For me a shroud.

Towers shake and the stars reel under,
Skulls are heaped in the Devil's fane;
My feet are wrapped in a rolling thunder,
Jets of agony lance my brain.

What of the world that I leave for ever?
Phantom forms in a fading sight—
Carry me out on the ebon river
Into the Night.

De Camp continues, "What was the battle, the dreary noise and prattle, whereof he was weary? [a reference to Howard's poem *The Tempter*, shown earlier] But we know the pain was there. Perhaps the gods who hammered out his personality were careless in their handiwork, for they neglected the hardening process that endows a man with a love of life despite all its trials and disappointments."

To some, the answer seems clearer, and it likely starts with Hester Howard herself. She was four when her mother died and five when her father remarried. Her departed mother, Sarah Jane Martin, had lived through the privations of the Civil War, and struggled through several resettlements of address as her health continued to fail. Her marriage lasted twenty years and produced ten children for her husband Colonel George Washington Ervin. But by the time of the tenth birth, mother and child were so weakened that both perished. Within a year her father married a Missouri woman, Alice Wynne Ervin. The family moved to Lewisville, Texas and Alice gave birth to Hester's new sister Coralie. The ever-changing atmosphere in which Hester developed likely left her with feelings of inadequacy, rejection and dependence. Her new mother expected her to help with future siblings, and soon two more children were born. Her father sired a total of sixteen.

Hester's southern family regarded her as a selfless, kind, giving woman to those she loved. She spent a good portion of her youth helping relatives who were suffering through a variety of sicknesses, and it is during this long stretch of service that she contracted tuberculosis, possibly early enough to have been from her mother. When her father passed in 1900 and her stepmother took sole control of the family's affairs, Hester moved to Mineral Wells, Texas to care for additional family members who had tuberculosis. It was here that she would meet and marry Doctor Isaac Mordecai Howard in 1904, who was enrolled at the Gate City Medical School in Texarkana. Texas, the first state to establish a board of medical examiners, would soon impose more stringent licensing requirements, and Isaac, who previously may have fallen victim to a medical "diploma mill" (a fly-by-night organization, quite common, that offered limited training and quickly awarded diplomas,) wanted to assure the validity of his medical career.

One of the ironies that wore on Hester was that she had spent the last twenty years caring for other people's children, and now that she was married, she feared her health would not be sufficient to have a child of her own. Childbirthing mortality was so high on the frontier that women were known to have made their own shrouds along with their layettes. And the drain that a woman with tuberculosis would suffer during childbirth would greatly compound the risk (in 1900 tuberculosis was second only to pneumonia as a major cause of death.). It was not even clear that Hester would be able to become pregnant. Knowing this, Isaac was in the process of appealing to his brother David, who would sire twelve children, to allow the Howards to adopt his most recent son Wallace. It was during these negotiations that Hester discovered she was pregnant.

This, she likely felt, would be her one chance to bestow upon a child of her flesh and blood all the kindness and love and attention that she herself had longed for as a youth. The prospect filled her heart with hope and happiness, but reality tempered it with fear and concern, and Hester was known to accompany Isaac everywhere, somewhere in her mind always grateful to be in the presence of a doctor. She was determined that her baby would be afforded every possible advantage. Neighbor and friend Kate Merryman related a story which exemplifies her commitment to her son: As an infant Robert had a bout of illness and he would cry continuously unless Hester sat beside his crib and rocked his bed. When Hester reached the point where she was too tired to push down on the mattress any longer, she got on the floor, lay under the mattress, and pushed up from below.

Their home in Dark Valley had two rooms, no plumbing, no electricity; only kerosene lamps and creek water (when the creek actually had water in it.) Just doing the laundry in the winter was enough to exhaust a healthy man, but Hester managed, and gave her every effort toward the unfailing nurturing of Robert. And during such times as his mother felt sad and even despondent over the hardships of life, Robert was there to see it. When he was eighteen months old Hester had a miscarriage, which threw her into a funk. He may not have been able to understand it, but he was able to absorb it. His mother's times of sorrow, hardship and reflection (again the term despondency has been used) would be impressed upon Howard to the point of him later attributing the melancholy to Dark Valley itself, a case of psychological transference. Howard related to Lovecraft in a February, 1931 letter that his inmost being had absorbed some of the valley's darkness during his infancy there. He described the enclosing cliffs, the shadows of the tall oaks, and the brooding silence. The real Dark Valley is but a shallow canyon where the hills are low. The darkness and the brooding came from somewhere else.

Chapter Four:
Confounded by the Crowd

The miscarriage confirmed Robert as Hester's one and only chance to shape and mold a child, and she became even more protective of him. Mark Finn said of this time in his biography *Blood & Thunder*: "Robert wanted to belong, to fit in, but that meant playing and roughhousing, and his mother wouldn't let him do that." To couple with this is de Camp's statement, "By protecting Robert from the rack of this uncaring world, his parents denied him the opportunity to achieve maturity." Finn's take on Dark Valley is essentially de Camp's take on Dark Valley. Compare the following two statements, first from the de Camp book: "Years later as an adult Robert Howard realized that his troubled spirit had its roots far back in the earliest experiences of his infancy. He was probably describing his reaction to his mother's despondency; but, being unaware of the source of the malaise, he projected his somber feelings on the landscape of Dark Valley." Twenty-three years after de Camp wrote this Finn wrote, "Dark Valley, as recorded in poetry and related in Robert's letters to Lovecraft, is Hester's depression, not Robert's." He seemed to think it was original, as he implied with his "cribbing ideas" statement in his aforementioned review of a previous draft of this book in *The Cimmerian*. Finn insinuated that I was "cribbing [his] ideas" about Dark Valley when, in Finn's elected vernacular, we both were cribbing de Camp's.

Howard told Lovecraft in December of 1930, "The shimmer and the filth were lacking in the old days, when men and women were more or less clean lived and primitively hardy... As for myself, neither idealism nor materialism appeals to me greatly. That life is chaotic, unjust and apparently blind and without reason or direction, anyone can see; if the universe leans either way it is toward evil rather than good, as regards life and humanity. That there is an eventual goal for the human race rather than extinction, I do not believe nor do I have any faith in the eventual superman. Civilization, no doubt, requires it, and peace of mind demands it, yet for myself I had rather be dead than to live in an emotionless world. The clear white lamp of science and the passionless pursuit of knowledge are not enough for me; I must live deeply and listen to the call of the common clay in me, if I am to live at all."

To live deeply in the oil boom and bust central Texas of the Twenties and Thirties would have brought Howard into contact with a changing panoply of characters which exposed some of the baser elements in human nature. He related to Lovecraft circa June 1931, "One of the cleanest stab-wounds I ever saw was in the body of a young cowpuncher who'd had a row with another cattleman. A long-bladed stockman's knife had been driven nearly to the hilt between the sixth and seventh ribs and left sticking in the wound. The victim had removed it himself, drawing it straight out. Had the wielder twisted it, it would have made a nasty wound. As it was, though dangerously near the vitals, the young fellow recovered quickly, and lived to be shot down by Mexican bandits south of the border.

"Another friend of mine got one of those long stockman's knives rammed into him—the blade went in under the collarbone and went nearly through him, just missing the arch of the aorta. Such power had the wielder of the knife put behind the blade, the sheer force of the blow knocked the victim out. He recovered after quite a long period, during which he imagined in his delirium that he had slain his foe and had his severed head under the bed to gloat over. Thinking perhaps that the victim might seek to put his dream into reality, the man who had stabbed him carried an automatic shotgun for years. He put it aside at last, and not many weeks ago his eldest son put it into play again—it figured prominently in an informal shotgun duel in which its wielder came out victorious, though he failed to finish his man."

Lest anyone wonder how a writer, even in such a place, would have opportunity to learn of and sometimes witness so many bloody events, Howard tells his *Weird* Tales editor Farnsworth Wright in a letter from the summer of 1931, "My boyhood was spent in the oil country—or rather oil came into the country when I was still a young boy, and remained. I'll say one thing about an oil boom; it will teach a kid that Life's a pretty rotten thing about as quickly as anything I can think of. I've worked several jobs, but wasn't a success at any of them; I've picked cotton, helped brand a few yearlings, hauled a little garbage, worked in a grocery store, ditto a dry-goods store, worked in a law office, jerked soda, worked up in a gas office, tried to be a public stenographer, packed a surveyor's rod, worked up oil field news for some Texas and Oklahoma papers, etc., etc., and also etc… Life's not worth living if somebody thinks he's in authority over you… Every now and then one of us finds the going too hard and blows his brains out, but it's all in the game, I reckon."

All of Howard's various jobs—some brief, other briefer—likely lent some remote aspect of themselves to his vivid imagination. At one point in the early 1920s Howard became keenly interested in the idea of having a career in music. He wrote to Wilford Blanch Talman circa September, 1931: "I graduated from high school at the age of seventeen and went to work in a tailor-shop—I was a solicitor—in other words I went out and euchered the customers into patronizing the shop, brought the clothes to the shop, cleaned them and delivered them—for which I got a third of the entire proceeds. Wearying of this I dallied—at the age of eighteen—with thoughts of a musical career and started taking violin lessons from a wandering old fiddler who'd gone on the rocks because of drink. But he took up with a wandering minstrel show and skipped the country, so I started taking lessons from an old Scotchman who led the local band. I took one lesson and then the Scotchman came to a sudden and violent end. I then made arrangements to continue my lessons with a German but before I could begin, he jumped town just ahead of the law, leaving a trail of deft swindles behind him." Howard inevitably took these instances as a bad sign for his potential musical career. Moreover, it likely exasperated him that he would need to be dependent on a teacher in any form. It wasn't very much in his nature to be the pupil.

Howard asked Lovecraft in September 1932, "Are the obligations of a laboring man to society different from those of the rich and powerful? If our laws are so blindly just, why do the wealthy seldom ever suffer by their enforcement? … Legislate—legislate—but what good will that do when the people are betrayed by everybody they put in office? … Now days if a man's hungry, he's a Red; if he wants a job, he's a Red; if he asserts his right to live, he's a Red; and should be clubbed on the head and dragged out as an enemy to organized society." The extensive examples and historic names Howard gave required a full eighteen footnotes of explanation for just three pages of writing in this section of the letter. From citing well-known cases such as the kidnapping and murder of the Lindbergh baby (more on this in Chapter Eleven as it possibly pertains to a dream Howard had) and the demise of Al Capone, to rarer historical gems such as disgraced Secretary of the Interior Albert Bacon Fall and the outlaw Micajah "Big" Harpe. Howard speculates, "…if revolution ever rises in America, the Southwest is the very last place where it will blaze up. The people of this section, especially the country people, are so inured to suffering and hardship that it would take a veritable cataclysm to cause them to rise. Their capacity for enduring hardship is incredible—more, it is appalling, because it only shows what their lives have been for generations." As an example of exploitation Howard states, "Gas produced almost in our backyards costs us $.75 a thousand, while that same gas is piped through a gigantic pipe-line to Chicago, there to be sold to the citizens at $.19 a thousand."

Many of Howard's extraordinary viewpoints were made the more so by the very environs to which he occasionally alludes.

The dying frontier and fading legends of the Old West, though often thought subdued by modernization, still had the ability to collide like a low pressure weather system with the high-pressured system of the oil business and its all too necessary evils. The kind of freedom Howard truly wanted was fading more as each rig was erected, each small town turned into a hectic way station for rowdy opportunists. Howard began to look upon himself as merely a minor writer, hacking and grinding his way through a cold, fickle, inscrutable literary world. His inner mind yearned for the careless release of duties and burdens, and he longed for the simple glory within athletic performance. He tells Lovecraft circa November 1932, "I, myself, was intended by Nature to be an athlete. If events had flowed smoothly and evenly from the time I first entered school, I would at this instant be engaged in some sort of professional athletics, rather than struggling at a profession for which I am not fitted. The chain of circumstances which altered the course of my life is too lengthy and involved to impose upon you. But I will say that I extremely regret those circumstances, and had rather have been a successful professional athlete than the very minor writer I have become—in honesty I will go further and say that I had rather have been a successful professional athlete than to be a great writer… The fact is that I believe I would have gotten more content out of an athletic career than I have out of this bitter grind, which I took up simply because it seemed to offer more freedom than anything else in the way of a job."

This outlook, if Howard maintained it, offers a glimpse into what may have led him to discount his career in his 1936 decision on suicide. This is not to say that Howard derived no pleasure out of life. In the same letter to Lovecraft he relates of his varied gastrointestinal proclivities: "Too bad New Orleans is going so modern. I'm glad I saw it before the vandalism had gotten completely under way. I was interested in your remarks concerning French food. I've encountered the 'poor boy sandwich' phenomenon in Galveston and similar places. I think if I were in the restaurant business I'd exploit a 'pauper's sandwich' which is going to be a necessity if things get any lousier. Too bad seafood disagrees with you. Now with me, as with many inland dwellers, it constitutes a rare delicacy. And the word 'rare' is quite descriptive. Oysters are about the only sort of sea-food which finds its way this far up-country.

"When I get in a sea-port town, I revel in oysters, shrimps, crabs, sea-fish, and the like, to my heart's content... I'm a big eater and I get a real kick out of gorging. Any kind of meat—fish, fowl, beef, turtle, pork; practically any kind of fruit; I'm not much of a vegetarian. Milk—I see people coaxing children to drink milk, and I can't understand their dislike for it. I always drank it in huge quantities, and believe it's one reason I was always so healthy. Cheese—give me limburger cheese, German sausage and beer and I'm content—yes, and a bit of what they call 'smear cake'—a rather unsavory name, for what we call cottage or cream cheese. Mexican dishes I enjoy, but they don't agree with me much. However I generally wrestle with them every time I go to the Border. Tamales, enchilados, tacos, chili con carne to a lesser extent, barbecued goat-meat, tortillas, Spanish-cooked rice, frijoles—they play the devil with a white man's digestion, but they have a tang you seldom find in Anglo-Saxon cookery... The last time I was on the Border I discovered one Pablo Ranes whose dishes smoked with the concentrated essence of hell-fire. I returned to his abode of digestional damnation until my once powerful constitution was but a shell of itself. I aided Pablo's atrocities with some wine bottled in Spain that kicked like an army mule, and eventually came to the conclusion that the Border is a place only for men with cast-iron consciences and copper bellies."

Howard also retained many scattered fragments of traditional American folk songs, many now long lost, which he had heard the old-timers sing in his travels as a child. His memory was such that he could go to a library, select a mound of books, quickly scan each, and then quote whole passages from them. He worked with the head of the Library of Congress folk song archive, Robert Winslow Gordon, to preserve the song "Sanford Burns," and his correspondence reveals fragments of many other folk songs about heroes, soldiers, presidents, cowboy laments, and even one about Lake Pontchartrain:

> '*Twas one bright March morning, I bid New Orleans adieu,*
> *And on my way back to Jackson, where I was forced to go,*
> *'Twas there my Georgia money no credit did me gain,*
> *And it filled my heart with sadness on the lakes of the Pontchartrain.*
>
> *Through swamps and alligators, I wound my weary way,*
> *O'er railroad ties and crossings, my weary feet did stray,*
> *Till the shadows of the evening, some higher ground did gain,*
> *Twas there that I met this Creole, on the lakes of the Pontchartrain.*
>
> *"Good evening, fair young maiden, my money to me is no good;*
> *If it wasn't for the alligators, I'd sleep out in the wood."*
> *"Oh, welcome, welcome, stranger, for though our home be plain,*
> *We never turn away a traveler from the lakes of the Pontchartrain."*

"Slavery is far from being extinct in this country today," wrote Howard, "though of course its present form has nothing to do with whole-sale enslavement... But if peonage, where a man gets a Mexican, a Negro, or even a white man, in debt to him, and keeps him toiling for years to pay out that debt, isn't slavery, then I don't know what is...such things do exist, and are no credit to our boasted civilization."

Howard often felt a keen sense of injustice when he closely examined many parts of his world. Local and regional law enforcement was one of his particular gripes. He tells Lovecraft, "Let me say one of my kicks at law-enforcement is the difficulty to convict an officer of the law for any thing he may do. Let me quote a case in point. In a certain town where I happened to be staying, an officer had trouble with a certain private citizen. There was no question of law enforcement. It was a private matter, involving family affairs. According to general opinion, the citizen was in the right of it. The officer came up to him suddenly on the street one day and shot him down without a word. I did not see the affair, but my room-mate did, and he said it was cold-blooded murder; he said the officer approached his victim without a word and suddenly drew and dropped him without warning. The murdered man was unarmed; he made no threatening move of any kind. The officer later said the man had threatened his life; I don't believe that. I was well acquainted with the murdered man and a more harmless, inoffensive mortal never lived."

Partially as a result of this and many other examples, reinforced throughout his formative years by classic tales of the Old West, and partially due to his natural inclination to prefer the plight of the outsiders (whether they be rebels or barbarians,) Howard was a sometimes admirer of outlaws such as John Wesley Hardin. To say that the outlaw typifies how Howard viewed himself within the literary world may be a bit too glib, but few reasonable observers could deny the veins of similarity. He related to Lovecraft, "There was one man prison could not break. I make bold to say no prison-system in the United States, or anywhere else could have broken him, for in those days Texas prisons were hell on earth. John Wesley Hardin. He was a bloodthirsty killer, a murderer—what you will. Yet I respect him more than I respect some of the men that hunted him. He did his own killing. For only one of these killings was he tried—that of Deputy Sheriff Webb. I have little sympathy for Webb. He met Hardin in a social way, and sought to take advantage of him, for the sake of the reward. The sheriff of another county than Webb's, a friend of Hardin, introduced the men in a saloon. Webb went for his gun and dropped with Hardin's bullet through him.... Hardin drew twenty-five years in the penitentiary. But he refused to work. He wasn't lazy. He'd done harder work rustling cattle and hazing them up the trails than any of the prison guards had ever dreamed of. But he was unconquerable. They could rob him of his liberty. They couldn't make a slave of him. And they didn't. It was because of no softness or sentimentality they failed. All that they could do, they did. They beat him in a manner that would have killed a lesser man. They hanged him by his thumbs. They starved him. They threw him into a dark cell to rot on moldy bread and stale water. A softer man would have died or given in. Not John Wesley Hardin… Finally they put him in a vat, where he had to pump water or drown. He didn't touch the pump. The water rose over his head and the prison officials lost their nerve."

Such fantastic trials and feats of sheer will and endurance would well set the stage for many of Howard's Conan tales, including one in which the barbarian survives crucifixion. But in a deeper sense, the qualities which Howard most admired about Hardin were qualities which Howard himself possessed and wished to strengthen, just as he had built his body to a point where no man looked easily upon picking a quarrel with him. There was the time Howard and his parents were entering a restaurant or boarding house for a meal, and a seated man was blocking their path to an available spot. After politely asking the man to move twice and getting no acknowledgement, Howard picked the chair up with the man still sitting in it, moved it aside and dumped the man onto the floor. Then he solemnly waved his parents through. But to possess the greater strength was not equal to having attained the superior will. In his amateur boxing endeavors Howard refused to go down, just like the fabled Iron Men of which he wrote. But to himself he may have wondered if he had truly achieved the same level of mental indomitability that he attributed to Hardin. It was one thing to be strong, stubborn and hardy, and quite another to be indomitable.

He still worried about his heart, and had even taken digitalis after his earlier car accident. Somewhere in the more guarded parts of his consciousness Howard may have known that his love of his mother was his Achilles heel, and it would forever stand as a barrier between the reality of his actions and the potential of his spirit. Love separated him from John Wesley Hardin. Even if he were more inclined to the dangerous life and inscrutable moral code of Hardin, Howard would have reasoned that he could not care for his mother from behind prison bars. If he were more inclined to the way of the naturalist and traveler such as John Muir, Howard would have known that such travel would place his mother in physical and emotional peril. He knew that Hester Howard had invested all she had in him, and he was compelled to repay the debt, out of a deep and wordless love and dependency which all of his characters and heroes would never know.

It would have been easier if Howard had not been such a thin and rather sickly child, bound to suffer the malicious jabs of his peers. But in some accounts he is portrayed as not being this way (childhood friend Earl Baker of Burkett reported Howard "was comparatively big and strong for his age,") so it is with caution that we should wholly believe some of de Camp's admitted speculation on Howard's childhood. It is more solidly believed (as told by Kate Merryman) that Howard may have been unwell between the ages of one and two. *Dark Valley Destiny* extrapolates liberally: "Frail, introverted, and looking to his mother for protection, Robert was a natural butt for bullies... He could not leave his yard for fear of being set upon." He did not enter the first grade until he was eight, and it is strongly suspected he had suffered childhood tuberculosis, which differs from the adult disease as it is more likely to attack the bones and joints. It was often misdiagnosed as rheumatic fever.

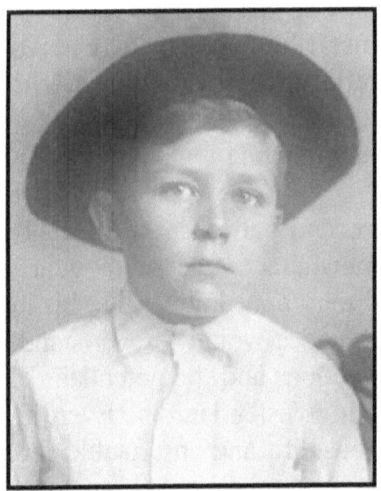
REH approx. age 5

REH approx. age 8 or 9

A surviving photo from when Howard was eight shows a thin, troubled looking child, barefoot and a little dirty, standing outside in front of some tall greenery, dressed as an Indian (Howard had an uncle by marriage on his mother's side who was a Native American.) The photo stands in stark contrast to the studio portrait of a somewhat plump-faced and healthy-looking Howard at the age of five. Howard scholar Rusty Burke suggests in *The Iron Harp*, "Is it possible this boy has recently had a bit of a growth spurt and hasn't filled out yet?" His sickly period, if it can be called that, would ultimately serve to greatly increase his dependence on his mother, and Hester enjoyed reading poetry to him during their time together. Howard was able to read before he entered the first grade, but in the rural Texas of that time, such intellectual ability was usually met with scorn and contempt by other children, and often their weapons of choice when faced with such disconcerting abilities were the easy and plentiful weapons of rocks and manure.

The enemies to which Howard would later refer (and arm himself against) may have been an adult continuation of the attitudes his peers exhibited toward him as a child. A man who could make his living by writing fanciful tales in the middle of a hard-working, scantily educated labor town would naturally be bound to garner suspicion and even contempt from certain individuals of the populace who, for lack of a better term, may justly be dubbed as ignorant. Hazing rituals among local children of the time included ganging up on the child considered to be smart or awkward or shy or weak (Howard at the time might have qualified for all of these, depending on which accounts you believe) and putting them head-first into the business end of an outhouse, as reported by Larry McMurtry from Archer County, although again the documentation of this in *Dark Valley Destiny* has been criticized as attempting to suggest this particular indignation happened to Howard specifically. The parallel drawn is Howard's incorporation of such treatment into his Conan tale *Rogues in the House*:

> "His captive whimpered and twisted, renewing her importunities. Conan glanced down into the muck and slime of the alleys below...then he dropped her with great accuracy into a cesspool. He enjoyed her kickings and flounderings and the concentrated

venom of her profanity for a few seconds, and even allowed himself a low rumble of laughter."

It was Robert's father who did him a great service by introducing him to the more well-mannered children of some of his patients and colleagues, and once these children got to know Howard, they appreciated his imagination and enthusiasm for creative play. He would often assign characters and roles for elaborate outdoor adventures, and early during the First World War young Howard decided he was completely for the Allies, and would thereafter refuse to pretend to be a German soldier when at play with his friends. His stubbornness would be both his strength and his downfall in his later interpersonal dealings with relative outsiders such as Novalyne Price, for Howard tended to equate compromise with loss of freedom. Even in the case of his first accepted story by *Weird Tales*, "Wolfshead," Howard became depressed when he got the galleys and saw the inevitable editorial corrections (and errors) which so many underpaid underlings tend to emit like an acrid haze, proffered to their boss as evidence that their small salaries are justified and their low places on the totem pole of literature regrettably secure. Even the artist assigned to do the image for Wolfshead mishandled the manuscript, and Farnsworth Wright wrote Howard on January 20, 1926: "I hope you have a carbon copy of WOLFSHEAD. If so, will you please forward it to me at one by special delivery? ...so far the artist has not sent me the manuscript...I wired him to rush the manuscript to me...I cannot possibly substitute another story for it now...I do not know that he has lost it, but it should have been in my hands last week...I will be grateful if you will rush the carbon copy to me..."

Howard did not possess a carbon copy. He responded on January 23rd (the day after his twentieth birthday) saying, "I have no carbon copy of 'Wolfshead.' I wrote this story while engaged upon a longer one, which I have not yet submitted to you, and I failed to make an extra copy. I certainly hope that the mss. is not lost, but am today beginning to re-write it from memory. Kindly let me know whether the story is lost, immediately upon receiving this letter. If necessary, I can mail you the re-written ms. within twelve hours from the time I hear from you." Many biographers have chosen to use the *Post Oaks* story version of Howard's reply to Wright, which was that the carbon copy of *Wolf Skull* was incomplete but that 'Steve Costigan' would complete it and forward it to *Bizarre Stories* (this biographer almost used this account until a reprinted copy of Howard's actual reply was located, right in the back of the first edition *Post Oaks* hardcover published by Donald M. Grant in 1990.) In any case, Howard would work through the night to complete the rewrite, only to receive another message from Wright saying the manuscript had been found, all except for the first page, which they would substitute with Howard's resubmitted work. The young author may have wondered if this sort of thing was going to happen with every story of his which got accepted, and he soon took a job at the Cross Plains Drug Store, working slavishly from about nine-thirty in the morning until one or two in the morning, serving ice cream, mixing syrups, selling medicine, and jerking soda. The manager was known to avoid the rowdy night crowd and leave Howard there alone to fend for himself. Then the manager would complain that Howard was too generous with his portion sizes in his absence. The rough and tumble oil rig workers which the establishment attracted like a beacon at night were both needed customers and troublesome pariahs. Many were the times Howard had to restrain his temper with both the manager and the customers, and eventually the stress and long hours wore on his health and dropped his weight.

In *Post Oaks and Sand Roughs* Howard recounts one particular drugstore episode where a local heavyweight prize fighter has just tucked a magazine under his shirt...

> "Steve thought weakly—let the fellow go—no use to be beaten up over a magazine which was, after all, somebody else's. If Gus didn't have the guts to stay and watch his own stuff...Suddenly Steve realized that his reasonings were false and dastardly. The magazine did not matter—it was only a symbol. What did matter was

that his self-respect was at stake."

Howard recounts how he held an ice pick in his right hand concealed under a towel, being at the ready to kill the would-be thief. He asks the much larger man, "Are you pregnant?" and he is able to diffuse the situation, but "He had been keyed up for murder, swift and without warning…it left him with the firm conviction that if he worked very much longer at this hellish job, he would, in a moment of semi-insanity, either kill or be killed." This kind of social tension never seemed to flow far from the surface of Howard's thoughts while he was in public situations. Years later when he was invited as a party guest to the home of Lexie Dean Robertson, a regional poet of some renown, Howard reported that he "was confounded by the crowd of strangers" and moped through the entire event and either spoke with only one word or a grunt when spoken to. Sociability while in the midst of an unfamiliar group eluded Howard as it does so many, even though Harold Preece said of Howard's one-time hostess in a January, 1965 letter to Lenore Preece, "…I regarded Lexie as a nice, big fat gal with cultural interests rather than as a poet. Yet, who couldn't help but liker her?" The scene that night at the Robertson house can almost be pictured in the mind's eye.

It is interesting to note that Robertson's 1928 book of verse is titled *Red Heels*, and both she and Howard wrote a similarly themed and metered version of *Recompense* (found at the beginning of the first chapter is Howard's version, and below is Lexie's.) Howard scholar Rusty Burke asks in *The Iron Harp* (vol. 2, no. 2) "So, I wonder—is it possible Bob's poem might have been written as a sort of response to Lexie Dean's?" Also interesting is the similarity of title between *Red Heels* and Howard's Conan tale *Red Nails*, which first appeared in *Weird Tales* in July, 1936.

Recompense
by Lexie Dean Robertson

I have not known the sweep of far blue seas
Where silver gulls lift wings to blown salt spray,
And suns come crashing through the long grey curve
Of rosy mist that marks the edge of day;
But I have known a sea of rippled green
Where wheatfields stretch beyond earth's limpid hem,
And I have seen its hot waves kissed to bronze
By winds that whispered undulant through them.

I have not seen the dawn from thin high peaks
Where mountain fingers clutch at heaven's blue,
And frail cloud vapors spread a chiffoned veil
To make a cruel beauty softly true;
But I have seen a quiet brown-fringed pool
Where redbirds stop to drink as they flash by,
And leaning there I've felt my heart lift up,
For its smooth mirrored depths reflect the sky.

I have not flung afar some flaming torch
To kindle valor in the hearts of men,
Or blaze a way of splendor to the goal
Where shackles loose and freedom's paths begin;
But I have made my cottage hearthfire glow
To warm a dreary heart grown sad and chill,
And I have left it burning through dark nights,
And I have lit a candle on my sill.

I have not merited the world's acclaim
Here in my little house close by the sod,
But I have walked through open doors to love,
And I, on bended knees, have talked with God.

Chapter Five:
Yellowed Leaves

As a young man of about twenty Howard did make one bold attempt to break away from his parents. While staying at a rooming house in Brownwood while he completed bookkeeping courses at Howard Payne College (the same rooming house where, earlier mentioned, he had sleepwalked straight out of a first floor window,) the family proprietors of the house, the Powells, saw their young daughter come down with a particularly virulent case of the measles, which was sweeping through Brownwood in epidemic proportions. The little girl died, and when Howard's parents heard of this they rushed down to Brownwood to remove their son (who had never had the measles) from the infected household…but Howard did not wish to leave. When his parents insisted and emphasized the risk, Howard stubbornly marched into the bathroom that was used by the little girl and drank out of her glass. Then he buried his face in her towel and rubbed it around. This, he hoped, would force his parents to leave him quarantined in the house of the Powells, or at least in Brownwood.

It did not.

His father would still have been an imposing figure at that time, taller than Howard and possessing the piercing ice blue eyes which Howard later lent to his notable Cimmerian. Together his parents prevailed and took him back home, where he quickly came down with an acute and intense case of the measles, causing him to be confined for two months and effectively ending what was likely his strongest attempt at rebellion. In fact, during this time Howard would have been severely dependent upon the care provided by his parents. Moreover, upon his recovery he learned that the college bursar's office refused to refund his fall tuition or even to credit it against a second term, and he would need to start the course over again from scratch.

Perhaps the greatest benefit during this period was the steady publication of Howard's regular contributions to the college student paper, *The Yellow Jacket*. Here he could transform what he later described to Lovecraft as the "fierce melancholy" which sometimes overwhelmed his personality into short stories which were full of humor and slapstick. From *Dark Valley Destiny*: "In the issue for January 13, 1927, ran *The Thessalians*, a short skit about [stage manager Hipurbilee Jones and] the havoc wrought during a play by [a thrown cat, a boneheaded stagehand, a hornet, and a skunk.] *Cupid vs. Pollux*, which appeared on February 10, tells of a boxing match in college between 'Steve' and 'Spike,' the names Robert gave himself and Lindsey Tyson in *Post Oaks*. [Tyson, perhaps the most intriguing and certainly the longest of Howard's local friends, will be discussed later.] There were other contributions, too, among them *Ye College Days*, an amusing satire on a college football game." Howard would refer to attending the college's football games in *Post Oaks*, changing the college name of Howard Payne to "Gower-Penn."

The amount of local activities in Cross Plains would not have held a candle to Brownwood, but the third Monday of every month was known as "Trade Monday" or "Horse Monday" in the Cross Plains of old. As Howard explains to Lovecraft circa June 1931, "On that day the streets and alleys were full of men swapping horses and mules. For three or four days before 'trade's day' the roving brotherhood would begin to arrive—the people who went about making their living by horse trading. They were generally a seedy and disreputable lot, who moved about in wagons, with a string of lean, mangy cayuses, lived from hand to mouth and camped wherever night found them. Trade's Day would find them camped at the edge of town, sometimes a dozen families together, and they would plunge into the business at hand. Farmers would come to town with equally worthless nags and the noise of arguments, assertations and refutations must at times have equaled the clamor in an Oriental bazaar. How anybody ever made anything out of most of those swaps is more than I can see. It always looked to me as if both parties got gypped."

Trade Monday in San Augustine, 1943. Waiting for the opening of the cattle auction.
Library of Congress, Prints & Photographs Division, FSA-OWI Collection

Some of the rowdy and nomadic peoples which populate the fringes of a small portion of Howard's tales may have been loosely based upon the horse traders and their kin. He continues to Lovecraft, "The wandering horse-traders were more or less a nuisance; they were thievish, quarrelsome—though not particularly courageous—and the men would invariably get drunk and beat their wives so the women would howl until it was a scandal to hear. After Prohibition came in their favorite drink was fruit extracts, and the amount they imbibed was a caution to behold. I used to work in a grocery store and the amount of lemon extract, etc. I've known some of them to buy in one day would startle me. I particularly remember a couple who were generally together most of the time: a big red-whiskered brute and a horrible hunchback, a stunted monstrous giant of the most sinister aspect I ever saw in any man. He seldom talked, and I never heard him speak above a menacing whisper. Generally Red-whiskers did all the talking for the pair, prompted by the hunchback's uncanny whispers."

One can only speculate if this "couple" to which Howard refers were related by blood or perhaps even a bond of taboo love, as the state of being a hunchback leaves one moreso at the mercy of affections which the times deemed unnatural. At any rate, the monthly visitations of such folk as Howard describes would have been a potential, if not subliminal, source of inspiration for minor characters and general atmosphere in tales of far-off adventure. The famous lesbian scene in Howard's novel "Red Nails" may have, in addition to the Sapphic influences sometimes found in the racier pulps of the time, drawn upon inferences from the lives of the wandering horse traders. The strong parallel of one woman cruelly whipping another in "Red Nails" ("...the whistle and crack of hard-woven silken cords on naked flesh...her body writhed and quivered...") and Howard's firsthand account of a horse trader whipping his young son is striking: "I remember once I heard a most outrageous outbreak of noise and clamor—howls, blows, bellowings and the drum of flying hoofs—and saw Red-whiskers careering down the street in high state. He was lying hog-drunk in the bed of a wagon, roaring at the top of his voice and slashing his son—a kid of ten or twelve—with a rolled-up slicker. The kid was screaming at the top of his voice, standing upright and pouring leather into the mules. The old man was beating the boy, the boy was beating the mules, and the mules were at a dead run. Why the wagon didn't come to pieces, I don't know, for it was just hitting the high spots."

The type of liquor being imbibed during Prohibition, as a general rule, steadily decreased in quality and even safety. "When I used to work in a law office I saw a good deal of good whiskey," Howard relates to Lovecraft, "but for the past few years it's been getting rottener and rottener until it's risky to even smell a cork. The stuff don't make men drunk; it maddens them." This is another factor to consider when weighing the atmosphere in which Howard lived. With virtually no consumer protection laws, persons desperate for alcohol during prohibition were known to drink almost anything that smelled strong or had similar chemical properties as alcohol, and the maddening which Howard describes may have been poisoning in many cases. Add to the mixture that nearly every household had at least one unlocked gun, and it is ironic for the modern observer to conclude the "Old West" was still somehow alive at that time, when Howard was too close to the shadow of the real thing to realize it, no matter how desperately he longed for it.

"What I want is impossible, as I've told you before," he wrote to Lovecraft circa May/June 1933. "I want, in a word, the frontier—which is compassed in the phrase, new land, open land, free land—land rich and unbroken and virgin, swarming with game and laden with fresh forests and sweet cold streams, where a man could live by the sweat of his hands unharried by taxes, crowds, noise, unemployment, bank-failures, gang-extortions, laws, and all the other wearisome things of civilization." This longstanding dream of Howard's is one that most every person can relate to; the unspoiled land, full of promise, hearty trials and rewards. If he could he would have escaped to this place, to live a lusty life and write ten thousand tales deep within the uninterrupted wilderness. He continued, "Failing in that, I want as much personal freedom as is possible under this system, and if I can't have at least as much as I have now, I don't want to live at all."

I cannot believe in a paradise
Glorious, undefiled,
For gates all scrolled and streets of gold
Are tales for a dreaming child.

I am too lost for shame
That it moves me unto mirth,

> *But I can vision a Hell of flame*
> *For I have lived on earth.*
>
> –*Visions*, REH

"What constitutes human suffering?" he asked Lovecraft. "The German barbarians had their feuds and tribal wars; we have strikes, child labor, sweat shops, unemployment, gang-rule. And I doubt if a larger number of Germans were bumped off in tribal wars than are smashed up by autos and machinery in civilization. It strikes me as rather extreme to judge the people of a former epoch by the standards of this, and conclude that all were miserable and wretched... You said war is merely a hangover from barbarism. According to that, modern wars are planned and instigated by those among us who are least civilized, according to the intellectual standard. Yet I hardly think that the facts would prove that our wars are caused by day-laborers, cowboys, prize fighters, soda-jerkers, farmers, and other despised types. As near as I can figure it out, they are planned and started and carried out by the men who represent the very highest type of civilization—statesmen, politicians, kings, lords of finance, and diplomats. If it is absurd, as you say, to attribute war to civilization, it seems to me that it is no less absurd to blame all the defects of this system on the survivals of barbarism. If our present civilization is possessed of so many virtues, why all this unrest and turmoil? Why isn't everybody happy? Why are we some twelve million people out of work and on the verge of starvation?"

A picture begins to develop of the many factors along the periphery of Howard's short life, and the ifs begin to compound as we ponder his early exit from this world. If any one major factor had been changed, would we now be privy to the full breadth of the work which Howard would likely have continued? If Novalyne had stayed and acquiesced to Howard's idea of a wife, if the Great Depression had not struck his soul with such profundity, if he had made a successful break during his college days in Brownwood, if Weird Tales had paid him the massive amount of money it owed for publishing his stories (more on this later,) if the illness which gripped his mother were less severe... Would any one of these things, if changed, equate to a full life for Howard, or was it the very nature of his character to fear the decline of his strength and faculties which older age would entail? He told August Derleth shortly before his suicide, "I don't want to live to be old. I want to die when my time comes, quickly and suddenly, in the full tide of my strength and health."

Of course, every day before his very eyes was proof of the cruelty the advancing years and decline of health could have on a person, and as Howard and his father increasingly performed the various and time-consuming ministrations which his ailing mother required, there was no cleaner wedge to drive between Howard and his full potential. Perhaps he envisioned himself in a similarly enfeebled state, except with no children or spouse to provide love and care. Perhaps he ultimately saw some feared hereditary condition prevail over his very ability to create. Would he have pulled that trigger if he had known the tales he so often discounted would ultimately be acknowledged as the birth of a new and much loved sub-genre of literature?

It seems probably so.

The brooding which gripped Howard was not only artistic melancholy, but somehow it was connected to the very formation of his thought patterns. Friends who knew him best, such as Truett Vinson and Tevis Clyde Smith, were well aware that the counterpart to Howard's warm, articulate and creative side was an aloof, flighty and dark side whose appearance could never quite be predicted. There is the story of the bus trip to San Antonio Howard took with Vinson just after graduating from Howard Payne. Forgetting to bring his pocket knife put Howard in an uncomfortable mood, and although he quickly purchased a replacement before the train left the station, he spent nearly all of the 192 mile journey stropping the knife against his left shoe and talking with the bus driver instead of his friend.

In possible explanation of a situation such as this Howard later told Lovecraft that after he had spoken with a noted poet, he "found relief and pleasure in exchanging reminiscences with a bus driver who didn't know a sonnet from an axle hub." But for a man such as Howard things like relief and pleasure were fleeting. In November of 1930 he would confide to friend Harold Preece, "I am haunted by the realization that my best days, mental and physical, lie behind me. And God knows my past life has not been so happy that I can look upon the future with any hope. A small thing, trivial in itself but significant—I put on the gloves the other day for the first time in months, and, for the first time in my life, found myself staggering and holding on to avoid being knocked out, and unable to inflict any punishment on my opponent. My legs never failed me before, but this time—well, I've slipped a long way, in every way. I'm just a shell of a man."

Slow shift the sands of Time; the yellowed leaves
Go drifting down an old and bitter wind;
Across the frozen moors the hedges stand
In tattered garments that the frost have thinned.

A thousand phantoms pluck my ragged sleeve,
Wan ghosts of souls into darkness thrust.
Their pale lips tell lost dreams I thought mine own,
And old sick longings smite my heart to dust.

I may not even dream of jeweled dawns,
Nor sing with lips that have forgot to laugh.
I fling aside the cloak of Youth and limp
A withered man upon a broken staff.

That was the verse he included with the letter.

Much akin to the writing of the nineteenth century French poet Jules Laforgue, Howard often reflected on his youth as a thing which had passed. (Laforgue was an influence on Ezra Pound. Both he and his wife Leah died of tuberculosis.)

When we consider that Howard was only twenty-three years

old when he wrote this, part of us may want to think that time itself somehow flowed differently for the man, but more likely is the reason that his innate sadness was slowly getting the best of him. Many people he went to school with were married with children or living independently, their incomes becoming as stable as the era allowed. While he yielded to the sedentary dictates of his chosen craft, men several years younger than himself were working the oil rigs and developing great physical stamina. While he spent the evening thinking of stories in the back room of his parent's house, others his age were on the town entertaining members of the opposite sex. Howard may not have enjoyed leading quite so exuberant a life as they, but the knowledge that it wasn't even an option for him must have trapped a part of his soul so tightly that it festered into depression. For a man who so cherished freedom, knowing that circumstances beyond his control prevented him from being able to truly become one of the locals for a day, must have struck a deep and grinding blow.

A portion of *Post Oaks* which is quoted from in *Dark Valley Destiny* to describe the inner turmoil of Howard is this: "Bewildered and baffled by life, full of savagery he could not control and knew not where to direct, hurling his ferocity at random against what seemed to him to be obstacles, battered and beaten, never winning, never admitting defeat, doomed to go down that rough road forever." The rest of the scene sees Howard's alter ego Costigan bidding his two local friends adios as he embarks on a bus headed out of Lost Plains. He refuses their charity, saying, "Thanks, but no; be a hell of a note if I started my pilgrimage on borrowed money. I sold my new suit to the second hand clothes man, and I got enough to leave town in style on. Then I don't know and I don't give a damn." And in this we may have a glimpse into Howard's attitude at death, his bravado toward it, not outwardly fearing it but rather looking at it as an opponent with which to spar for a while. Leaving the broken place he knows and dislikes equates to him literally leaving the world. The bus driver serves as Charon the ferryman as the final scene unfolds:

The bus came to a halt, and Steve swaggered to the door. He walked with an arrogant assurance, his cap was drawn low over his eyes; his whole bearing was that of a thug.

He climbed in, spat on the floor, and looked for a seat. The few passengers eyed him askance.

"Kick in with the dough, friend," said the bus driver crisply. "You pay in advance."

"Aw, go to the devil," Steve snarled, sinking into the cushions. "Don't try to run no bluff with me, kid, see? Get goin' before I take the guts outa this can; I pay when we get to where I'm started!"

"And where is that?" asked the amazed bus driver, as he started the bus, and the white road began to spin beneath them, the fence posts to flash by.

"To hell."

If we take what is implied here a step further, we could surmise that Howard, though not religious but perhaps closer to the Methodist faith than any other, is acknowledging that if the hereafter exists, any conventional heaven is not likely to accept souls who have committed suicide. Just prior to his departure in the book he alludes to "breaking rocks" for the rest of his life if that is to be his fate. Breaking rocks, a predominantly pointless task, is often perceived as one of the myriad possible punishments for lost souls in the afterlife, along with such things as digging endless ditches and stoking furnaces. He refuses money from his friends, and not paying the bus driver is, of course, an allusion to the belief that if a soul did not pay Charon the ferryman, they had to wander the desolate banks of the Acheron/River Styx for one hundred years, a task which in essence equates to purgatory. Even the described act of spitting as he enters the bus suggests an expulsion of the obolus (the coin traditionally used to pay Charon,) as this coin was customarily placed under the tongue.

To carry these afterlife/religious symbols into the field of fantasy writing was generally avoided, as Poul Anderson said in his famous 1978 essay *On Thud and Blunder*: "The Church raises the subject of religion in general, which is little used in our field. Oh, yes, we may get a hero swearing by his particular gods and perhaps carrying through a small rite, equivalent to stroking a rabbit's foot. We certainly got plenty of obscene ceremonies in honor of assorted toad-like beings." So for Howard to place some stronger, more obvious mythic suggestion at the end of *Post Oaks* would not have been in keeping with the unfolding of his story. As it is, the end of the book is the part which is least likely to parallel anything that might have happened in Howard's life. He never left Cross Plains for good, never called his boss a "son of a whore" and punched him in the face as he quit his job, but perhaps he *wanted* to do both these things. He may also have wanted to convey something more with the ending of *Post Oaks* than just a bus ride out of town.

While it is debatable that Howard consciously meant to imply these things (he once modestly told Lovecraft that he lacked the guile to use symbolism in his writing,) there are not many other readily available interpretations which aptly fit. Although completed some seven years before his suicide, the ending of *Post Oaks* nonetheless leaves one feeling it was on his mind even then. More recent biographers such as Mark Finn (*Blood & Thunder: The Life and Art of Robert E. Howard*) have shed greater light on the environmental factors present in Texas at that time which influenced the formation of many of Howard's beliefs and opinions. *Blood & Thunder* offers imaginative passages as they might have been seen through Howard's eyes. Although the first four paragraphs of the introduction to the Finn book use the word "Texas" a full twenty times (try reading or writing four short paragraphs that use the same proper noun twenty times and you'll see why this can be off-putting,) the linear breakdown of the chapters in correlation to Howard's life offers straightforward perspective and insight. Ignoring the back cover material, which claims that Howard "lived all of his thirty years in the small town of Cross Plains," the book offers a laudable and solid depiction, presents new outlooks, and is well worth reading.

"As absorbing as Kull's Atlantis and as detailed as Conan's Hyborian Age are for modern readers, the roots of these fantastic places are in Texas," Mark Finn states. "The story of Robert E. Howard is the story of twentieth-century Texas." Now, for some this might be fine, but to suggest that Howard's extensive reading of history and his vivid imagination of distant shores would still cause him to use Texas as the basis for everything from Kull to Conan seems, by and large, a little too neat and tidy.

The Finn book downplays the amount of bullying Howard may have received as a child, as L. Sprague de Camp's passages regarding this issue in *Dark Valley Destiny* suggest. Finn wrote in a Howard forum on November 9, 2006: "The Bully issue was one that I wanted to specifically take away from the de Camp argument. The way that de Camp wrote *DVD*, and using (for example) the Larry McMurtry quotes judiciously out of context, he made it seem as if Howard himself was specifically tormented to the point of madness." In response to this another Howard scholar of note, Rusty Burke, wrote, "'Established fact' is that he SAID he was bullied. Note that even Dr Howard didn't say 'Bob was bullied as a boy,' he said that Bob *told him* he was bullied."

What is known is that Lyon Sprague de Camp was bullied as a child, and as a fan of Howard and the single most important finisher of many of Howard's uncompleted stories (including of course the Conan works,) de Camp may have stressed the bully issue to feel more closely identified to Howard as his biographer in *Dark Valley Destiny*. De Camp's story *Judgement Day* (which bears a striking similarity to Howard's *The Supreme Moment*—more on this Howard piece later) was first published in the August 1955 issue of Astounding Science Fiction and later reprinted by Ballantine Books in *The Best of L. Sprague de Camp*. Its main character is Wade Ormont, who spent his childhood as a skinny, sickly, intellectual kid who was severely bullied and teased. De Camp said of *Judgement Day* in the afterword to the Ballantine collection, "...several incidents are taken straight out of my boyhood. It was, as you can infer, not a very pleasant one." (Thanks to Gary Romeo for his research in *Sand Roughs*.) Thus we have a possible reason why many other Howard biographers have appeared somewhat stumped as to why de Camp (who pressed Kate Merryman five times to say that Howard was bullied and was five times rebutted) seemed so keen on incorporating into *Dark Valley Destiny* the image of Howard as a sickly and bullied child. And while it is certainly clear that Howard as a child was bullied to some extent, as Howard himself said, the frequency of these events is murky.

What is clear is that Howard's perception of the injustices around him and especially those he believed were inflicted upon him had a distinct and cumulative psychological effect, far moreso than any one case of physical trauma or bullying. As a young man he was more willing to question his perception, and far more open to such ideas as reincarnation (partially attributable to his father's many studies and fancies.) The letters from his teenage years reflect this. When he was nineteen he wrote Tevis Clyde Smith, "I've been thinking. What is reality and what is illusion? One cannot say that our thoughts are abstract and our actions concrete, for then we are reduced to the level of thoughtless machines. Do our thoughts, as soon as born, assume some unseeable, intangible, yet concrete substance? Or, are your thoughts really born? Or is it that they merely enter your mind from the outside? Is man no more than a vessel for formless, yet tangible, thoughts? Is it that we do not really think and control ourselves by our thoughts, but that some outside influence controls us? The Hindus, as you know, believe that all things are without beginning. That thoughts are but symbols, concrete evidence of past lives, wandering through space, anon taking up their abode for a time in the human mind. But are thoughts either the creation of the mind, or substances without beginning, lasting forever, or are they influences of some higher, intangible outside power? What if we were but puppets, dancing on the strings of Destiny?"

Much later he expounds upon this in a letter to Clark Ashton Smith circa January 1934: "I agree with you that little is actually known about the sources of human motivation. I've wondered if, in a thousand years or so, people wouldn't regard present day psychologists as we regard the alchemists of the middle ages; some phases of their work, anyway. It certainly does seem that certain individuals occasionally get in contact with forces outside themselves; something like cog-wheels grinding away in their spirits, that suddenly, perhaps only momentarily, slip into the notches of gigantic, unseen cog-wheels of cosmic scope. Maybe that's what is meant by getting 'in tune with the infinite.' Sometimes it seems to me that the interlocking of unseen cog-wheels lifts a man on to heights he would never have attained by his own efforts. This would explain the fact that a mediocre man sometimes attains great success and fame; explain also the unexpected and unexplainable catastrophes that often startle mankind in the fall of a great one. Some say cosmic law causes these cog-wheels (I can think of no better name for it) to work together for a space, the wheels within perfectly matching the wheels without. Some man happens to be placed in a position where he is lifted by the turning of the wheels. Apparently by his own efforts, but really blindly, he mounts to dizzy heights; he is acclaimed and praised, dazzled by his own glory. Then the same cosmic law that locked the wheels, unlocks them, leaving him in the gap. Dazed, stunned and helpless he comes down crashing in the ruins of his glory, and neither he nor anyone else ever understands why this man who seemed so invincible the day before, seemed so unable ultimately to avert the final disaster." At this point we cannot help but think of Howard's ultimate fate. He continues, "This is mere supposition, of course, and not even any attempt to put forward a theory. But I have seen, and have read of, so many mediocre men in high positions, and wondered how they ever got there; and there are so many cases where men who had reputations for greatness finally made the most stupid blunders, and acted in a manner so inconsistent with their former actions—well, it just set me meditating."

If Howard was occasionally inclined to ponder sudden and unexpected downfalls, what would he have said about slow and steady ones? The deep resonating chord which quick and fatal twists of fate tend to strike is one that held more appeal and understanding to Howard, for it was clear and sharp and decisive, and these qualities are possessed by his best characters. It may be said that in many ways, life to Howard was like a boxing match: you may have it right where you want it in the early rounds, but its inexhaustible stamina is steadily leading you on the path to suffer a knockout. Living and dying were not the vague imponderables which poets struggled to make sense of, but rather they were brothers—the two snakes which are eating each other's tail. To fear one and not the other, or to praise one and not the other, was simply out of balance. Each presented different opportunities. Thusly, the line between life and death did not necessarily define their boundaries. A man could be alive but dead inside, and in such a case, was it not more merciful and even honorable to spare onself the inevitable decline?

The haunting words of "there are so many cases where men who had reputations for greatness finally made the most stupid blunders" are ones which linger around the state of depression Howard had entered at the end of his life. "Dazed, stunned and helpless he comes down crashing in the ruins of his glory, and neither he nor anyone else ever understands why this man who seemed so invincible the day before, seemed so unable ultimately to avert the final disaster." It is a striking prediction.

"Death to the old is inevitable, and yet somehow I often feel it is a greater tragedy than death to the young," he wrote August Derleth in May of 1936. "When a man dies young he misses much suffering, but the old have only life as a possession and somehow to me the tearing of a pitiful remnant from weak old fingers is more tragic than the looting of a life in its full rich prime." Howard was doubtless reflecting on his mother's state, and heavily thinking about his own. By this time such thoughts were like an old companion to him, and his attitude toward the business practices of death gives one the impression that he strongly wished to give death a beating. It would have been grand if Bob Howard had crossed the threshold and snapped the bones of the grim reaper, breaking femurs and tibulas over his knee, using the black robe like a garbage sack to tie the remnants. Doubtless he would have given it a go if such an opportunity had awaited him.

As he sat in his slender narrow room in the back of the house, with his heavy writing desk facing a small bank of windows which overlooked a wide scrubby back yard, behind him there would have been a bureau for clothes with books on top (two of his favorite authors were Harold Lamb and Jack London,) and to his left was his small single bed next to a trunk for his papers kept against the far wall. Project Pride of Cross Plains, who restored Howard's home, notes "In opening the Howard house, we cannot duplicate all the furnishings. Instead, friends in the community have graciously donated furnishings of the 1920's and 1930's. Above all, we have tried to capture the mood and spirit of the environment of the home and the period. In Howard's room, however, we have stayed as close as possible to the type of furnishings and to the crowded conditions, in which Howard lived and worked." The room was perhaps only six feet wide and little more than ten or eleven long, and there was an inside window next to his bed which overlooked his mother's room, with its colorful vertical floral patterned wallpaper. By contrast Howard's walls were unadorned white planks; his floorboards were reminiscent of a ship's deck. The one bit of color in his room was his bedspread, which he did not likely purchase. His typewriter and an armless chair were the centerpieces of the room, with an arcing black metal desk lamp on the far right corner of his desk and a bare bulb in the ceiling above. As a combination bedroom/office, it left little room for dressing, save for a small square between Howard's bed and the outside wall. It was here that he would by function get dressed, smack dab in front of the window to his mother's room, whose height was almost level to the bed itself, so that she would have seen his lower half as he slept, for no blinds or curtains were kept on this window by either party. A visitor to the home today is prevented from entering the room by a thin white chain, but little save technicality is missed.

Where life is more terrible than death, it is then the truest valor to dare to live.
--Thomas Browne

This small area served as Howard's ultimate retreat from the clamors of the world. Here only his mother could see his most private moments. On hot quiet nights the windows stood open and the two could hear each other breathe. For countless nights his mother must have fallen asleep to the tapping of Howard's typewriter keys, and when their neighbors the Butlers complained about the clickety-click sound at all hours of the night, Hester removed them from her list of friends. It was as if Howard himself were telling them to go to hell. The two defended each other, and simply being in each other's company lent both a sense of comfort and security. Caring for each other lent each a sense of purpose. What wordless understanding they must have shared. From earlier times when Hester would enter the small space to silently serve the young writer meals upon a tray, to the reversal of roles as Robert suspended his activities to administer patient care, the nature of the disease made some days better than others. During the times his mother seemed to rally, Howard's demeanor could be quite ebullient, cheerfully singing as he made his way around the house. It must have made her downward spells all the harder for him to take. He, who created worlds whose shamans, priests and sorcerers possessed the ability to cure such a trivial thing as tuberculosis, was ever reminded of the reality that in this life, prayers usually go unanswered. For all the grim gods his mind spawned, they were *active* gods—gods who reacted, smote, punished, and, sometimes, if the plea was worthy and it amused them, spared.

Chapter Six:

The Stoic

Oftentimes when Howard rested at home he would swing on the front porch and bellow out songs. One of his favorites to sing on such occasions was *Bye Bye Blackbird:*

Pack up all my care and woe
Here I go, singing low
Bye Bye Blackbird
Where somebody waits for me
Sugar's sweet, so is she
Bye Bye Blackbird
No one here can love and understand me
Oh, what hard luck stories they all hand me
Make my bed and light the light
I'll arrive late tonight
Blackbird, Bye Bye!

—*Bye Bye Blackbird (chorus)*
1926. Lyrics by Mort Dixon.

Howard would often improvise the lyrics to suit his mood.

He frequently walked into town to get the mail and the groceries from the small market owned by Annie Newton Davis and her husband, and these long walks, coupled with the weight of the family's groceries, built and maintained his strength. "We didn't have much in common," Cross Plains newspaperman Jack Scott said in a 1996 interview with Brian Bethel of The Abilene Reporter. "He didn't play ball, he didn't go to dances, he didn't do most of the things that guys his age usually did." To further develop himself he also chopped wood and pounded a log with a sledge hammer for hours at a time. He drank large quantities of milk and he loved pancakes for any type of meal. Many mistook this successful focus on bodybuilding as Howard's attempt to become a bully in his own right, but this is not the case. It was further made easy to confuse his intentions by the large number of weapons he began collecting.

His collection included a Civil War cavalry saber, two fencing foils, a Latin American machete, a World War I trench knife with a scalloped knuckle guard, a long French double-curved bayonet, and an untold number of pocket knives and daggers. And of course he had guns, stashed in a closet. His home décor attempts began and ended with him displaying some of his collection on the bathroom walls. It must have been a rather intimidating setting for visitors to conduct their ablutions.

From an early age he had specific tastes in books and authors. He writes to Tevis Clyde Smith in February, 1928: "I never look for perfection in anything, but merely an approach to perfection as measured by my paltry standard. And my standard means Force, Power, Strength—that's what I say is Near Perfection—Strength. I have carefully gone over, in my mind, the most powerful men—that is, in my opinion—in all of the world's literature and here is my list: Jack London, Leonid Andreyev, Omar Kayyam, Eugene O'Neill, William Shakespeare. All these men, and especially London and Kayyam, to my mind stand just so far above the rest of the world that comparison is futile, a waste of time. Reading these men and appreciating them makes a man feel life not altogether useless."

It was the conflicting nature of Howard to both seize and condemn life. Good authors flared his imagination and made him dream of the possibilities for adventure in the world, but when he faced that world with his shoulders squared he could not help but focus on the flaw and corruption of it all. Most of the time he dealt with it in stride, and he employed certain mannerisms and ways of communicating (what other biographers have simply dubbed acting) as buffers between himself and reality. In *Post Oaks* he mentions how he's played so many roles that it's hard to bring out his true self. When he met poet and prominent Catholic layman Benjamin Francis Musser (1889-1951) in early 1933, Howard made no effort to drop his adopted local dialect. He later told Lovecraft, "I once met a noted poet, who had been kind enough to praise my verse most highly, and with whom I'd had an enjoyable correspondence. But I reckon I didn't come up to his idea of what a poet should be, because he didn't write me, even after he returned East, or even answer the letter I wrote him. I suppose he expected to meet some kind of intellectual, and lost interest when he met only an ordinary man, thinking the thoughts and speaking in the dialect of the common people." There is no question that Howard had the ability to impress a "noted poet," but much like his invitation to Lexie Robertson's soirée, something about Howard's general demeanor undermined these opportunities.

Part of what we know about Howard suggests that these supposedly intellectual opportunities tended to strike a false chord within his gut, and the inherent aspects of public relations and self-promoting which dubiously manifest in both large and small literary gatherings were something which Howard preferred to avoid. It was one thing if a beginning writer was asking for his opinion, and quite another if a supposed peer were drawing similarities between his own work and that of H.L. Mencken, Oliver Goldsmith, or Charles Dickens, authors which Howard mostly despised. Howard said of Dickens, "He gets on my nerves, not so much by his tedium as by the spineless cringing characters he portrays." He called Goldsmith's *The Vicar of Wakefield* "one of the most abominable books ever penned." He mentions this to Lovecraft in a letter dated November 2, 1932: "I read this abomination [The Vicar of Wakefield] as a part of my high-school work, and in writing my report, I let myself go the only time I ever did in school, and gave my own honest opinion in my own honest words, allowing myself the freedom of frothing at the mouth. I expected to flunk the course, so many teachers being slaves of the established, but that particular teacher was a black-headed Irish woman who evidently entertained similar ideas on the subject to mine, and she gave me a good grade instead of the tongue-lashing I expected."

Of the writing life he said to Lovecraft circa May/June 1933, "It seems to me that many writers, by virtue of environments or culture, art and education, slip into writing because of their environments. I became a writer in spite of my environments. Understand, I am not criticizing these environments. They were good, solid and worthy. The fact that they were not inductive to literature and art is nothing in their disfavor. Never the less, it is no light thing to enter into a profession absolutely foreign and alien to the people among which one's lot is cast; a profession which seems as dim and faraway and unreal as the shores of Europe. The people among which I lived—and yet live, mainly—made their living from cotton, wheat, cattle, oil, with the usual percentage of business men and professional men. That is most certainly not in their disfavor. But the idea of a man making his living by writing seemed, in that hardy environment, so fantastic that even today I am sometimes myself assailed by a feeling of unreality. Never the less, at the age of fifteen, having never seen a writer, a poet, a publisher or a magazine editor, and having only the vaguest ideas of procedure, I began working on the profession I had chosen. I have accomplished little enough, but such as it is, it is the result of my own efforts. I had neither expert aid nor advice, I studied no courses in writing; until a year or so ago, I never read a book by anybody advising writers how to write. Ordinarily I had no access to public libraries, and when I did, it was to no such libraries as exist in the cities. Until recently—a few weeks ago in fact—I employed no agent. I have not been a success, and probably never will be. But whatever my failure, I have this thing to remember—that I was a pioneer in my profession, just as my grandfathers were in theirs, in that I was the first man in this section to earn his living as a writer."

Plainly Howard isn't counting journalists among the writing profession, for if he were he may have recalled a family connection. From a January, 1966 letter from Harold Preece to Glenn Lord: "...Bob's cousin, Maxine Ervin, whom I met at TCU before I'd even heard of Bob. I happened to mention Maxine when I met Bob and Truett for the first time at the Stephen F. Austin Hotel in Austin town during the summer of 1927. Maxine and her sister, Lesta, later became my friends in Dallas and were two of the genuine Texas ladies I've known over a lifetime. Originally, they were from Big Spring where their father had been a pioneer newspaperman." Also, to be fair to Howard's parameter of "this section," Big Spring is about 150 miles west of Cross Plains, on the road to Midland and Odessa, which are not far from the Arizona border.

Railroad yard at Big Spring, TX, home of Howard's cousins Maxine and Lesta Ervin. 1940.
Library of Congress, Prints & Photographs Division, FSA-OWI Collection

The Austin meeting mentioned by Preece included Preece's friend Booth Mooney. Preece and Mooney had been members of the Lone Scout organization (mentioned earlier in relation to Herbert Klatt.) In the Glenn Lord letter Preece states of his writing at that time, "...most of my output at that time was for the Lone Scout amateur publications, and I first knew Bob and Truett through a Lone Scout contact [Mooney]." The meeting of the four men succeeded to the point of them deciding to create a round-robin literary publication, *The Junto*, whose first issue would appear around mid-1928. In it they could exchange ideas, thoughts, criticisms, and stories. It would become both an outlet and a kind of inside joke.

One of Howard's favorite paintings was called *The Stoic*, and in a letter to Lovecraft circa July 25, 1935 he describes the scene of an Indian going about his daily tasks, scourged by his own hand in response to the grief he feels at the loss of his son. Howard saw this harsh model as an ideal for survival. In the Native American he saw an indomitable life force, determined to prevail in spite of the trials which life had flung upon him. In it he saw stubbornness and pride in the face of grimness, a rally when the tide of spirit is low. He saw dignity maintained, and sheer will prevailing through the struggle that is the continuation of life under harsh circumstances. In it he saw a standard which he himself would struggle to maintain, and perhaps he felt a red glimmer in his mind as he gazed upon the image of a man who would not commit suicide when faced with the loss of his family. Howard knew that to struggle bravely onward took more strength than any other option.

To be the first man in his region to make a living as a creative writer (journalists, despite great inventiveness, were still meant to report news and not create it) was a reservoir of pride that could never be deep enough to sustain a man like Howard. Ever seeking to justify his thinking and defend his positions when writing to the elder Lovecraft, perennially downplaying the importance of his literary impact, leery of enemies about town whom he felt resented his lifestyle, unwilling and uncomfortable to exhibit his true intelligence on the rare occasions he found himself among highly literate acquaintances and strangers, Howard had built a wall around himself which just a handful of people could access by invitation only. One wonders if things could have been changed during a brief window when he was younger. When he was seventeen he wrote Tevis Clyde Smith, "I have lived here for four years and so far I have gone my way, unhampered by girlish attentions. And so far as I know I will continue so." The first sentence is not so uncommon, but the second one reveals a sort of predetermination. He continues, "No, I'm not a girl-hater. I have the highest respect for the feminine sex. I just prefer other amusements as a general rule. I'm no lady's man." He directs that the girl question should be shoved into obscurity. Later he writes, "I wish you would come and see me. I don't know whether I could show you as good a time as you showed me, but I could try. If you have a desire for exploration, there are several places that might interest you. There are a lot of good swimming places. If you wanted action of the fighting kind, you could find two or three dozen persons who would be glad to oblige you, any way you might wish. (The majority of the inhabitants being different from me, who am a peaceful guy as you know.) You might desire the society of the fair sex; if so, I think your desire might be gratified to a certain extent. (Beyond which extent I would not advise anyone to trespass.) At least, if you come and visit me, I will do my best to entertain you. I certainly hope you will come."

This early example of a young Robert E. Howard who is all but begging for companionship (at the end of the same letter he writes, "I wish you would come…") is very different from the Howard we see in the 1930s. His father was long aware of the gap in Howard's interpersonal growth, with his mother serving as sole companion throughout much of childhood. Isaac wrote to his friend and colleague Frank Torbett (whose son Thurston was friends with Howard) on June 22, 1936 of how he had little time to "cultivate and shape" the course of his son's emotional development through the years of his absences due to necessary travel as a country physician. It was ironic that now, after he had moved his practice to his own home, it was too late to make a truly vital connection with his son. Instead the elder Howard seemed to accept the fatalistic side of his son's personality, and the decline of his optimism as it was paced by the decline of his mother's health. Howard was moving further and further away from the life essence portrayed in *The Stoic*.

In many of his stories, the theme of the untamed wilderness, dark and dangerous, ran a strong parallel with the theme of Howard's soul. The untamed people within these wild environs could be likened to Howard's untamed thoughts. They crouched in the blackness, full of cunning and verisimilitude—knowledge of the deadly ways of life. Few gray areas existed in their thinking, and they exulted in the tactile, the straightforward, the challenge of life with no pretense. Sometimes they made forays into civilization, when hunger or vengeance demanded or they simply wanted to revel in the pleasures of raiding and striking back at what they saw as a growing virus upon the world. Oftentimes civilization is suggested as having defiled something, or taken something away, which the angry soul of the wild wished returned. From Howard's *The People of the Black Circle*: "He stood silently facing the dark towers that loomed through the trees, his eyes slits of blue bale-fire. Desire for the yellow-haired woman vied with a sullen primordial rage at whoever had taken her. His human passion fought down his ultra-human fears, and dropping into the stalking crouch of a hunting panther, he glided toward the walls, taking advantage of the dense foliage to escape detection from the battlements."

What compassion that lurked in the untamed heart of Howard's stories was usually best demonstrated as a kind of wild kinship and understanding, rather than taking its accustomed setting within the prim bounds of civilization. From Howard's *Red Nails*: "The exhibition of primordial fury chilled the blood in Valeria's veins, but Conan was too close to the primitive himself to feel anything but a comprehending interest. To the barbarian, no such gulf existed between himself and other men, and the animals, as existed in the conception of Valeria. The monster below them, to Conan, was merely a form of life differing from himself mainly in physical shape. He attributed to it characteristics similar to his own, and saw in its wrath a counterpart of his rages, in its roars and bellowings merely reptilian equivalents to the curses he had bestowed upon it. Feeling a kinship with all wild things, even dragons, it was impossible for him to experience the sick horror which assailed Valeria at the sight of the brute's ferocity."

These examples of unburnished freedom and wild thrilling danger had their own ironic carryover into Howard's personal finance situation. In a letter to *Weird Tales* editor Farnsworth Wright dated May 6, 1935 Howard relates his grim predicament: "For some time now I have been receiving a check regularly each month from Weird Tales—half checks, it is true, but by practicing the most rigid economy I have managed to keep my head above the water; that I was able to do so was largely because of, not the size but the regularity of the checks. I came to depend on them and to expect them, as I felt justified in so doing. But this month, at the very time when I need money so desperately bad, I did not receive a check. Somehow, some way, my family and I have struggled along this far, but if you cut off my monthly checks now, I don't know what in God's name we'll do…

"I do not feel that my request is unreasonable. As you know, it has been six months since 'The People of the Black Circle' (the story the check for which is now due me) appeared in Weird Tales. Weird Tales owes me over eight hundred dollars for stories already published and supposed to be paid on publication—enough to pay all my debts and get me back on my feet again if I could receive it all at once. Perhaps this is impossible. I have no wish to be unreasonable; I know times are hard for everybody. But I don't believe I am being unreasonable in asking you to pay me a check each month until the accounts are squared. Honestly, at the rate we're going now, I'll be an old man before I get paid up! And my need for money now is urgent.

"Of course, I sell to other magazines from time to time, but these sales are uncertain; to make markets regularly requires much time and effort, and for years most of my time and effort has been devoted to the stories I have written for Weird Tales. I may not—may never be a great writer, but no writer ever worked with more earnest sincerity than I have worked on the tales that have appeared in Weird Tales. I have grown up in the magazine, so to speak, and it is as much a part of my life as are my hands and arms. But to a poor man the money he makes is his life's blood, and of late when I write of Conan's adventures I have to struggle against the disheartening reflection that if the story is accepted, it may be years before I get paid for it.

This is a statement of my case, spoken in the only way I know how to speak, that is to say frankly. I trust that my bluntness has given no offense. Necessity drives me. A monthly check from Weird Tales may well mean for me the difference between a life that is at least endurable—and God alone knows what."

Weird Tales would go on to owe Howard a total of $1350 for published stories, all unpaid at the time of his death thirteen months after the letter to Wright. During the Depression this was simply a gigantic sum. By comparison, Howard had purchased his car for $350, and the magazines for which he wrote had a newsstand price of between a dime and a quarter per issue. Having the extra money in 1935 would almost undoubtedly have meant more Conan stories, and it would have put some of Howard's worries concerning the medical bills of his mother in an easier state. Although he did have savings in a Postal savings account, having the extra money might have put Howard at more liberty to travel (he regretted not having enough money to meet Lovecraft when he traveled to New Orleans, and he spoke with eagerness about sampling the unprohibited liquors of Quebec, and seeing the countryside of Rhode Island) or simply to afford something from which he derived enjoyment. The sense of financial desperation which Howard conveys to Wright cannot be dismissed or underestimated, for in it is the underlying root of the betrayal of contract and Howard's powerless position. He hated feeling powerless, and the near begging tone of that letter must have sent tremors through his soul. The irony of having his Conan tales be among the most popular and not getting paid for them must have appeared to him as another soul-testing contrivance of life, and it came at a time when his concern for his mother's health was taxing his ability to cope.

Howard used an allegory to describe the situation with Wright, as chronicled by Novalyne Price Ellis in *One Who Walked Alone*: "One of our goats is bigger than the other one," he said. "I have to watch her closely. She won't let the little one eat. She gobbles up most of her food, then moves over and runs the little one off and begins on her food. It's the nature of animals to dominate the ones they can. I understand that. Human beings are the same way. They dominate the ones they can dominate. Wright won't pay me what he owes me, because he's got the upper hand. His salary is assured; therefore, I can work my guts out, and it doesn't mean a damn to him. He's the dominant one. It's the animal in him. We're one ... man and animals."

Throughout the years one of the psychological mechanisms Howard used in order to feel more in tune with the world was adopting the hearty belief that he had been many other people throughout history, from a soldier in the army of Vortigern, king of the Britons, to an artisan of ancient Gath, to a rider with Jenghiz Khan. Novalyne recounts:

> *He described the land, the colors of Jenghiz Khan's robes, the horse he rode. As I listened, I knew what Jenghiz Khan experienced and thought. But I understood as one who plays a part in a play; you study the man... You study the role... You try to understand and experience him; then you try to reveal him to an audience. But in the final analysis, on stage, you create the illusion of reality. Bob was not acting. He was there. At that moment, he was Jenghiz Khan, the barbarian, conqueror of an empire.*
>
> *It overwhelmed me. "How do you know so much about him—Jenghiz Khan? History books don't tell you these things. History books don't describe. They recount."*

"I was there, girl." Exultantly. "I rode with Jenghiz Khan."

By contrast, real life always seemed to hold some underlying accusations toward Howard, and even his father, as this next Howard quote from Novalyne's book suggests:

> "These damn pseudo-scientific writers of today who try to explore a man's inner mind ain't worth a damn. Evil, they say, lurks inside a man. I hate the damn bastards who write stuff like that, because every decent impulse a man has is given a dirty meaning by these damn sons-of-bi— guns. A man loves his poor old sick mother, and those damn bastards call it the 'Oedipus complex.' A doctor goes to see an attractive sick woman, and it's portrayed as lust."

This last sentence likely refers to the situation with nearby neighbors of the Howards, the Newtons. Mrs. J.W. Newton was a patient of Isaac's, and her attractive unmarried daughter Annie lived with her. Isaac took to the habit of drawing his water from the Newtons' cistern, saying that theirs tasted better to him. He would go there in the evening, and if he saw lights on in the parlor, he would often knock on the door. Mr. Newton was a farmer and always in bed early. He felt uneasy about the doctor's nighttime visitations with two women, but his wife's healthcare needs prevented him from protesting directly.

Dr. Howard himself would years later confirm the sensitivity Robert had to things which were negative and critical. And considering Howard's oft-stated belief that life was a struggle, full of a shapeless kind of malevolence which seeks to constantly test the mettle of people, it becomes easier to see how attuned Howard had become to the negative forces which sometimes grip a person's heart, or cast their shadow over a situation. In a letter dated June 21, 1944 Isaac wrote E. Hoffman Price: "He was so sensitive to things of a depressing nature that his mother and I never mentioned anything of a depressing nature in his presence. It had been thus with him since childhood. His dog died when he (the dog) was 12 and Robert 24. He raised the dog from the time it was a wee thing, before his eyes were barely open, through the life of the dog. The dog was an inseparable companion to Robert. It was often fed from the table as Robert ate, sitting down by Robert's chair. When Robert helped himself, before eating a bite, he helped Patch to food...

Howard and Patch playing in the yard

"Robert loved animals of all kind. You could not by any amount of persuasion have induced him to shoot a bird or a jackrabbit or any kind of animal. He had a dog, a mixed-breed, half-collie, half-Walker foxhound. His association was so close with this dog until the dog seemed to develop a perfectly human understanding of not only Robert, but Robert's mother and myself. Also, when the dog was 12 years old, he sickened to die. Robert knew his dog was going to die. He packed his grip, opened the gate, walked out, and said 'Mama, I am going.' He went to Brownwood and stayed until his dog died, which was two or three days. But each morning he phoned and asked his mother if Patch (that was the dog's name) was still alive; finally on the third or fourth morning, his mother told him she thought the Patch dog would not last longer than 12 o'clock. He always spoke thus: 'Mama, how are you?' When his mother would reply, he would say: 'How is Patch?' After the fourth day when his mother told him the dog was going, he never inquired any more; he knew the dog would soon die. Therefore he never spoke of him again. I had the dog buried in a deep grave in the back lot, then had the lot plowed deeply and then had them take a big harrow and harrow it deeply all over to destroy every trace of the grave, so sensitive was he to the loss of the dog. And only once did he ever allude to the death of his dog again. He said to his mother one day: 'Mother, did you bury Patch under the mesquite tree in the corner of the lot on the east side?' She said yes, and the matter was never mentioned by any of us again."

Some studiers of Howard such as Patrice Louinet have suggested that the death of Patch sparked, probably unbeknownst to Howard himself, a kind of reincarnation of the dog within Howard's fiction. The first and clearer example is Mike, the white bulldog companion of Sailor Steve Costigan (also the name Howard gave himself in *Post Oaks*, minus of course the sailor part) in the popular series of boxing adventures by Howard. In the series Mike is the truest and most loyal companion to Steve, just as Patch was to Howard. The timeline for the appearance fits well, as the bulldog Mike makes his first showing very close to the time of Patch's passing. In some stories the name of Mike is changed to Spike (in cases where Howard already had a story appearing in the same magazine, slight alterations to author and character names were made so as not to appear overly gauche) and the bulldog is even called Bill in *The Sign of the Snake* (Action Stories, June 1931) although Steve Costigan remains the owner. The second and much looser relation occurs years later in 1934. In Howard's *Beyond the Black River*, the character Balthus has a dog named Slasher, but this comparison seems thinner, although in *One Who Walked Alone* Novalyne Price refers to Howard as describing this story as, "The triumph of a dog and the barbarian." Also it should be noted that loyal animal companions in Howard stories could take other shapes than dogs, as Breckenridge Elkins' remarkable horse Cap'n Kidd proves. (Incidentally, while pondering Howardian nomenclature, it's interesting to note that Breckenridge, Texas is just fifty miles north of Cross Plains.)

It is suspected Dr. Howard, who wrote the letter to E. Hoffman Price less than five months before his death on November 12 in Ranger Texas, may have been slightly off with the age of Howard at the time the dog died, for a local named Elsie Burns wrote a recollection of meeting Howard as "a lad of about ten" out in the countryside with his dog, and Howard recounts in *The Last Celt* that he spent a great deal of time "wandering about the countryside" as a boy. *Dark Valley Destiny* further muddles the issue by pulling from seemingly thin air the date of Christmas, 1917 as when Howard received the dog. Patrice Louinet contends, "De Camp doesn't give any source that could indicate Howard got the dog as a Christmas present for 1917. For the simple reason that very likely no such source exists. Undoubtedly De Camp invented the fact that Howard got the dog as a Christmas present, only arriving at his December 1917 date by subtracting twelve years from his supposed date of death of Patch, i.e. December 1929 or January 1930." The archive of L. Sprague de Camp, containing manuscripts for twenty-five novels as well as research, correspondence, family records and business files, and hundreds of letters from major authors and editors, is kept at the Harry Ransom Center at the University of Texas at Austin.

What is best to remember from all this is an existing photo of Howard and Patch, taken when Howard was an adult. He and the dog are outside on the grass. Howard is wearing his usual khaki pants and white short-sleeved shirt. He is standing over the dog, bending down to playfully grip Patch by the ribs. The dog has its head tilted and appears to be in a fine state of happiness, and more importantly, so does Howard. The photo is perhaps the best example of Howard actually smiling, and this supercedes all the facts, figures and speculation about the details of Patch. Like his fictional dog Mike (Spike, Bill,) Patch clearly has some of the same white coloration which Howard notes in his stories. The bond was beautifully simple, and it stood as a bastion against the tide of cruelty and violence Howard saw within the world.

Chapter Seven:
Interlude: Stories from Brownwood

A sack of grain on the bumper of a farmer's car in Brownwood, 1939.
Library of Congress, Prints & Photographs Division, FSA-OWI Collection

While researching Robert E. Howard's Texas, I came across many interesting manuscripts from the Federal Writers' Project, a work program started by FDR to supply needed jobs during the Great Depression. These manuscripts can be found in the American Life Histories section at the Library of Congress. Although accounts from a town as small as Cross Plains in the 1930s were able to escape my detection despite numerous searches (it is likely none are available within the collection), Brownwood is a different story.

Howard writes appreciatively of his travels through the area, and how the early morning clouds and mist were "Not grey and damp and depressing, but purely white, with almost a rosy tinge, through which the sky peeped here and there, with a rare and delicate blue." (Letter to HPL, 12/35) Lake Brownwood was created by damning the Pecan Bayou, and just two years after Howard's death the 538-acre Brownwood State Park would open.

During Howard's time Brownwood was a place where he and Truett Vinson and Tevis Clyde Smith could catch a movie or have or soda, gas up with Indian brand fuel, and sometimes even purchase chickens and turkeys for a hearty holiday meal at the Brownwood Poultry Cooperative. What seemed to really interest Howard, however, were the legends and history of an older time.

Before rooming with Lindsey Tyson at 417 Austin Avenue in Brownwood during college, Howard had stayed at 316 Wilson Street while a high school senior in Brownwood. His mother insisted on keeping house for him, and Isaac was only able to visit on weekends. Located a few blocks south of the center of town, Howard would have had opportunities to hear stories of an older Brownwood, and the pioneer days which interested him. He would later use the mobility afforded him by his automobile to seek out such stories from old timers living in the area.

Farmers frequented Brownwood's agricultural supply store as well as dropping off future squawking dinners at the poultry cooperative. Many of them had been on the land at the turn of the century, and had witnessed the changes which swept West Texas.

Brownwood agricultural supply store in 1939.

Courtesy LOC, FSA-OWI Collection.

Rich and vivid are the stories from Brownwood's past, told in the words of the people who lived them as America was entering the 20th Century. Perhaps Howard himself listened to some of these stories from the very same pioneers which are documented below.

Brownwood Stories

We start with Andrew Jackson Hale, born in Greenville, Hunt County, Texas, May 20, 1856. Known as "Uncle Jack," he was 82 years old when interviewed. He recalls an incident that happened near Brownwood:

"In '82, I went up the trail with a man named Tom King. He was a big, cattle man and a banker. We had one-thousand head of cattle and were moving them from Greenville to Jones and Shackelford County in East Texas. Mr. King had bought a big ranch there and this herd was cows and calves. He was taking them to grass. I drove the chuck wagon and cooked for the outfit but rode too when it was necessary. There were about fourteen men in all.

"I remember one day I was shoeing a mule while we were resting the cattle at noon. Part of the men were standing guard and the rest were eating dinner. Charley Moore rode up while I was holding the mule's foot between my knees. The mule, being a fool, wouldn't stand. Moore came up behind him and gave him a kick to make him stand up. The mule reared and jumped, jerking me down. The nails in the shoe were sticking out and very sharp. They cut a gash in my leg about seven or eight inches long and real deep. I carry the brand there yet.

"When I got up, I was mad as the devil. I knew that Moore had done this on purpose for he and I had been on terms that were none too good for several days. I came up with a rasp in my hand that I had been using to shoe the mule and I threw it at Moore's head with all the force I had. I hit him on the nose and cut the end of his nose off and it dropped down on his mouth. The boss was standing there looking on. My leg was bleeding badly and King says, 'Well, we've got to sew that leg up for Jack is going to bleed to death.' All the kind of thread they had was a spool of ordinary, sewing thread and that's just what he used. He took about twelve or sixteen stitches in my leg and put a wet pack on it to get the blood stopped. Then he turned to Moore and sewed his nose back on but it was always crooked afterward. It was the boss' time to talk then. He said, 'Moore, you knew that mule was a fool. Why did you do that?' Then he turned to us both and says, 'Now you fellows renew this and I'll set you both afoot out here in this lonely country.' It was fifty miles or more between ranches.

"Well, we started on and everything went all right till we got to Brownwood. He had a lot of cows that were given out -- road-foundered -- and would fight a man on a horse or afoot either. They had the road brand on them and King's brand, also. When they got too bad, we would just leave them beside the trail and the next man who came along with a herd would pick them up and find out who they belonged to and turn them over to King.

"One day, we had just eaten dinner and was within a short distance of Brownwood. I was behind, driving the chuck wagon. One of the cows on ahead was mad and fighting. We met a young man and a little girl in the road. They were coming from school, I suppose. The man was well dressed. The little girl saw this cow and thought it was a gentle milk cow and ran ahead to scare her. The cow knocked the child down and had her between her horns on the ground. The young man ran and caught the cow by the horns and the little girl jumped up and climbed up on a fence close by. The cow was so weak the man could manage her very well, although she was churning him around considerably. I knew when they came in sight what would happen, but I was too far away to prevent it. When I finally got to where they were, the man says, 'Mister, come and help me. I'm in a hell of a shape!' I says, 'Turn her loose and run and jump on the fence like the little girl did.' He said, 'No, the cow will catch me and kill me. I wont risk that.' I said, 'Hell, stand there and hold her all day. I'll drive around.' Then I got out of the wagon and went and examined the little girl. She wasn't hurt but scared to death. I finally got her quiet and over some of her scare and turned to the man with language that won't do to repeat and I says, 'Now, I am going to let you out of this. I'll take this cow and hold her till you get a start and then I am going to turn her loose.'

"So I caught the cow by the horns and gave him a kick in the seat of the pants. He made about two jumps and hit the fence and landed on the other side. I says, 'Now, I'll show you how to handle a cow.' I caught the old cow by the horn and the jaw and with a little twist, threw her down. He was very angry and said, 'Mister, I'll kill that cow before morning.' Sure enough he did. She was missing next morning and the boss sent one of the boys back to look for her and he found her with two bullet holes in her head. The boss said he didn't blame him, he would have done the same thing."

Mr. E.F. Forsgard, born in Waco in 1870, tells a real-life story of cowboys and Indians in the area of Brownwood:

"My father was a member of the Ranger force, and one time he and about two hundred rangers were sent after a bunch of Indians that had made a raid at Comanche. They caught up with the Indians over about Brownwood, and killed some of them. They then killed a cow to get rawhide strips to tie rocks to the bodies of the Indians so they could sink them in the bayou over there so as not to leave any sign, for other Indians, I suppose.

"Sometimes cowboys from over in Bosque county or somewhere else would drive in several head of cattle they had stolen and sell them to a butcher here in Waco for money enough to go on a spree. They would tell the butcher it was 'jumping stock', and was to be killed at once so it wouldn't be found.

"The cowboys would come in with herds and stop here and get drunk and shoot and yell around some, but nobody paid any attention to them. If they shot out any show windows in the stores their boss man would go around to the merchants and ask them what the damage was and pay it. If the cowboys got to shooting too much, the storekeepers would put up heavy wooden shutters before the windows, and then the boys wouldn't see any glass to shoot at."

Next we have a Brownwood native, L.M. Cox, who settled in Brownwood in 1880. He spent the bulk of his life as a rancher.

"The cowboy's life as we know it was certainly lacking in the glamour which we see on our screens today. I have known cowboys to ride one hundred miles per day. I know this sounds unreasonable but they were off before daylight and rode hard until after dark. Their usual day's work was to be off as soon as they could see how to catch their horses, throw the round-up together around 10 o'clock then work cattle or brand until dark and often times stand guard one-third of the night after that.

"The usual ride was sixteen hours per day. No Union hours for them. It was from daylight until dark with work, and hard work as that. [...] Each cowboy had his mount, which usually consisted of ten or twelve horses and he rode four each day. Many of the horses were remarkably trained and like their owners, had their good and bad points. My own horse would tell his age by pawing
on the ground and I have been criticized for saying that he could tell marks and brands but I know he could.

"There were few buffalo left, but there were antelopes in vast herds on both sides of the Pecos. I have seen hundreds of them on one drove, also black-tail deer. We could rope the deer but not the antelope. They were too swift on foot, faster than our fastest horses.

"In the late 80's and early 90's came the covered wagons and then the sheepman. We stood the covered wagons pretty well but it took a long time to get on friendly terms with the sheepman. They were sure enough trespassers in the cowman's eye. One sheepman got his flock located on some good grass and the cowmen came along and ordered him off their premises. 'I can't go now,' the sheepman complained, 'I have lost my wagon wheel.' Cowboys always had a heart and tried to be lenient but they also hated deception. One of the cowboys who had heard this gag before, looked around a bit and found the missing wheel hidden away in some mesquite bushes. The sheepman was hustled away in a hurry.

"Early days were hard on all stockman. With sheep selling at 75¢ per head, wool at .04¢ and cattle no better, a panic seemed evident. Neglect of herds caused lots of cattle rustling, stealing, burning of brands, etc. Many tales were told of mysterious increases in herds, one fellow had an old red cow that fruitfully produced twenty mavericks in one year. Another with a yoke of oxen reported an increase of twenty-six in a short time.

"We never heard much complaint about hard times. People thought about a lot of things more than they did money then, 'cause it didn't take so much money to live. No cowpuncher ever talked much. Ride further and talk less, few words and fast action, were rules which they followed pretty close."

Charles W. Holden was born April 3, 1865 and retired to Fort Worth after a life spent settling on the range in Brown County. He spoke of a tremendous grasshopper infestation which befell the earlier settlers. But grasshoppers were not their greatest worry:

"Among the troubles that the settlers had to contend with was the Indian hoss thieves. About two weeks after we arrived, some Indians sneaked up and stole two of John Cooper's hosses.. Then they tethered all the hosses with a rope, near the camp, but one night the Indians again sneaked in, cut the ropes and stole two hosses from Brown. Then the men bought chains and padlocked a loop around the animal's neck and the other end around a tree, which stopped the hoss stealing.

"The settlement was never raided and the only one that had any trouble with Indians, while living at the settlement, was my father. He had made a trip to Round

Mountain after a critter for beef. Three Indians took after him and run him to within 200 yards of the camp. It happened at the time he was riding a fast hoss, instead of a mule, and that saved his scalp from dangling at an Indian's belt.

"The Indians got Tom Brown's family, but not at the settlement. He moved to some school land which he took up, five miles west of Brownwood. All the settlers advised him not to make the move and live off there alone, but he did. He had two children around five and six years old and an infant about three months old, at the time.

"Brown went to Brownwood one day and when he returned home he found his wife, dead and scalped, in the cowpen. The milk pail was on the ground, which indicated that she had gone there to milk. The infant was found dead in it's cradle. The child had been scalded with hot water from a kettle which was on the stove heating. Brown told how his wife always heated a kettle of water before starting to do the milking, which she used to scald the milk pail. The kettle was found setting on the floor; and the cradle clothes, also the child's, was soaking wet. The two older children were gone and were never heard from afterwards, so far as I have ever learned.

"There was a hunting party, made up of cowhands from the various ranges, but the boys had to give up the hunt when they completely lost the trail after two days of trailing."

Robert Lindsey was born about 1869. His father was a cattle dealer. For a time he was employed on the Payne Ranch in Denton County, but he settled on Brownwood.

"I bought me a pool hall in Brownwood, and quit the ranch. It wasn't so big anyway, and there wasn't enough money for all of us since there were only 1,000 sheep, and a 150 cattle on about 1800 acres of land.

"In a pool hall, you have time to sit around and talk about things. In fact, that's almost all you do when you have one. One of my customers was a W.S. Bill Foscett. Old Bill didn't talk much to anybody, and it took me several years to break him down to talking. I knew that he'd been somebody because you could tell it in his eyes, and his bearing. He'd look at you, and you'd feel like he knew your very thoughts. That caused me to sort of cater to him, and try to win his confidence without ever letting him know I was a-doing it.

"One day, I was talking about the Dalton ranches in Palo Pinto county, and a-wondering if they had any connections with the Dalton outlaws. I was talking about Bob Dalton, and asked Bill if he ever heard of him. He said, 'Yes, I knew him well. Truth of it is, I outlawed with him a little'.

"Being a pretty fair hand a poker playing, I didn't let my face tell what I felt, and I just let him talk on. He said, [...] 'There was one thing that happened to me though, where I really should have lost my life. If it hadn't been for my early training on my dad's ranch in Kansas when Kansas was the wildest place in the world, with a good many desparadoes running around, I'd never have been able to stand up to this experience. My dad had a saying, 'That a man can only die once, and he might's well die a man.' That's the way I felt.

'This time come about when I decide to visit a friend of mine, that was sheriff in a town after Oklahoma was a State. I'll send you a clipping from the Kansas City Star that tells a heap of it, but I'll tell you right now how I recall it. You know, in fast gun action, with your life in danger every minute, a lot goes on that you just nacherly don't recall.

'Well, when I reached the outskirts of this little town, I heard a lot of shooting start. I whipped my hoss up, and saw a gang of men split up, and go in three bunches to'ards some buildings. As I rode in, I saw two or three men on the ground, and I figured it was a holdup. Since I didn't see my friend anywhere, I figured that they'd already got him. I filled both fist with six shooters, and rode to the center of the town, where I could shoot at all three
gangs at the same time when they showed.

'What they was really doing, was robbing three places. Two banks, and a big store. Well, I stood in the middle of the street, and everytime one of 'em showed, I cut down on him. I was so bust that I never noticed what I was doing, but I did feel queer that I hadn't felt a shot yet. They were shooting at me from both ends of the street and the store in the middle. After about 15 minutes, which seemed like a month, the shooting stopped and the rest of the men came out with their hands in the air.

'When the count was taken, I'd [accounted?] for 13 of 'em. 13 of 'em dead, and me without a scratch. I tell you Bob, I've really got no claim on my life because the law of averages ought to have taken it then.'"

Chapter Eight:
The Supreme Moment

"When a nation forgets her skill in war, when her religion becomes a mockery, when the whole nation becomes a nation of money-grabbers, then the wild tribes, the barbarians drive in... Who will our invaders be? From whence will they come?"

--REH to Tevis Clyde Smith, July 1923

Howard enthusiast Larry Richter wrote in *Pale Rider*: "I think that Howard realized that most of the peace and progress which the world enjoyed were based on perversely engineered uses of violence, or unexpected and unpredicted results of raw, simple, violence. This is a view that is expensive to hold, a very high priced truth. It means that even in it's most benign aspects, the world is only a pinprick away from madness, and that madness is what the world is built of and on. This suggests that his best commercial character, the dangerous but surprisingly uncruel Conan, is perhaps a sane man in an insane world. This line of ideas is not a bond-builder among men."

In Howard's story *Delcarde's Cat* (which Howard refers to by the title *The Cat in the Skull* in a 1929 letter to Tevis Clyde Smith,) King Kull is told, "You are at the center of the universe as you are always. Time, place, and space are illusions, having no existence save in the mind of man, which must set limits and bounds in order to understand. There is only the underlying reality, of which all appearances are but outward manifestations, just as the upper lake is fed by the waters of this real one. Go now, king, for you are a true man even though you be the first wave of the rising tide of savagery which shall overwhelm the world ere it recedes."

This "rising tide of savagery" should not necessarily be confused with Howard's ideas of the morals and codes prevalent in primitive society. Savagery is a different breed of animal from barbarism, although civilization tends to make little distinction. To Howard such a distinction would have made a great difference, so that when he read the newspaper or walked down Main Street at night, reports or actual sightings of crimes would not be barbaric, but savage, which implies a kind of inherent degeneracy of morals, decency and tact, rather than a separate and different set of ethics. If his mind's eye could foresee or at least perceive an impending decline of civilization (the cyclic properties of history being well entrenched in his thoughts,) it may have been less of a struggle to contemplate death. Similar quandaries must have weighed upon his mind as he wrote *The Supreme Moment*, a story whose climax is suicide by a gunshot to the head.

This, one of Howard's rare forays into science fiction (the novel *Almuric*—not to be confused with the character name Amalric which appears in both the Conan tales *Drums of Tombalku* and *The Hour of the Dragon*—being the longest and most known) was on the surface written as a response to an increasing interest in sci-fi stories by some of the pulps. Howard himself did have some aptitude with science and biology; as he told Lovecraft, circa January 1934, "In high school I showed something of a knack for biology; certainly my science grades were infinitely higher than my English and literature grades. I have reason to believe that I had more capacity for biology than I have for literature. My teacher—who detested me as a human being but seemed to appreciate my laboratory work—suggested that I take up biology as a career." But of course Howard wasn't interested in buckling to such career constraints.

In July 1933 he told Lovecraft, "My biology class was the biggest in the school, and all the unruly spirits that could got in there. The teacher was a poor misfit who didn't know his stuff; that is, he was a good biologist, but he couldn't handle students. They gave him hell. The very last day of school, for instance, while he was trying to lecture to the class, certain unregenerate spirits kept galloping past the door, firing various objects at him, such as old shirts wadded up and soaked with water, to the hilarious enjoyment of the class. At last he shut the door, and then they locked it from the outside and he had to telephone down to the janitor to come and open it. I had no part in harassing the poor devil; but he never gave me a square deal if he could help it, so I didn't much give a damn what they did to him…

"…I had a hell of a time with mathematics. I blundered through algebra, geometry and trigonometry without learning a blamed thing about any of them. The only reason I passed my last year's math was a combination of luck and a teacher's laziness. The final exam was split in half, part to be taken one day and part the next, the results to be added on the basis of 100; thus, if a scholar made 100 on the first exam, he was given 50, etc. the results of both exams to be added. I made 60 on the first exam, and came in the next day to take the rest of it. The teacher was there alone, to my surprise, leaning back with his feet on a desk. I told him I was there to take my exam. He asked me what I made; I told him; he said then my grade was really 30, and asked me if I could improve that in another exam. 'Hell, no,' quoth I; 'I worked the only problem in the book I could work, yesterday.' He then asked me what grades I made in other subjects — they ran something like this: English 80, science 100, economics 85. He allowed that we'd let it go and say nothing; and call my mathematics grade 60, which would pass me."

It is quite interesting to note that Howard's science grade was 100. He adds, "I had a short course in agriculture once, which interested me immensely, and I made very high grades in it, as well as in its various branching, such as the grafting of trees, etc.." And although Howard claimed to have forgotten most of what he learned, enough seemed to remain for him to construct a believable biological element for *The Supreme Moment*.

The Supreme Moment was unpublished in Howard's lifetime, and most likely its political content prevented it from being published in the decades immediately following Howard's death. Its first known printed appearance was in 1984, in *Crypt of Cthulhu* issue 25, and later in Joe Marek's *The New Howard Reader* issue 1, both issues now very rare. And although other Howard works feature suicide, such as in the climax to his detective story *The House of Suspicion*, where suicide is committed using a rigged explosion, *The Supreme Moment* is remarkable in its striking parallels to aspects of Howard himself.

As the story opens, five wealthy and powerful business magnates are trying to convince a small and deformed man to save the human race. A new and unstoppable fungus which destroys all vegetation is spreading across the world, leaving barren fields in its wake and bringing starvation and death wherever it goes. The small and deformed man whose work has finally garnered the attention of these titans of industry is scientist Zan Uller, an expert on parasitic plants.

Zan's heart is touched little by the plight of the world. He recounts the story of his life, of being an impoverished child in a London tenement, with his mother thrown into prison for stealing. When he was 10 he was forced to work in a looming mill, which damaged his health. Savage beatings by his employer left him partially mutilated and crippled. He became a newsboy, and soon learned that other newsboys were willing to fight for their territory. And as he struggled to survive, the thing that kept him going was his interest in science.

Greater adversity awaited him once he became a true scientist. A rival purposely caused an explosion in his laboratory which impaired his vision. He wrote a book on evolution only to suffer fierce attacks from religious zealots. He continued to struggle, eventually gaining enough success to allow himself to live a relatively undisturbed life. Years earlier he had discovered the harmful effects of the fungi but his efforts were mocked by his peers in the scientific community. Undaunted, he started to work on a fungicide.

Once completed, Zan refuses to check the growth of the cataclysmic strain. He watches the world move closer to the brink, unwilling to save the people who had tortured him. Finally the five business tycoons catch him and corner him:

> *"If I should refuse to give you the formula, you will torture me?"*
>
> *Five voices answered assent.*
>
> *"But what if I do not refuse? Is it not godlike to forgive? Who am I to leave the world to destruction?*
>
> *"Gentlemen, this is my vengeance, this the supreme moment!"*

Zan reaches for a gun and before anyone can stop him he blows his brains out, with the echoes of his shot "rebounding through the room like mocking, devilish laughter."

(Note the parallel to Zan in the character of Zahn as played by Virginia Hey in the sci-fi series *Farscape*. Zahn is an expert in herbal medicine who sacrifices her life/commits suicide to save her friends.)

The theme of a pioneer in his field who is unappreciated by his peers, toiling slavishly for years with little reward—any writer who had worked as hard as Howard might have felt that way. In Rusty Burke's June 11, 1999 presentation at the Robert E. Howard Day Banquet in Cross Plains, he said that Howard's massive writing production included 1,533 pages of Conan stories that were completely discarded, and speculated, "If Howard's 250 other completed stories resulted in the same number of discarded pages, that would be another 22,500 pages thrown away. Try to imagine how many hours of typing that involves, on an old Underwood manual." (Incidentally, the combined figure comes out to about 4,000 hours if we allow ten minutes per page.) Frequently known to spend eighteen hours at a time at his desk, Howard's production remains a marvel, and each story contained that little piece of himself which made it stand out. Yet for all this work Howard's writing was still rejected far more often than it was accepted.

Perhaps he had hoped that more would come of it—that the dedicated pounding at the typewriter would continue to make both sales and stories come easier. It undoubtedly seems that in the following excerpt from *One Who Walked Alone* Howard was daunted to a greater degree than one might expect:

> [...] he talked about the crash of his career, and I said it seemed to me he was making sales, some to new markets too.

> At that, he became impatient. "Your career falls in ruins when you go on producing, knowing the well is running dry," he said loudly. "How much more time you have to produce before it dries up, you don't know. You've got to watch that, Novalyne, when you start writing full time."

> [...] "You start in to write," he said one day, "and, at first, you write day and night. Many days, eighteen hours. Sometimes, if things are going right, you may write twenty-four. But the constant production finally gets you. If you try to settle down to eight to ten hours a day steadily, if you devote your whole life to breaking into the writing game, you should be mighty careful that you don't burn yourself out before you write the big book."

Another stress which was constantly building and boding heavy on his writing output was the condition of his mother. Even the people who were hired to help around the house were prone to continually interrupt Howard while writing to ask how various things should be done. From Novalyne's book:

> His real feelings came out. He'd been able to sell Argosy a couple of yarns, and he had two or three other western heroes going to other magazines. There he was, trying to write and getting interrupted every few minutes! It wasn't, he said, that he didn't want to do whatever his mother needed. She came first in his life, but those people they'd hired to help out couldn't turn around without coming in and asking him how to do it. He glared accusingly at me, as if I'd hired them and sent them there.
>
> He said he didn't want to try to write anything but westerns, nowadays, which he guessed would please me. But he was going absolutely crazy the way people interrupted him. His mother never called him in the middle of a scene he was just getting right. She understood that a man has to be left strictly alone when he's trying to write.

Little has been said concerning the impact increasing interruptions had on Howard. Some writers can handle interruptions much better than others. Journalists are frequently interrupted when they are working in a newsroom. They have a telephone at their desk and many times they actually want it to ring! Next in general would have to come writers of nonfiction, whose stages of constant research are themselves an interruption to the flow of writing. And of the writers who tend to dislike interruption the absolute most, you have fiction writers. Unlike journalists or nonfiction writers, they don't have as clear a mental bookmark for resuming their story, and if a thought is lost there is little chance it will be regained in a reference book or through a confidential source (although the idea of a novelist who has lost his train of thought in mid-sentence suddenly getting a call from Deep Throat to arrange a meeting in an underground parking garage wherein the clue to finishing the sentence will be given is whimsical.) And of fiction writers, some can mildly tolerate interruptions and others can't stand them. Howard couldn't stand them, and Novalyne suggests he had fantasies of strangling those who interrupted him: "For a moment it seemed to help Bob to find someone who knew how badly he wanted to strangle people who interrupted him. He talked about them and about the rest of the world-damn fools who thought sitting down at the typewriter and pounding your guts out was not the kind of job a man ought to work at." This strangling business is a good meter of Howard's level of frustration with his reduced writing privacy. From Novalyne's book:

> Finally, I interrupted him. "Bob, you keep talking about stories I might write. What about you? Why don't you write all these things you're telling me to?"
>
> He walked impatiently away from the cistern. "I can't write anything anymore," he said harshly. "No time. Never any time. I get started; I have to stop."
>
> He began to pace up and down the yard, rubbing a hand across his forehead. "I'm burned out. You pound out yarn after yarn—sometimes ten or twelve thousand words a day. You work your damn guts out. Finally, you know you're burning out—that the time is coming fast when there won't be anything left. Nothing at all."

In some ways, Howard may have felt that even a best-case scenario for him would entail his mother living longer, but continually dependent on the kind of home care which would provide a constant source of interruptions for him. Logically it would seem that the only reasonable way Howard might have suffered fewer interruptions was if he had married Novalyne and the couple had found their own prerequisite love nest. It would not have been practical to expect Howard to move out without such incentive (although the image of Howard conducting his nuptials in his little single bed beside his mother's window, with the lower halves of the bride and groom perfectly framed in said window, is one that may have had more potential than anyone would care to admit.) But of course, aside from the possibility that he may have had a whole new set of interruptions from Novalyne with which to contend, he still would have felt compelled to make steady trips to his mother. These trips may have even lessened in time if Howard were able, by sheer conditioning if nothing else, to detach himself from the intensity of interdependence which loomed so predominantly between them. Hester wouldn't have liked such a thing at all, but if she saw her son married and comparatively content, a certain well of grace which she did indeed possess may have allowed her to accept such an arrangement, albeit grudgingly.

Earlier Howard had written in *Ambitions By Moonlight*, which appeared in the round-robin monthly *The Junto*: "I'd like to be the strongest man in the world….I want to know all the hidden, secret things….I want to delve into all the secret cults and demoniac mysteries….I want to write dark and forbidding books which will freeze the blood and burn the ears of men….And I'd like to have about four hundred women who thought they understood me." The challenge here seems to be to take Howard at his word, and picture his fantasy self as a frighteningly bemuscled dark mage who somehow finds himself allotted with four hundred damsels who confidently have the wrong impression of him. With such a quantity of attention, it seems he would be left with little time for delving into arcane abominations, much less writing coronary-inducing, ear-incinerating literature (or even pamphlets.) Although to his credit he does not say that the women have to be attractive, and perhaps having a stable of four hundred ugly women would have given Howard just the right incentive to tirelessly pursue his other interests, and do some bodybuilding between memorizing ancient death spells and laying waste to the central nervous systems of his readership. Suffice to say that even this confessed ambition does not truly reveal his heart's desire.

What Howard would have likely loved, simply, was to be able to produce stories which satisfied his interests as well as his readership, and to be promptly paid for those stories. Novalyne had continually urged him to write of the American West, of its history and people, as Howard had expressed great interest in doing full-time but had postponed the impulse. Reader reaction to stories such as *Sowers of the Thunder*, which appeared in the winter 1932 issue of *Oriental Stories*, gave Howard a positive boost. He wrote to Tevis Clyde Smith circa May 1932: "Did you notice what a hand I got in 'The Souk' [the letters section of *Oriental Stories*] on 'The Sowers of the Thunder'? I'm sincerely amazed. I knew it was a pretty good yarn, but I didn't have any idea the readers would go for it like they seem to have done. There must be more folks interested in historical episodes than is generally thought. Kirk Mashburn, a damned good writer, wrote and told me I should have sold it to *Adventure*—of which he says he hasn't missed a copy since he found one in a deserted stretch of Florida Everglades many years ago. But if I'd sent it to *Adventure*, they'd have returned it unread, same as usual."

Slicker magazines such as *Adventure* and *Argosy* seemed to be just the type of markets for Howard, yet they rejected his work most of the time. In February 1929 Howard sent an account to Clyde Smith of some of the stories he had submitted to various magazines and their acceptance or rejection. By Howard's account from 1921 to 1928 he sent 20 submissions to these two magazines alone (with slight overlap) and was not accepted once. Some of the stories named are known to exist while others are presumed lost. The names are, *Bill Smalley and the Power of the Human Eye, Lal Singh—Adventurer, The Feminine of the Species, The Crimson Line, Windigo! Windigo!, The Hand of Obeah, John Morrissey—Adventurer, Skulls in the Stars, Spanish Gold on Devil Horse, The Isle of Pirates' Doom, The Spirit of Tom Molyneaux, The Weepin' Willow, The Right Hook, The Touch of Death, Skulls and Orchids,* and *The Charming Gong*. Howard notes that he included a "long letter" with his submission of *The Hand of Obeah* to *Adventure* magazine, yet was still rejected. Howard was also asked to rewrite R. Fowler Gafford's novel *West of the Rio Grande* but upon completion of the task a publisher could not be found for it.

Howard tells Lovecraft circa May/June 1933, "I was eighteen when I wrote 'Spear and Fang,' 'The Lost Race,' 'The Hyena'; nineteen when I wrote 'In the Forest of Villefere' and 'Wolfshead.' And after that it was two solid years before I sold another line of fiction. I don't like to think about those two years. I wrote my first story when I was fifteen, and sent it—to *Adventure*, I believe. Three years later I managed to break into *Weird Tales*. Three years of writing without selling a blasted line. (I have never been able to sell to *Adventure*; guess my first attempt cooked me with them for ever!) I haven't been any kind of a success, financially, though I have managed to get by."

What Howard did not fully realize was that *Weird Tales* itself was just barely getting by, although some would call it floundering. "*Weird Tales* always had trouble staying alive," Marvin Kaye wrote in his December 1987 introduction to a *Weird Tales* anthology book. "During its long, intermittent run from 1923 till the present, it has changed size, staff and physical headquarters; several times, it went out of business…only to return from the grave again and again." Volume One, Number One of *Weird Tales* appeared in March of 1923 under the umbrella of Rural Publications, which also launched its less famous sister magazines *Mystery Stories* and *Real Detective Tales*. The first issue was a whopping 192 pages, cost twenty-five cents, and featured two dozen stories, including contributions by both Farnsworth Wright and Otis Adelbert Kline, who were on the magazine's staff at the time. Wright was formerly a Chicago music critic, and Kline would eventually become Howard's literary agent. Financial problems were quick and swift, but co-owner Jacob Clark Henneberger felt strongly about keeping the magazine afloat, and he sold his other holdings to his partner John M. Lansinger to keep *Weird Tales* all to himself.

H.P. Lovecraft was offered the editorship of the reorganized magazine in 1924, but Lovecraft politely declined. Next

Henneberger offered the job to Wright, who held it until his death in 1940.

It is interesting to note that while Howard admittedly had to scrimp and save in order to get by, his great barbarian Conan did nothing of the sort when he found gold in his purse, freely spending it on drink and women. The lifestyle of Conan ranged from lavish during those brief periods he had coin, to lean and hardy for much of the remainder. While it may be a bit excessive to equate Conan's financial ups and downs to Howard's mood swinging high and low, the theme of fluctuation without balance is certainly present in both Howard's life and his writing. It's the same for many writers, to feel very close to happy when you've worked out a good story, and very close to depressed when you are between stories and unsure of what will come next. Howard worked in spurts, sometimes producing ten thousand or more words in a day (thirty thousand has been mentioned,) and sometimes going for days or even weeks without writing much; another microcosm of extremes. The nature of his mother's illness caused her to rally to near normal at times, only to climb down hill again. The nation's finances went to the negative extreme, and even the weather in Texas during this period went from periods of great harvests to hard droughts and bitter winters; as recounted by Howard in a letter to August Derleth from July 1933: "There's one hell of a drouth burning this country up right now. The cotton looks pretty good, but the grain crops suffered savagely, and the corn wasn't worth a curse." We could continue, and say that here was one of the most well-paid men in his region living in a confined, near prison cell-like space, who went on and off with ideas about becoming engaged to Novalyne, on and off with moods while with friends. But rather than agree with those who have speculatively diagnosed Howard's condition as a bi-polar disorder, it seems more logical to argue that any writer so heavily entrenched in his craft is far more likely to experience such states. Intense writing is often indicative of an intense writer, who might possess any number of unusual quirks and oddities, plus Howard's only known concerns for his health were physical and not mental. Aside from aforementioned heart concerns, which did not seem to be serious, the condition of Howard's eyesight required him to wear glasses while working, and although no picture is known to exist of Howard wearing glasses, he writes to R.H. Barlow circa June 1934, "Thank you very much for your kind comments concerning 'The Queen of the Black Coast,' and I am sorry about your eyes. I strained mine at a comparatively early age, and have been forced to wear glasses while reading or working for a number of years now." Later that month in a reply to Barlow's letter Howard said, "Yes, my eyes are poor; started when I was a kid, sitting out on the woodpile and reading until after dark. The condition hasn't been improved by getting a large number of boxing gloves stuck in my eyes and bounced off my temples."

It is hard to picture Howard in glasses—hitting a log with a sledgehammer, yes; wearing glasses, no. And it seems clear he didn't want himself pictured that way, regardless of whatever literary connotations spectacles provide.

> "At my best I am a jovial companion, neither smart nor witty, but friendly at least; at my worst I am merely moody and taciturn, desiring only solitude in which to brood over the melancholy images which haunt a gloomy mind." —Robert E. Howard to H. P. Lovecraft, August 9, 1932.

Moving out of his twenties it seems likely that Howard became more entrenched with daily reality. When he completed his studies at Howard Payne, the young author made an agreement with his father that if he could not support himself by writing in one year's time, he would pursue other endeavors. Much later in his well running dry conversation with Novalyne, Howard intimates it is becoming harder to make the connection to the imaginative ("...at first you write day and night...but the constant production finally gets to you...you should be mighty careful that you don't burn yourself out...") and it seems certain that he is no longer as close to some of the viewpoints that a younger man or teenager would hold. It is hard to maintain raw anger and other emotions without having them wane or morph or graduate into something different. For all their regional dialect, Howard's more sophisticated western stories, generally written later in his life, have a different flavor to their driving force. It is quite possible Howard saw this change not so much as any maturation, for his work was usually excellent whether he admitted it or not, but rather as a signpost on a road whose destination was uncertain to him. We've all had that quavering feeling as we see a sign that makes us question our route. Perhaps the changing flavors in Howard's later writing gave him just such a feeling, amplified to a degree by the knowledge that his main publisher, Farnsworth Wright, was laying out a debt and nonpayment situation which demanded Howard find other markets, plus an increasing general interest in science fiction did not play to Howard's strongest points. Novalyne's dislike of the subject matter made her unwilling to read more than the first paragraph or two of many of Howard's *Weird Tales* writing, and these things put together must have amounted to a situation which he could hardly consider desirable. After all, who would not be somewhat disturbed if the source of their bread and butter income became insufferably delinquent and their significant other usually couldn't stomach their work? Novalyne cited nightmares, and it seems safe to speculate that part of Howard would have preferred she have them, and be witness to the impact of his writing. But Novalyne favored more mainstream and tamer literature.

Howard at Fort McKavett, 1933

Chapter Nine:

Secrets of the Silver Key

> "...there is absolutely no justification for literature unless it serves to release the imagination from the bounds of everyday life."
>
> --Clark Ashton Smith to HP Lovecraft, October 1930.

As an example of a truly thought-provoking story, Novalyne recalls in *One Who Walked Alone* of Howard telling her, "Now, a friend of mine wrote a yarn a few years ago. It was one of the greatest yarns I ever read. I think about it a lot. Sometimes when I finish a yarn and am getting another one ready, I think about that yarn of his, and why I think it was good. Sometimes I sit at my typewriter and think about it. I think about it on my way to and from the post office. Why, girl, I even think about that yarn when I go out to milk the cow. As I think about it, I begin to have my own thoughts and ideas. Maybe there was something I believe about life that he didn't say."

Research suggests that man was H.P. Lovecraft, and that story was *The Silver Key*. From Glenn Lord's *The Howard Collector*, in a letter to Lovecraft from July 1933 Howard said, "I remember 'The Silver Key'—yet remember is hardly the word to use. I have constantly referred to that story in my meditations ever since I read it, years ago—have probably thought of it more than any other story that ever appeared in Weird Tales. There was something about it that struck deep. I read it aloud to Tevis Clyde Smith, some years ago, and he agreed with me as to its cosmic sweep."

The Silver Key was written in 1926 and published in the January, 1929 *Weird Tales*. Farnsworth Wright first rejected the story in 1927, but then asked to see it again. After publication Wright told Lovecraft the story was "violently disliked" by readers (*An H.P. Lovecraft Encyclopedia*, S.T. Joshi and David Shultz.) It's character of Randolph Carter appears in several stories, the sequence being *The Dream-Quest of Unknown Kadath, The Statement of Randolph Carter, The Unnamable, The Silver Key* and its sequel *Through the Gates of the Silver Key*.

Its beginning of "When Randolph Carter was thirty he lost the key to the gate of dreams" parallels Howard's loss of life at the age of thirty. Since more than seventy years have passed since Lovecraft's death, and for other reasons, his work is in the public domain and partially available through Project Gutenberg and manybooks.net. August Derleth's *Arkham House* had represented itself as having rights to Lovecraft's fiction (presumably with the 1941 Morriss-Lewis agreement and the 1947 *Weird Tales* agreement,) but if these rights existed at all, they effectively ended when Arkham House abandoned its copyright claims in order to withhold royalties from Derleth's associate and publishing partner Donald Wandrei (formerly with E.P. Dutton,) as related in *The Black Seas of Copyright* by Chris Karr, who elegantly presents these three factors:

1.) None of the copyrights to any of the individual Lovecraft stories were renewed in the 1950's as required by that time's copyright laws. Arkham House did renew the copyrights to their Lovecraft compilations, but these renewals protect the arrangement of the works and not the individual stories within. For more details, see "A Report on the Copyright Renewals of the Works of H.P. Lovecraft".

2.) The copyrights to the issues of Weird Tales containing Lovecraft stories were renewed. However, in 1947, Weird Tales sold their rights to the Lovecraft materials to Arkham House. It is unclear what rights that Weird Tales actually owned, but it is believed that after 1926, Lovecraft began reserving the full rights for himself. It is also unclear whether the Weird Tales renewals applied to the rights that Arkham House purchased.

3.) After the death of August Derleth in the 1970's, his partner Donald Wandrei sued his estate for royalties and rights due to him as a consequence of the partner's death. During the course of the litigation, the attorney overseeing both Derleth's estate and Arkham House testified that Wandrei was not owed anything because the Lovecraft works entered the public domain due to the lack of copyright renewal.

So, this long-winded preface is meant to set the stage for the following presentation of Lovecraft's *The Silver Key* in its known entirety. As the *Weird Tales* story which Howard said he probably thought of most and "constantly referred to" in his meditations because it struck such a deep chord within his mind, it deserves to be presented here so that readers may share it and gain an essential glimpse into something which Howard liked and thought of so much. It offers a wealth of comparisons with Howard beliefs which will be touched upon at the story's conclusion.

The Silver Key
by Howard Phillips Lovecraft

When Randolph Carter was thirty he lost the key of the gate of dreams. Prior to that time he had made up for the prosiness of life by nightly excursions to strange and ancient cities beyond space, and lovely, unbelievable garden lands across ethereal seas; but as middle age hardened upon him he felt those liberties slipping away little by little, until at last he was cut off altogether. No more could his galleys sail up the river Oukranos past the gilded spires of Thran, or his elephant caravans tramp through perfumed jungles in Kled, where forgotten palaces with veined ivory columns sleep lovely and unbroken under the moon.

He had read much of things as they are, and talked with too many people. Well-meaning philosophers had taught him to look into the logical relations of things, and analyse the processes which shaped his thoughts and fancies. Wonder had gone away, and he had forgotten that all life is only a set of pictures in the brain, among which there is no difference betwixt those born of real things and those born of inward dreamings, and no cause to value the one above the other. Custom had dinned into his ears a superstitious reverence for that which tangibly and physically exists, and had made him secretly ashamed to dwell in visions. Wise men told him his simple fancies were inane and childish, and even more absurd because their actors persist in fancying them full of meaning and purpose as the blind cosmos grinds aimlessly on from nothing to something and from something back to nothing again, neither heeding nor knowing the wishes or existence of the minds that flicker for a second now and then in the darkness.

They had chained him down to things that are, and had then explained the workings of those things till mystery had gone out of the world. When he complained, and longed to escape into twilight realms where magic moulded all the little vivid fragments and prized associations of his mind into vistas of breathless expectancy and unquenchable delight, they turned him instead toward the new-found prodigies of science, bidding him find wonder in the atom's vortex and mystery in the sky's dimensions. And when he had failed to find these boons in things whose laws are known and measurable, they told him he lacked imagination, and was immature because he preferred dream-illusions to the illusions of our physical creation.

So Carter had tried to do as others did, and pretended that the common events and emotions of earthy minds were more important than the fantasies of rare and delicate souls. He did not dissent when they told him that the animal pain of a stuck pig or dyspeptic ploughman in real life is a greater thing than the peerless beauty of Narath with its hundred carven gates and domes of chalcedony, which he dimly remembered from his dreams; and under their guidance he cultivated a painstaking sense of pity and tragedy.

Once in a while, though, he could not help seeing how shallow, fickle, and meaningless all human aspirations are, and how emptily our real impulses contrast with those pompous ideals we profess to hold. Then he would have recourse to the polite laughter they had taught him to use against the extravagance and artificiality of dreams; for he saw that the daily life of our world is every inch as extravagant and artificial, and far less worthy of respect because of its poverty in beauty and its silly reluctance to admit its own lack of reason and purpose. In this way he became a kind of humorist, for he did not see that even humour is empty in a mindless universe devoid of any true standard of consistency or inconsistency.

In the first days of his bondage he had turned to the gentle churchly faith endeared to him by the naive trust of his fathers, for thence stretched mystic avenues which seemed to promise escape from life. Only on closer view did he mark the starved fancy and beauty, the stale and prosy triteness, and the owlish gravity and grotesque claims of solid truth which reigned boresomely and overwhelmingly among most of its professors; or feel to the full the awkwardness with which it sought to keep alive as literal fact the outgrown fears and guesses of a primal race confronting the unknown. It wearied Carter to see how solemnly people tried to make earthly reality out of old myths which every step of their boasted science confuted, and this misplaced seriousness killed the attachment he might have kept for the ancient creeds had they been content to offer the sonorous rites and emotional outlets in their true guise of ethereal fantasy.

But when he came to study those who had thrown off the old myths, he found them even more ugly than those who had not. They did not know that beauty lies in harmony, and that loveliness of life has no standard amidst an aimless cosmos save only its harmony with the dreams and the feelings which have gone before and blindly moulded our little spheres out of the rest of chaos. They did not see that good and evil and beauty and ugliness are only ornamental fruits of perspective, whose sole value lies in their linkage to what chance made our fathers think and feel, and whose finer details are different for every race and culture. Instead, they either denied these things altogether or transferred them to the crude, vague instincts which they shared with the beasts and peasants; so that their lives were dragged malodorously out in pain, ugliness, and disproportion, yet filled with a ludicrous pride at having escaped from something no more unsound than that which still held them. They had traded the false gods of fear and blind piety for those of license and anarchy.

Carter did not taste deeply of these modern freedoms; for their cheapness and squalor sickened a spirit loving beauty alone while his reason rebelled at the flimsy logic with which their champions tried to gild brute impulse with a sacredness stripped from the idols they had discarded. He saw that most of them, in common with their cast-off priestcraft, could not escape from the delusion that life has a meaning apart from that which men dream into it; and could not lay aside the crude notion of ethics and obligations beyond those of beauty, even when all Nature shrieked of its unconsciousness and impersonal unmorality in the light of their scientific discoveries. Warped and bigoted with preconceived illusions of justice, freedom, and consistency, they cast off the old lore and the old way with the old beliefs; nor ever stopped to think that that lore and those ways were the sole makers of their present thoughts and judgments, and the sole guides and standards in a meaningless universe without fixed aims or stable points of reference. Having lost these artificial settings, their lives grew void of direction and dramatic interest; till at length they strove to drown their ennui in bustle and pretended usefulness, noise and excitement, barbaric display and animal sensation. When these things palled, disappointed, or grew nauseous through revulsion, they cultivated irony and bitterness, and found fault with the social order. Never could they realize that their brute foundations were as shifting and contradictory as the gods of their elders, and that the satisfaction of one moment is the bane of the next. Calm, lasting beauty comes only in a dream, and this solace the world had thrown away when in its worship of the real it threw away the secrets of childhood and innocence.

Amidst this chaos of hollowness and unrest Carter tried to live as befitted a man of keen thought and good heritage. With his dreams fading under the ridicule of the age he could not believe in anything, but the love of harmony kept him close to the ways of his race and station. He walked impassive through the cities of men, and sighed because no vista seemed fully real; because every flash of yellow sunlight on tall roofs and every glimpse of balustraded plazas in the first lamps of evening served only to remind him of dreams he had once known, and to make him homesick for ethereal lands he no longer knew how to find. Travel was only a mockery; and even the Great War stirred him but little, though he served from the first in the Foreign Legion of France. For a while he sought friends, but soon grew weary of the crudeness of their emotions, and the sameness and earthiness of their visions. He felt vaguely glad that all his relatives were distant and out of touch with him, for they would not have understood his mental life. That is, none but his grandfather and great-uncle Christopher could, and they were long dead.

Then he began once more the writing of books, which he had left off when dreams first failed him. But here, too, was there no satisfaction or fulfillment; for the touch of earth was upon his mind, and he could not think of lovely things as he had done of yore. Ironic humor dragged down all the twilight minarets he reared, and the earthy fear of improbability blasted all the delicate and amazing flowers in his faery gardens. The convention of assumed pity spilt mawkishness on his characters, while the myth of an important reality and significant human events and emotions debased all his high fantasy into thin-veiled allegory and cheap social satire. His new novels were successful as his old ones had never been; and because he knew how empty they must be to please an empty herd, he burned them and ceased his writing. They were very graceful novels, in which he urbanely laughed at the dreams he lightly sketched; but he saw that their sophistication had sapped all their life away.

It was after this that he cultivated deliberate illusion, and dabbled in the notions of the bizarre and the eccentric as an antidote for the commonplace. Most of these, however, soon showed their poverty and barrenness; and he saw that the popular doctrines of occultism are as dry and inflexible as those of science, yet without even the slender palliative of truth to redeem them. Gross stupidity, falsehood, and muddled thinking are not dream; and form no escape from life to a mind trained above their own level. So Carter bought stranger books and sought out deeper and more terrible men of fantastic erudition; delving into arcana of consciousness that few have trod, and learning things about the secret pits of life, legend, and immemorial antiquity which disturbed him ever afterward. He decided to live on a rarer plane, and furnished his Boston home to suit his changing moods; one room for each, hung in appropriate colours, furnished with befitting books and objects, and provided with sources of the proper sensations of light, heat, sound, taste, and odour.

Once he heard of a man in the south, who was shunned and

feared for the blasphemous things he read in prehistoric books and clay tablets smuggled from India and Arabia. Him he visited, living with him and sharing his studies for seven years, till horror overtook them one midnight in an unknown and archaic graveyard, and only one emerged where two had entered. Then he went back to Arkham, the terrible witch-haunted old town of his forefathers in New England, and had experiences in the dark, amidst the hoary willows and tottering gambrel roofs, which made him seal forever certain pages in the diary of a wild-minded ancestor. But these horrors took him only to the edge of reality, and were not of the true dream country he had known in youth; so that at fifty he despaired of any rest or contentment in a world grown too busy for beauty and too shrewd for dreams.

Having perceived at last the hollowness and futility of real things, Carter spent his days in retirement, and in wistful disjointed memories of his dream-filled youth. He thought it rather silly that he bothered to keep on living at all, and got from a South American acquaintance a very curious liquid to take him to oblivion without suffering. Inertia and force of habit, however, caused him to defer action; and he lingered indecisively among thoughts of old times, taking down the strange hangings from his walls and refitting the house as it was in his early boyhood - purple panes, Victorian furniture, and all.

With the passage of time he became almost glad he had lingered, for his relics of youth and his cleavage from the world made life and sophistication seem very distant and unreal; so much so that a touch of magic and expectancy stole back into his nightly slumbers. For years those slumbers had known only such twisted reflections of everyday things as the commonest slumbers know, but now there returned a flicker of something stranger and wilder; something of vaguely awesome imminence which took the form of tensely clear pictures from his childhood days, and made him think of little inconsequential things he had long forgotten. He would often awake calling for his mother and grandfather, both in their graves a quarter of a century.

Then one night his grandfather reminded him of the key. The grey old scholar, as vivid as in life, spoke long and earnestly of their ancient line, and of the strange visions of the delicate and sensitive men who composed it. He spoke of the flame-eyed Crusader who learnt wild secrets of the Saracens that held him captive; and of the first Sir Randolph Carter who studied magic when Elizabeth was queen. He spoke, too, of that Edmund Carter who had just escaped hanging in the Salem witchcraft, and who had placed in an antique box a great silver key handed down from his ancestors. Before Carter awaked, the gentle visitant had told him where to find that box; that carved oak box of archaic wonder whose grotesque lid no hand had raised for two centuries.

In the dust and shadows of the great attic he found it, remote and forgotten at the back of a drawer in a tall chest. It was about a foot square, and its Gothic carvings were so fearful that he did not marvel no person since Edmund Carter had dared to open it. It gave forth no noise when shaken, but was mystic with the scent of unremembered spices. That it held a key was indeed only a dim legend, and Randolph Carter's father had never known such a box existed. It was bound in rusty iron, and no means was provided for working the formidable lock. Carter vaguely understood that he would find within it some key to the lost gate of dreams, but of where and how to use it his grandfather had told him nothing.

An old servant forced the carven lid, shaking as he did so at the hideous faces leering from the blackened wood, and at some unplaced familiarity. Inside, wrapped in a discoloured parchment, was a huge key of tarnished silver covered with cryptical arabesques; but of any legible explanation there was none. The parchment was voluminous, and held only the strange hieroglyphs of an unknown tongue written with an antique reed. Carter recognized the characters as those he had seen on a certain papyrus scroll belonging to that terrible scholar of the South who had vanished one midmght in a nameless cemetery. The man had always shivered when he read this scroll, and Carter shivered now.

But he cleaned the key, and kept it by him nightly in its aromatic box of ancient oak. His dreams were meanwhile increasing in vividness, and though showing him none of the strange cities and incredible gardens of the old days, were assuming a definite cast whose purpose could not be mistaken. They were calling him back along the years, and with the mingled wills of all his fathers were pulling him toward some hidden and ancestral source. Then he knew he must go into the past and merge himself with old things, and day after day he thought of the hills to the north where haunted Arkham and the rushing Miskatonic and the lonely rustic homestead of his people lay.

In the brooding fire of autumn Carter took the old remembered way past graceful lines of rolling hill and stone-walled meadow, distant vale and hanging woodland, curving road and nestling farmstead, and the crystal windings of the Miskatonic, crossed here and there by rustic bridges of wood or stone. At one bend he saw the group of giant elms among which an ancestor had oddly vanished a century and a half before, and shuddered as the wind blew meaningly through them. Then there was the crumbling farmhouse of old Goody Fowler the witch, with its little evil windows and great roof sloping nearly to the ground on the north side. He speeded up his car as he passed it, and did not slacken till he had mounted the hill where his mother and her fathers before her were born, and where the old white house still looked proudly across the road at the breathlessly lovely panorama of rocky slope and verdant valley, with the distant spires of Kingsport on the horizon, and hints of the archaic, dream-laden sea in the farthest background.

Then came the steeper slope that held the old Carter place he had not seen in over forty years. Afternoon was far gone when he reached the foot, and at the bend half way up he paused to scan the outspread countryside golden and glorified in the slanting floods of magic poured out by a western sun. All the strangeness and expectancy of his recent dreams seemed present in this hushed and unearthly landscape, and he thought of the unknown solitudes of other planets as his eyes traced out the velvet and deserted lawns shining undulant between their tumbled walls, and clumps of faery forest setting off far lines of purple hills beyond hills, and the spectral wooded valley dipping down in shadow to dank hollows where trickling waters crooned and gurgled among swollen and distorted roots.

Something made him feel that motors did not belong in the realm he was seeking, so he left his car at the edge of the forest, and putting the great key in his coat pocket walked on up the hill. Woods now engulfed him utterly, though he knew the house was on a high knoll that cleared the trees except to the north. He wondered how it would look, for it had been left vacant and untended through his neglect since the death of his strange great-uncle Christopher thirty years before. In his boyhood he had revelled through long visits there, and had found weird marvels in the woods beyond the orchard.

Shadows thickened around him, for the night was near. Once a gap in the trees opened up to the right, so that he saw off across leagues of twilight meadow and spied the old Congregational steeple on Central Hill in Kingsport; pink with the last flush of day, the panes of the little round windows blazing with reflected fire. Then, when he was in deep shadow again, he recalled with a start that the glimpse must have come from childish memory alone, since the old white church had long been torn down to make room for the Congregational Hospital. He had read of it with interest, for the paper had told about some strange burrows or passages found in the rocky hill beneath.

Through his puzzlement a voice piped, and he started again at its familiarity after long years. Old Benijah Corey had been his Uncle Christopher's hired man, and was aged even in those far-off times of his boyhood visits. Now he must be well over a hundred, but that piping voice could come from no one else. He could distinguish no words, yet the tone was haunting and unmistakable. To think that "Old Benijy" should still be alive!

"Mister Randy! Mister Randy! Wharbe ye? D'ye want to skeer yer Aunt Marthy plumb to death? Hain't she tuld ye to keep nigh the place in the arternoon an' git back afur dark? Randy! Ran... dee!... He's the beatin'est boy fer runnin' off in the woods I ever see; haff the time a-settin' moonin' raound that snake-den in the upper timberlot! ... Hey yew, Ran ... dee!"

Randolph Carter stopped in the pitch darkness and rubbed his hand across his eyes. Something was queer. He had been somewhere he ought not to be; had strayed very far away to places where he had not belonged, and was now inexcusably late. He had not noticed the time on the Kingsport steeple, though he could easily have made it out with his pocket telescope; but he knew his lateness was something very strange and unprecedented. He was not sure he had his little telescope with him, and put his hand in his blouse pocket to see. No, it was not there, but there was the big silver key he had found in a box somewhere. Uncle Chris had told him something odd once about an old unopened box with a key in it, but Aunt Martha had stopped the story abruptly, saying it was no kind of thing to tell a child whose head was already too full of queer fancies. He tried to recall just where he had found the key, but something seemed very confused. He guessed it was in the attic at home in Boston, and dimly remembered bribing Parks with half his week's allowance to help him open the box and keep quiet about it; but when he remembered this, the face of Parks came up very strangely, as if the wrinkles of long years had fallen upon the brisk little Cockney.

"Ran ... dee! Ran ... dee! Hi! Hi! Randy!"

A swaying lantern came around the black bend, and old Benijah pounced on the silent and bewildered form of the pilgrim.

"Durn ye, boy, so thar ye be! Ain't ye got a tongue in yer head, that ye can't answer a body! I ben callin' this haff hour, an' ye must a heerd me long ago! Dun't ye know yer Aunt Marthy's all a-fidget over yer bein' off arter dark? Wait till I tell yer Uncle Chris when he gits hum! Ye'd orta know these here woods ain't no fitten place to be traipsin' this hour! They's things abroad what dun't do nobody no good, as my gran'-sir knowed afur me. Come, Mister Randy, or Hannah wunt keep supper no longer!"

So Randolph Carter was marched up the road where wondering stars glimmered through high autumn boughs. And dogs barked as the yellow light of small-paned windows shone out at the farther turn, and the Pleiades twinkled across the open knoll where a great gambrel roof stood black against the dim west. Aunt Martha was in the doorway, and did not scold too hard when Benijah shoved the truant in. She knew Uncle Chris well enough to expect such things of the Carter blood. Randolph did not show his key, but ate his supper in silence and protested only when bedtime came. He sometimes dreamed better when awake, and he wanted to use that key.

In the morning Randolph was up early, and would have run

off to the upper timberlot if Uncle Chris had not caught him and forced him into his chair by the breakfast table. He looked impatiently around the low-pitched room with the rag carpet and exposed beams and corner-posts, and smiled only when the orchard boughs scratched at the leaded panes of the rear window. The trees and the hills were close to him, and formed the gates of that timeless realm which was his true country.

Then, when he was free, he felt in his blouse pocket for the key; and being reassured, skipped off across the orchard to the rise beyond, where the wooded hill climbed again to heights above even the treeless knoll. The floor of the forest was mossy and mysterious, and great lichened rocks rose vaguely here and there in the dim light like Druid monoliths among the swollen and twisted trunks of a sacred grove. Once in his ascent Randolph crossed a rushing stream whose falls a little way off sang runic incantations to the lurking fauns and aegipans and dryads.

Then he came to the strange cave in the forest slope, the dreaded "snake-den" which country folk shunned, and away from which Benijah had warned him again and again. It was deep; far deeper than anyone but Randolph suspected, for the boy had found a fissure in the farthermost black corner that led to a loftier grotto beyond - a haunting sepulchral place whose granite walls held a curious illusion of conscious artifice. On this occasion he crawled in as usual, lighting his way with matches filched from the sitting-room matchsafe, and edging through the final crevice with an eagerness hard to explain even to himself. He could not tell why he approached the farther wall so confidently, or why he instinctively drew forth the great silver key as he did so. But on he went, and when he danced back to the house that night he offered no excuses for his lateness, nor heeded in the least the reproofs he gained for ignoring the noon-tide dinner-horn altogether.

Now it is agreed by all the distant relatives of Randolph Carter that something occurred to heighten his imagination in his tenth year. His cousin, Ernest B. Aspinwall, Esq., of Chicago, is fully ten years his senior; and distinctly recalls a change in the boy after the autumn of 1883. Randolph had looked on scenes of fantasy that few others can ever have beheld, and stranger still were some of the qualities which he showed in relation to very mundane things. He seemed, in fine, to have picked up an odd gift of prophecy; and reacted unusually to things which, though at the time without meaning, were later found to justify the singular impressions. In subsequent decades as new inventions, new names, and new events appeared one by one in the book of history, people would now and then recall wonderingly how Carter had years before let fall some careless word of undoubted connection with what was then far in the future. He did not himself understand these words, or know why certain things made him feel certain emotions; but fancied that some unremembered dream must be responsible. It was as early as 1897 that he turned pale when some traveller mentioned the French town of Belloy-en-Santerre, and friends remembered it when he was almost mortally wounded there in 1916, while serving with the Foreign Legion in the Great War.

Carter's relatives talk much of these things because he has lately disappeared. His little old servant Parks, who for years bore patiently with his vagaries, last saw him on the morning he drove off alone in his car with a key he had recently found. Parks had helped him get the key from the old box containing it, and had felt strangely affected by the grotesque carvings on the box, and by some other odd quality he could not name. When Carter left, he had said he was going to visit his old ancestral country around Arkham.

Half way up Elm Mountain, on the way to the ruins of the old Carter place, they found his motor set carefully by the roadside; and in it was a box of fragrant wood with carvings that frightened the countrymen who stumbled on it. The box held only a queer parchment whose characters no linguist or palaeographer has been able to decipher or identify. Rain had long effaced any possible footprints, though Boston investigators had something to say about evidences of disturbances among the fallen timbers of the Carter place. It was, they averred, as though someone had groped about the ruins at no distant period. A common white handkerchief found among forest rocks on the hillside beyond cannot be identified as belonging to the missing man.

There is talk of apportioning Randolph Carter's estate among his heirs, but I shall stand firmly against this course because I do not believe he is dead. There are twists of time and space, of vision and reality, which only a dreamer can divine; and from what I know of Carter I think he has merely found a way to traverse these mazes. Whether or not he will ever come back, I cannot say. He wanted the lands of dream he had lost, and yearned for the days of his childhood. Then he found a key, and I somehow believe he was able to use it to strange advantage.

I shall ask him when I see him, for I expect to meet him shortly in a certain dream-city we both used to haunt. It is rumoured in Ulthar, beyond the River Skai, that a new king reigns on the opal throne of Ilek-Vad, that fabulous town of turrets atop the hollow cliffs of glass overlooking the twilight sea wherein the bearded and finny Gnorri build their singular labyrinths, and I believe I know how to interpret this rumour. Certainly, I look forward impatiently to the sight of that great silver key, for in its cryptical arabesques there may stand symbolised all the aims and mysteries of a blindly impersonal cosmos.

11 quotes from *The Silver Key* which likely resonated with Howard

1.) "Well-meaning philosophers had taught him to look into the logical relations of things, and analyse the processes which shaped his thoughts and fancies. Wonder had gone away, and he had forgotten that all life is only a set of pictures in the brain, among which there is no difference betwixt those born of real things and those born of inward dreamings, and no cause to value the one above the other."

2.) "…the blind cosmos grinds aimlessly on from nothing to something and from something back to nothing again, neither heeding nor knowing the wishes or existence of the minds that flicker for a second now and then in the darkness."

3.) "Once in a while, though, he could not help seeing how shallow, fickle, and meaningless all human aspirations are, and how emptily our real impulses contrast with those pompous ideals we profess to hold. Then he would have recourse to the polite laughter they had taught him to use against the extravagance and artificiality of dreams; for he saw that the daily life of our world is every inch as extravagant and artificial, and far less worthy of respect because of its poverty in beauty and its silly reluctance to admit its own lack of reason and purpose."

4.) "In the first days of his bondage he had turned to the gentle churchly faith endeared to him by the naive trust of his fathers, for thence stretched mystic avenues which seemed to promise escape from life. Only on closer view did he mark the starved fancy and beauty, the stale and prosy triteness, and the owlish gravity and grotesque claims of solid truth which reigned boresomely and overwhelmingly among most of its professors; or feel to the full the awkwardness with which it sought to keep alive as literal fact the outgrown fears and guesses of a primal race confronting the unknown. It wearied Carter to see how solemnly people tried to make earthly reality out of old myths which every step of their boasted science confuted, and this misplaced seriousness killed the attachment he might have kept for the ancient creeds had they been content to offer the sonorous rites and emotional outlets in their true guise of ethereal fantasy."

5.) "They did not see that good and evil and beauty and ugliness are only ornamental fruits of perspective, whose sole value lies in their linkage to what chance made our fathers think and feel, and whose finer details are different for every race and culture."

6.) "Calm, lasting beauty comes only in a dream, and this solace the world had thrown away when in its worship of the real it threw away the secrets of childhood and innocence."

7.) "He walked impassive through the cities of men, and sighed because no vista seemed fully real; because every flash of yellow sunlight on tall roofs and every glimpse of balustraded plazas in the first lamps of evening served only to remind him of dreams he had once known, and to make him homesick for ethereal lands he no longer knew how to find."

8.) "He decided to live on a rarer plane, and furnished his Boston home to suit his changing moods; one room for each, hung in appropriate colours, furnished with befitting books and objects, and provided with sources of the proper sensations of light, heat, sound, taste, and odour."

9.) "…he despaired of any rest or contentment in a world grown too busy for beauty and too shrewd for dreams."

10.) "Randolph had looked on scenes of fantasy that few others can ever have beheld, and stranger still were some of the qualities which he showed in relation to very mundane things."

11.) "There are twists of time and space, of vision and reality, which only a dreamer can divine…"

From Wikipedia: "'The Silver Key' is thought to have been inspired in part by Lovecraft's visit to Foster, Rhode Island, where his maternal ancestors lived. The character Benijah Corey from the story seems to combine the names of Emma Corey Phillips, one of Lovecraft's relatives, and Benejah Place, a farmer who lived across the street from the home where Lovecraft stayed. Carter's search for meaning through a succession of philosophical and aesthetic approaches may have been inspired by J.K. Huysmans' *A rebours* (1884), whose main character undertakes a similar progression."

It is worthwhile to note the similarity between Howard's "cog-wheels" theory of cosmic fate mentioned earlier in this volume in his letter to Clark Ashton Smith circa January 1934 and Lovecraft's grinding of the blind cosmos from nothing to something and back again as covered in Quote 2. Later *The Silver Key* offers what might be an accurate summation of Howard's general attitude toward religion in Quote 4.

Of particular interest is Quote 7, which although it describes Carter, it might as well have been written to describe Howard himself when states of depression gripped him such as the "burned out" discussion he had with Novalyne.

The part about furnishing different rooms to suit different moods (Quote 8) must have both intrigued and mocked Howard, whose confines were monk-like. Quotes 9-11 can be applied to Howard's view of the world and his power of imagination.

It becomes easy to see why *The Silver Key* made such a connection with REH.

Howard (with sword) and Truett Vinson

Howard's famous studio portrait for Novalyne

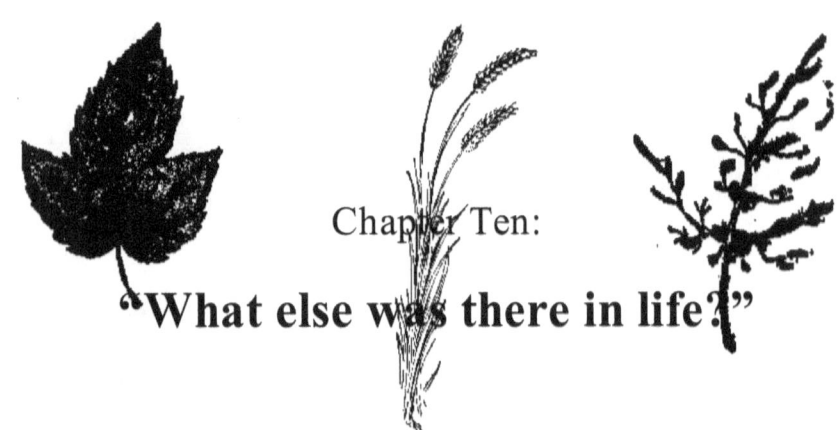

Chapter Ten:

"What else was there in life?"

"Whether my mother ever recovers or not possibly depends on the kind of care and attention I am able to give her, and that in turn depends on the money I am able to earn....Poverty is no new tale to me. I've gnawed crusts all my life. But the hardships I've suffered in the past may be picnics to what confronts me if Weird Tales discontinues my monthly checks."

--REH to Farnsworth Wright, May, 1935 (from *The Howard Collector*)

In a letter dated July 22, 1944, E. Hoffmann Price (who had visited Howard twice and was able to gain a very accurate perspective on him from so brief a time) wrote to Francis T. Laney, "...REH at the age of 30 had that same dismay and despair that one might expect of a child who has lost his mother....and with growing up, he had also acquired a lot of grown-up grimness, a lack of which would have made his act impossible....With all affection and respect, I repeat what is my conviction: that it was the act of a 5-year-old's emotion driving a grown and rugged man accustomed to firearms and violence; and that while mere absences from home would not have changed his emotional set-up, the normal keen interests which inevitably make most of us finally see home as a pleasant memory rather than as that without which there is no use living, would have saved REH..."

"This dark and brooding attitude was at the core of Howard's creative impulse," Don Herron wrote in *The Dark Barbarian* (whose title comes from a line in the poem *A Word from the Outer Dark*, copyrighted in 1974 by Lin Carter.) "His artistic leanings toward the poetic and the romantic, his compulsion for violence, his interests in history, myth and adventure all fell easily into this shadow of barbarism....The fact that Howard committed suicide underlines this intensity, this impulsive drive through personal destruction. He acted in life: his dark urgings were real. This powerful chord is reflected in Howard's art, and many people find it appalling."

Many more found it captivating. Howard told Lovecraft in a missive from December 1930, "I'm no philosopher, but resignation isn't in my blood. I wish it was. It isn't necessarily a hope to win that makes a man rebel against the infamies of life, vainly. Defeat is the lot of all men, and I come of a breed that never won a war. Men and women, too, of my line have fought for hopeless lost causes for a thousand years. Defeat waits for us all, but some of us, worse luck, can't accept it quietly."

In some ways, in Howard's mind, defeat even stretched to encompass the land which surrounded him. He wrote Lovecraft in June 1931, "Take this land around here; most of it isn't worth anything. Yet forty years ago, it was rich and fertile. But the men who farmed it knew nothing about crop-rotation, fertilizing the land, or anything else. They planted cotton till they wore the land out. Drouths baked all the moisture out of the soil and floods washed it away. This land washes amazingly in rains seasons. Terracing would have saved it—would have kept the fat dirt from washing away and held the moisture in the land. But it's only recently that any terracing has been done and now it's too late." This viewpoint of a cyclic continuation of ruination between the people and the land was ill lightened by the gloom of the Depression. Much of its flavor left Howard dreaming about other times, such as when he wrote Lovecraft in September 1932, "...if I were to be reborn in some earlier age and grow up knowing no other life or environment than that, I would choose to be born in a hut among the hills of western Ireland, the forests of Germany or the steppes of Southern Russia; to grow up hard and lean and wolfish, worshipping barbarian gods and living the hard barren life of a barbarian—which is, to the barbarian who has never tasted anything else, neither hard nor barren."

Drought refugees from Abilene in 1936. "The finest people in the world live in Texas, but I just can't seem to accomplish nothin' there. Two year drought, then a crop, then two year drought and so on. I got two brothers still trying to make it back there, and there they're sitting," said the father of these children.
Courtesy LOC, FSA/OWI

It is suggestive of a certain degree of contradiction when Howard discounts his challenging environs in the early 1930s as less of a test of the mettle of a soul (and less of a vibrant chord within the great iron harp of life) than the baser quandaries of more primitive lifestyles. It is likely not so much a case of the grass being greener on the other side of the timeline as it is a case of Howard's inner restlessness and turmoil coming to the surface, which would have happened regardless of his setting.

> *"There comes, even to kings, the time of great weariness. Then the gold of the throne is brass, the silk of the palace becomes drab. The gems in the diadem sparkle drearily like the ice of the white seas; the speech of men is as the empty rattle of a jester's bell and the feel comes of things unreal; even the sun is copper in the sky, and the breath of the green ocean is no longer fresh."*
> – REH, *The Mirrors of Tuzun Thune*

It is hard to separate the man from his writing, and some would say it is even futile and counterproductive. These voices would contend that a biography of Howard should be very much about his literary characters (in essence a biography of his characters.) But voices such as Howard's longtime friend E. Hoffmann Price did not agree. "To hell with the blow to literature and/or fiction. I laugh that off," he passionately wrote to Lovecraft on June 25, 1936, after Lovecraft had sent him an airmail saying that Howard had shot himself "in a fit of despondence due to his mother's [impending] death." Of Howard's suicide Price continued, "…the loss of the man is so damned incomparably greater than the loss to anything as stupid as literature that I can hardly hold the two ideas in my mind simultaneously. Maybe, later, I'll acquire the mental agility….I did appreciate his writings, deeply and heartily, and often wrote him to that effect. I was deeply grateful for his encouragement when I went into the fiction writing business in 1932, and often told him so….What he wrote was a joy that lingers, and I have many a time re-read many of his tales—but what he wrote was so god damned insignificant compared to the man himself."

Countless collections of Howard's stories are now being published. Writers such as the veteran Darrel Schweitzer and Dale Rippke have already endeavored to chronicle Howard's Hyborian world (*Conan's World and Robert E. Howard*, and Schweitzer's newer collection of essays in *The Robert E. Howard Reader,* and Rippke's *The Hyborian Heresies,*) writers such as Paul Sammon have looked at Conan specifically (*Conan the Phenomenon*,) and writers such as Leon Neilsen (who died of cancer on July 6, 2007) and Damon C. Sasser have focused their attentions on the broader scope of Howard's many other creations (*Robert E. Howard: A Collector's Descriptive Bibliography*, which has twice the bibliographical information as *The Last Celt*.) Even the late Gary Gygax admittedly incorporated much of Howard's Hyborian world into his *Dungeons & Dragons* franchise. But fewer writers have endeavored to present a comprehensive biography of Howard the man. The "old guard" of this presentation was Lyon Sprague de Camp, who contributed valuable research and conducted interviews and captured data in the mid 1970s which would otherwise have been lost. But de Camp had a tendency to push incomplete amounts of information in directions which suited his project or even just his fancy, such as his picture of Howard being a sickly boy who was constantly bullied. Of de Camp Leo Grin wrote in 2007 in *The Cimmerian* that he could recommend de Camp's autobiography *Time and Chance*, saying that it shed light on many of de Camp's motivations. "Years ago, the first thing I was struck by after wading through its 400+ often charming pages is how barren de Camp was of any inclination towards the pose of *artist*. As he rolls through his life, highlighting what he thinks is important, we get hundreds of facts, jokes, anecdotes—but not a single expression of writing as a passion or a high calling, of wanting to use his stories to express something important to him." Grin states that when this attitude is compared with the perennially intense collected thoughts of writers like Howard and Lovecraft, it stands in exceptional contrast. While REH and HPL spent feverish hours pondering the great mysteries of the cosmos, de Camp seemed content to don a Viking helmet and down a stein of ale (as one black and white photo of him depicts.) Here was a man who could look at writing not as an all-consuming vortex which is slowly and inextricably pulling in the soul of the author, but rather as a nice job with flexible hours and lots of freedom. In short, de Camp seemed less concerned with how his craft would be seen by the ages, and more content with simply living a good life.

But not all of the newer Howard publications are worth purchasing, for publishers such as the UK's Dodo Press are putting out overpriced hackish volumes of Howard's public domain works just to squeeze fans. Of this subject Damon C. Sasser wrote in the April 2008 Publisher's Journal section of *REH: Two-Gun Raconteur*: "Like vultures picking a carcass clean, opportunistic POD publisher Dodo Press (a UK outfit) is churning out dozens of thin paperback editions consisting of two or three Howard stories (for $10.00 a pop!), each sporting a startlingly awful cover culled from some on-line warehouse of terrible paintings that seek (unsuccessfully) to match the content of the book it covers." Sasser goes on to state that hopefully Dodo Press will go the way of the actual dodo bird, for it seems hard to imagine why any Howard collector would choose to direct their funds at purchasing such "over-priced crap."

Of the new Howard scholars (Mark Finn's *Blood & Thunder* was mentioned earlier) Rusty Burke and Don Herron are the unquestioned standard bearers of Howardian knowledge, although Burke himself acknowledges in *The Robert E. Howard Bookshelf* that Glenn Lord is "still the foremost authority on Howard." (And it is Glenn Lord to whom every Howard fan owes an inestimable debt of gratitude for his careful preservation of Howard's surviving manuscripts.) Burke, a longtime social worker, resembles a "Rusty," which means one could picture him and his beard back in time, sitting on a front porch as a young Bob Howard stopped by with his Chevy to ask the "old timer" a few questions about the pioneer days. Burke's conclusions tend to exhibit the depth of the study that went behind them and they tend to make the most sense. But it is hard to find a middle ground between the old guard and the new. Leo Grin continues, "For well over a decade now Howard publishing has been dominated by what can loosely be referred to as an anti-de Camp faction. These are a group of guys who endured thirty years of his near-stranglehold on the perception of Howard in the broader fantasy marketplace, and who are now intent on methodically undoing the damage wrought over decades of judging REH by oftentimes reductive, frivolous, and catty standards. Whenever there is a call for someone to step up and say something about the creator of Conan, it is inevitably the new guard who now gets contacted, with de Camp's old acolytes relegated to an embarrassing, impotent bystander status."

This status formed its roots when Don Herron published the famous essay *Conan vs. Conantics* in 1976, in which he calls out de Camp and Lin Carter and their propensity to alter much of Howard's intentions as well as changing his actual work. Specifically Herron mentions the injection of "good gods" by de

Camp and Carter—gods which sometimes help the hero. Even the mighty and indifferent Crom is portrayed as being amenable to helping. From Herron's essay: "I personally feel that REH's treatment of Hyborian Age religion on a conceptual basis, with alien beings or beings from earth's prime acting as evil gods, is much more realistic than the simplistic antics in some of the de Camp-Carter efforts. Once a writer admits the existence of Good Gods who are willing and ready to help out the hero, he blunts all suspense with the overwhelming presence of deus ex machina. Of course, authors like J. R. R. Tolkien are able to use a good vs. evil conflict - without the presence of supreme beings - on various story levels and in various degrees to great achievement. A comparison of Tolkien to Carter, though, could only be facetious. Likewise, there is little reason to compare Howard with Carter with any degree of seriousness."

Of de Camp's positive influences Gary Romeo wrote in *Sand Roughs* in 2001: "Trying to understand L. Sprague de Camp is not the same as condemning him. De Camp, for whatever motivation, was the primary force behind the multi-million selling Lancer 'Conan' series. Robert E. Howard's reputation as a premiere fantasist and the creator of the sub-genre known as 'Sword & Sorcery' was cemented by this popular series. The Conan stories by Howard were clearly separated from the de Camp/Carter stories and De Camp's introductions pointed readers to Howard's other works as published by Donald M. Grant, Glenn Lord, and others. De Camp was clearly a Howard fan and was instrumental in getting Howard's stories (albeit in sometimes edited form) before the reading public."

A principle of unifying these old and new approaches to Howard study can well be guided by the sage words of Mahatma Gandhi: "Adaptability is not imitation. It means power of resistance and assimilation." The usefulness of both old and new scholars is unquestioned, and while earnestly endeavoring to chronicle Howard there is always the knowledge that you, like every chronicler before you, have to deal with a missing element whose total recovery is impossible and whose very content is very much guesswork. As published in Glenn Lord's *The Last Celt* Howard wrote "I will be kind to my biographers for assuredly the day will come when some line-faced scrivener will be glad of this information," Howard plays a kind of trick on us scriveners by proceeding to discuss World War I, Christopher Columbus, Leif Ericson, St. Brandon, John L. Sullivan, Diamond Jim Brady, Jack Dempsey, Oliver Cromwell, Sir Walter Raleigh, the great potato famine of 1842 (which happened long after his people had immigrated to America,) the Tartars and Mongols, Ptolemies, the Moors, Charlemagne, Rollo the Walker, Joan of Arc, Napoleon, the Duke of Monmouth, the Turks and the Armenians, etcetera. Finally the whole thing comes to an abrupt halt with a discussion of how France doesn't want Russia to have the Dardanelles: "So she and England look at each other over their shoulders and let the unspeakable one hold on to it; while each year the bloody smoke of helpless thousands go up to the skies, a befitting sacrifice to the great god of commerce, who is greater than his younger brother, war." To the unfamiliar reader it would appear to be the autobiography of a disembodied history teacher.

There is also a whopping contradiction in two accounts Howard gives. The first, which appeared as part of a pastiche autobiography in *The Last Celt*, features Howard's impersonal authorial tone in discussing his supposed reasons for writing. He tells us, "Literature is a business to me....My sole desire in writing is to make a reasonable living. I may cling to many illusions, but I am not ridden by the illusion that I have anything wonderful or magical to say, or that it would amount to anything particularly if I did say it. I have no quarrel with art-for-art's-sakers. On the contrary, I admire their work. But my pet delusions tend in other directions. I took up writing simply because it seemed to promise an easier mode of work, more money, and more freedom than any other job I'd tried. I would write otherwise. If it was in my power to pen the grandest masterpiece the world has ever seen, I wouldn't hit the first key, or dip the pen in the ink, unless I knew there was a chance for me to get some money out of it, or publicity that would lead to money." Howard again echoes these stated beliefs in a letter to Lovecraft circa May/June 1933, with a similarity of phrase which seems to indicate a prepared front.

Now consider the complete confession about the falseness of this attitude which Novalyne recounts withdrawing from him in *One Who Walked Alone*:

> He tried to explain it to me. His father damn sure wasn't as interested in money as he himself was. Part of the trouble was that his dad felt he had a mission to perform in a small town. Mission, hell! Did I think for one minute he'd slave long hours at the typewriter, if there weren't any money in it? If there weren't always the chance and the hope he'd make bigger money?
>
> He looked boyish then, and I felt sorry for him. "You can't fool me," I said. "You love sitting in there at the typewriter and shouting fantastic stories to the top of your voice. You were born to write. It's the only thing you want to do."
>
> He smiled, and I could see he was beginning to relax. "You're right. You're damn right. I wouldn't spend an hour doing anything else. Hack that I am."

Howard, perhaps, wasn't wholly ready to reveal the more personal details which are so highly prized by line-faced scriveners. Clearly he wants us to understand his grasp of history, and in his latter writings history (earth history) is more closely interwoven. At a time when C.L. (Catherine Lucile) Moore had newly completed the stories *Black God's Kiss* and *Black God's Shadow* featuring the fighting heroine Jirel of Joiry, a red-haired warrior-woman defending her castle (whose backdrop was fantasy,) Howard had written of Dark Agnes de Chastillon, the swordswoman whose hard adventures took place not in a fantasy realm but in Renaissance France. After reading Moore's work in

Weird Tales Howard sent her a copy of his *Sword Woman*, and she loved it and hoped there would be more.

In a letter by C.L. Moore to Howard dated January 29, 1935, she writes, "My blessings! I can't tell you how much I enjoyed 'Sword Woman.' It seemed such a pity to leave her just at the threshold of higher adventures. Your favorite trick of slamming the door on a burst of bugles! And leaving one to wonder what happened next and wanting badly to know. Aren't there any more stories about Agnes?" Yes. Two more Howard tales about Dark Agnes did exist, these being *Blades for France* and *Mistress of Death*, but they were incomplete. *Blades for France* had a finished first draft and an unfinished second, while *Mistress of Death* was an unfinished first draft which dwindled into a synopsis. Eventually it would be completed by Gerald W. Page.

Of course Howard also created the fighting femmes Belit (*Queen of the Black Coast*,) Valeria of the Red Brotherhood (*Red Nails*) and Red Sonya, not to be confused with the later Red Sonja. However, many look to Red Sonja as another Howard creation, but Tim Jansen writes in his review for *The Adventures of Red Sonja*: "Now one thing we should be clear on is that despite popular opinion, Conan creator Robert E. Howard did not create Red Sonja, at least not the Red Sonja we know today. This is explained in the introduction by Roy Thomas. Howard's Red SONYA was a character in one of Howard's many historical adventures, actually set in the 16th century. Roy Thomas is responsible for actually creating the Sonja of the Hyborian age using Howard's creation as a blueprint."

The Official Robert E. Howard Website makes the Sonya/Sonja issue even clearer: "The Red Sonya (with a "y") character was created in 1934 by Robert E. Howard. Howard's Red Sonya of Rogatino first appeared in the Howard story The Shadow of the Vulture. She was a 16th century Russian woman fighter who participated in the battle against the Turks in Vienna. She had absolutely nothing to do with Conan, or the Conan world of Hyboria. The Red Sonja (with a "j") character was created by

Roy Thomas in 1974 and was set in Conan's Hyborian Age. This Red Sonja was the heroine of the 1985 Film entitled Red Sonja and is featured in the current Dynamite Comic books."

Howard created his three great fighting women (Belit, Dark Agnes, Red Sonya—Valeria is minor compared with these) within about a year, and perhaps just as the ice blue eyes and tall imposing stature of Conan may have been a tribute to his father, the heart and persistence of these heroines could be a tribute to his mother. The tales were written at a time when Hester was requiring increased hospitalization, and, without delving into psychological realms in which we don't belong, it's a reasonable bet that it may have provided some amount of comfort to Howard to create these strong women who could overcome obstacles with skill and determination. But what would the markets think of them?

"Women who could do things were not very popular in fiction back in the thirties, particularly in the adventure story field," wrote Leigh Bracket in her 1976 introduction for Howard's fighting Dark Agnes, whose tale first saw book form with a 1977 printing by Zebra Books and then a 1979 Berkley edition, sparked to life not only by the resurgence of interest in Howard by also by the women's liberation movement (and looking at the cover illustration of the Berkley edition people of a certain age cannot help but note the resemblance of Dark Agnes to a busty and bemuscled Jane Fonda in thigh-high boots and armed to the teeth.) It is interesting to note that this Berkley edition did not contain the *Sword Woman* dedication which appears in the copy of the tale included in Glenn Lord's *The Second Book of Robert E. Howard* (it being, "To Mary Read, Graine O'Malley, Jeanne Laisne, Liliard of Ancrum, Anny Bonney, and all other sword women, good or bad, bold or gay, who have swaggered down the centuries, this chronicle is respectfully dedicated.") Leigh Bracket continues, "The accepted notion of the weak and helpless female has social rather than factual origins. Soft, submissive, uncompetitive women sold better in the marriage market. In addition, to be genteelly frail was a status symbol; it meant that you didn't have to work."

Howard was not fond of weak characters. The lusty pirate captain Belit, with whom Conan falls in love in *Queen of the Black Coast*, is another fine example (it can be noted that the overly used fantasy descriptive term of "black" was in the titles of the aforementioned C.L. Moore stories, and as a new writer in the field, Moore would likely have been familiar with Belit and Howard's *Queen of the Black Coast*, as it was published in the May 1934 edition of *Weird Tales* and the first printing of Moore's Jirel work was not until that October.) But not everyone understood the kind of strength with which Howard imbued his pirate queen. In what is the funniest conversation in Novalyne's book she recounts:

> "You have sex in the Conan yarns?" I said unbelievingly.
>
> "Hell, yes. That's what he did—drinking, whoring, fighting. What else was there in life?"
>
> I thought of a story he'd brought me a couple of months ago. I couldn't think of the name of it, and I hadn't read it closely. [*Queen of the Black Coast*] If he got technical and asked me what was in it, I wouldn't be able to tell him. About the only thing I remembered was there'd been a naked woman in it.
>
> "I don't see anything sexy about a naked woman dancing around on a ship."
>
> "You don't? For God's sake!" Bob barked the words out.
>
> "No," I said, and it was all I could do to keep from laughing.

He took an audible breath. "My God, she danced the mating dance. What could be more sexy?"

"I thought she was crazy," I said. "There she was captain of a pirate ship, and running around naked. Naked in front of all those slaves or whatever you call them—soldiers, sailors. Anyway, those black men around her....All eunuchs, I suppose."

Howard's use of black characters included leading men, such as the champion Ace Jessel in the boxing tales *Apparition in the Prize Ring* and *Double Cross*. His attitudes towards African Americans were more advanced than those of people like Lovecraft, and certainly more advanced than the average white man in his region, though the pervasiveness of prejudice was inescapable. In Callahan County where he lived (named for James A. Callahan who fought for Texan independence in the 1830s) a longstanding law stated that no Negro was allowed to stay overnight. From *Dark Valley Destiny*: "When in the 1920s an oil magnate came through in his limousine, his black chauffeur was allowed into the county only on condition that he stay in the car the whole time." Howard had told August Derleth in a letter circa February 1931 that if he wrote any chronicle of Texas, it would deal with Callahan County alone, in the time following his arrival and the "color, violence, and sudden change" sparked by the oil boom.

Howard well knew that greed and corruption came with an oil boom, and while these things made unpleasant neighbors, it was possible to use them to advantage in writing.

The royal purple is a moldy shroud;
The laurel crown is cypress fixed with thorns;
The sword of fame, a sickle notched and dull;
The face of beauty is a grinning skull;
And ever in their soul's red caverns loud
The rattle of the cloven hoofs and horns.

> *The poets know that justice is a lie,*
> *That good and light are baubles filled with dust—*
> *The world's slave-market where swine sell and buy,*
> *This shambles where the howling cattle die,*
> *Has blinded not their eyes with lies and lust.*

--excerpt from *Which Will Scarcely Be Understood*, REH

One of the more unusual Howard comparisons comes from Gary Romeo. In his journal *Sand Roughs* he compares Howard as an artist with Brian Wilson of the Beach Boys: "I suppose the first objection will be that Brian Wilson didn't commit suicide. Shouldn't Bob be Phil Ochs, Jim Morrison, or even Brian Jones? No. Brian Wilson created a sub-genre of pop music based on the modern myths of California and thus created sun and surf music. Bob Howard created a sub-genre of fantasy literature based on the ancient myths of Europe and thus created sword and sorcery fiction." There is also a floating opinion that Howard's most famous studio portrait of him in the city slicker hat (which he wore at Novalyne's behest to cover his short-shaved hair) bears a "separated at birth" type of resemblance to a similar photo of Al Capone. From Rob Roehn's *Cimmerian* article *Separated at Birth*:

> So, I'm at the local convenience store for my morning big gulp when some guy taps me on the shoulder and says, with a big grin, "Cool shirt." I look down at my REH Texas Tour 2006 t-shirt, the one with the famous studio portrait of REH on the front, and grin back at him. Could it be? Is there someone else in the Antelope Valley who shares my freakish obsession with Robert E. Howard? "You've heard of him?" I ask.
>
> "Sure," the man replies. "Everyone's heard of Al Capone." Sigh.

Expositions of this type serve as healthy demonstrations of the activeness the afterimage of Howard has in resonating deep beneath the fluffy surface of popular culture. In other words, just as Andy Warhol's multicolored Marilyn Monroe is one of the premiere images of the starlet, its very nature represents a morphed image, transcending whatever you might see in a newsreel. The various fanzines which have sprung up over the decades such as *Amra, The Howard Collector, The Cimmerian, Crypt of Cthulhu, REH Two-Gun Raconteur, The Cross Plainsman, The Dark Man* and others demonstrate a lasting cultural impact, but always beneath the surface, just as the long-held fear among many Howard fans was that the popularity of Conan was eclipsing that of the barbarian's creator. Some of the numerous finishers of Howard's incomplete tales (often converting pieces which were meant for other characters into Conan yarns) were often considered to be stretching thin the purity of Howard's work, while others did a better job of maintaining Howard's vision. "The Brian Wilson replacements Glen Campbell and Bruce Johnston are akin to Karl Edward Wagner and Robert Jordan," contends Gary Romeo. "They are talented individuals who had successes of their own."

Al Capone

REH

Robert Jordan was indeed able to capture much of the spirit of Conan's Hyborian realm, and anyone who has read his *Crossroads of Twilight* addition to his immensely popular *Wheel of Time* series, and witnessed the somnambulant marvels of a book full of Aes Sedai clutching their shawls and looking suspiciously at one another, or a chapter seemingly dedicated to picking weevils out of oats, may be thankful that he did not unremittingly milk the Conan series in such a fashion. *Crossroads of Twilight* has some truly horrible reviews on Amazon.com, and many if not most of them are from stout fans of the series. It would be ghastly to see such a devolution in the Conan series, and fear it has already happened was most humorously expressed in this sentiment by Boy of Tomorrow on gaygamer.net: "Seriously, Robert E. Howard must've been spinning in his grave at 1000+ RPMs when Conan The Destroyer came out in theaters." And while it is true that almost anyone could suggest the blasphemy of such a film sent Howard's remains spinning, it is rare that one finds the critical acuity in a reviewer to correctly estimate the RPMs.

Those who recall TSR's *Dragon* magazine of the mid 1980s may also recall consistent ads for the play-by-mail (and pay-by-mail) game *Hyborian War* from Reality Simulations. In it, human players controlled kingdoms within Howard's Hyborian world, and could issue a detailed set of military instructions each turn. Although the game has long since gone online and players can now email their instructions, in the mid 1980's players sat waiting at home for the snail mail to bring them long dot matrix printouts from the x86 super computers at Reality Simulations which told them the fate of their nation's maneuvers. I remember first choosing Argos as a country, but when it was taken my choice fell to Cimmeria. Eagerly I issued instructions for my brave Cimmerian warriors to conduct a raid on the Bossonian Marches to the south, as well as issuing instructions for spying. With my fee for that round paid I waited, and got a long printout informing me that the Bossonian raid had failed rather miserably, my spies were captured, and key Cimmerian warriors under my control had been stricken with wanderlust and simply deserted. Disheartened by the whole damned thing, I straggled on for a few more rounds with similar results. My Cimmerian wizards were as mystical as they were impotent, in-fighting further reduced my authority over my characters, warriors continued to simply wander away clutching their swords. Worst of all, Conan was nowhere to be seen within the realm (trapped in some licensing quandary, no doubt.) I kept thinking all the while that if this were truly Howard's game, the Cimmerians would at least administer a few choice ass-whoopings. How else could it be true to Howard's vision, right? But no, it had all the grimness of Cimmeria with none of the occasional triumphs (and not a single sacking of Venarium.) The barbarians were the jokes of the realm. (How many RPM does *that* concept induce?) I soon knew it was foolish of me to expect the computers at Reality Simulations to understand. To their fixed chips, Cimmeria was just another set of numbers and random variables.

In a similar fashion, some writers and readers are tempted to view Howard's worlds as merely a formula. Too much truly awful Sword & Sorcery has been written since Howard's death. Those ignorant of the difference in depth should be imparted with the greatest measure of shame, akin to treating Tolkien's intricate kingdoms as a mere amusement park, his created language as decorative scribbles. From the first Gnome Press reprinting of the Conan tales to the lavish Frazetta-illustrated mass market paperbacks to the Ballantine/Del Rey revival, the significance of Howard's art has not diminished. Harry Turtledove said, "Most of the fantasy of the past thirty-five years has two main wellsprings: J.R.R. Tolkien and Robert E. Howard. Tolkien himself, who had little use for most contemporary fantasists, rather liked the Conan tales. For headlong, nonstop adventure and for vivid, even florid, scenery, no one even comes close to Howard."

Part of Howard's ability to capture the scene can be attributed both to his excellent memory and his perception of the landscapes which surrounded him. "Why, by the time I was nine years old I'd lived in the Palo Pinto hills of Central Texas; in a small town only fifty miles from the coast; on a ranch in Atascosa County; in San Antonio; on the South Plains close to the New Mexican line; in the Wichita Falls country up next to

Oklahoma; and in the piney woods of Red River over next to Arkansas."

Howard continues, "If you'll glance at a map of Texas you'll note that covers considerable distance, altogether, and I didn't mention a few short stays in Missouri [to visit relative son his mother's side and sample peaches which he highly praised] and Oklahoma. I've lived in land boom towns, railroad boom towns, oil boom towns, where life was raw and primitive, and all I can say is: Texas is just too big for me to grasp," he told Lovecraft in a letter circa October 1930. "...I've seen towns leap into being overnight and become deserted almost as quick. I've seen old farmers, bent with toil and ignorant of the feel of ten dollars at a time, become millionaires in a week, by the way of oil gushers. And I've seen them blow in every cent of it and die paupers. I've seen whole towns debauched by an oil boom and boys and girls go to the devil wholesale. I've seen promising youths turn from respectable citizens to dope fiends, drunkards, gamblers and gangsters in a matter of months."

Sherman County, TX. Roughnecks on core drilling crew.

LOC, FSA-OWI Collection

Howard himself would write of hashish smoking in *Skull-Face*: "The horror first took concrete form amid that most unconcrete of all things—a hashish dream. I was off on a timeless, spaceless journey through the strange lands that belong to this state of being, a million miles away from earth and all things earthly; yet I became cognizant that something was reaching across the unknown voids--something that tore ruthlessly at the separating curtains of my illusions and intruded itself into my visions." Chapter Two of the story is titled "The Hashish Slave," and includes the interesting observation, "When I first began to experiment with hashish, I sought to find a physical or psychic basis for the wild flights of illusion pertaining thereto, but of late I had been content to enjoy without seeking cause and effect."

Also interesting is Howard's precise description of an opium pipe with accompanying pipe cleaner in the Costigan tale *Blow the Chinks Down!* In it he writes, "I looked into the case which laid open on the floor. They was a small pipe with a slender amber stem and a ivory bowl, finely carved and yellow with age, some extra stems, a small silver box of them funny looking Chinese matches, and a golden rod for cleaning the pipe."

It's worth noting the first-person narrative of *Skull-Face* as Howard continues, "I slew my red dreams in other dreams—the dreams of hashish whereby a man may descend to the lower pits of the reddest hells or soar into those unnamable heights where the stars are diamond pinpoints beneath his feet."

A third example in which one of Howard's characters uses a "mystical substance" is the case of the wizard Xaltotun and his fondness for the "black lotus" [likely opium but possibly hashish] in *The Hour of the Dragon*. From Howard's story:

> "From a carven green jade box he took a handful of shimmering black dust, and placed it in a brazier which stood in a golden tripod at his elbow. [...] A glance back, before the heavy, gold-bound teak door was closed, showed him Xaltotun leaning back in his throne-like chair, his arms folded, while a thin wisp of smoke curled up from the brazier. Conan's scalp prickled. In Stygia, that ancient and evil kingdom that lay far to the south, he had seen such black dust before. It was the pollen of the black lotus, which creates death-like sleep and monstrous dreams..."

Now the inevitable fact arises that Howard would have had access to hashish and especially its more natural form of marijuana, as it had been legal in the United States and relatively easy to obtain throughout Howard's lifetime. (It was not until the 1937 Marihuana Tax Act and the formation of the Federal Bureau of Narcotics that more severe regulation took place. Before that time the Uniform State Narcotic Act allowed state-level regulation and seizures, itself sparked by the wave of Mexican immigrants which came to the United States after the Mexican Revolution of 1910 and introduced the recreational use of marijuana.) Marijuana would have been even more prevalent when Howard made his forays, gastrointestinal and otherwise, south of the border.

We know that Howard brewed his own beer during the time of Prohibition, even though he had promised his mother he wouldn't imbibe. A photo Howard sent to E. Hoffmann Price comes to mind, of Howard sipping from a truly enormous glass of beer and his inscription, "Schlitz didn't pay a penny for this endorsement—and probably won't." And we are left to wonder how much of a leap it would have been for a lover of creative writing to try something as potentially beneficial to creative thought as marijuana. Plus, Howard's local friends would have had just as much access to it as he. We know he and they enjoyed relaxing on the shores of the man-made Brownwood Lake, and Howard had written to Lovecraft in May/June 1933, "That lake has a fascination for me. Some friends of mine and I have discussed tentative plans for building a fishing shack up in the hills, on one of the broad arms of the lake, in a secluded spot, but it takes money, and money is always short. I don't know whether we'll do it or not; probably not....If I had the money, I'd buy—but hell, what am I maundering about."

It is a rather unfortunate remnant of a less enlightened culture that still regards the artistic and even medicinal use of marijuana as a reflection that the user is a "dope fiend". Many in the writing community, including this author, have advocated the stance that responsible use of marijuana is less harmful and more beneficial than alcohol, and less harmful on the lungs than tobacco. In fact medically, marijuana has a lower toxicity rating than alcohol. At last check the entire region of Humboldt County in California permits marijuana use, as do countries abroad. Noted science fiction writer Arthur C. Clark (who died on March 19, 2008) moved to Sri Lanka in 1956, where marijuana is a feature in local ayurvedic medicine.

Add the possibilities of a secluded fishing shack to this scene described by Howard in a December, 1935 letter to HPL: "It was a clear, cold, frosty morning, the sun not yet up. As I drove out of Cross Plains, but little after dawn, I saw steam rising from the small lake where wild ducks swam by the hundreds. Then, many miles farther on, as I approached the valley of the Jim Ned, I saw what looked like a long bar of cloud stretching for miles across the horizon. Yet everywhere else it was clear. As I approached the Jim Ned, which runs between rugged hills, I saw that it was a heavy, white fog rising from the water, and filling the valley as far as I could see in each direction. This doubtless seems too common a thing to notice, to anyone accustomed to big rivers, but here in West Texas, where the streams are so small and the water so scarce, it constituted an occurrence so rare as to be unique, to the best of my knowledge. But the building of the Brownwood dam, ten miles below the spot where I crossed the Jim Ned, has backed water up the creek and made a real river out of it, big enough to send up a cloud of dense mist on such a morning as I have described. As I crossed the bridge I could hardly see the water beneath me, and the sky overhead was revealed only in irregular blue patches; the sun was about to rise and the fog seemed luminous, almost. Not grey and damp and depressing, but purely white, with almost a rosy tinge, through which the sky peeped here and there, with a rare and delicate blue. As I drove out of the valley and looked back, I saw the river hidden by the fog which nowhere rose over a hundred or so feet high. Far away to the east the long line of fog grew into a gigantic billowy cloud that hung over the lake, invisible from that spot. And the fog had sent out questing fingers that floated up every creek and branch that ran into the river. When I got to Brownwood, which stands in a basin traversed by Pecan Bayou, the town too, was veiled with the mist. It seems a strange thing, somehow, that we should have a body of water in this country so big that it emanates a regular fog."

This vivid description of a moment—the rugged hills on a clear frosty morning, the fog enshrouding the river, giving the impression along the horizon of a long bar of cloud—is reminiscent of T.S. Eliot's moment of Silence while at Harvard in June of 1910: "...the indescribable Silence in the midst of the clatter of graduation, the exhortations of practical men, the questions of parents, the frivolity of millinery and strawberries in the Yard. Suddenly able to shed the world, he experiences a fugitive sensation of peace that he would try all his life to recapture." (*Eliot's Early Years*, by Lyndall Gordon)

Suspension bridge on Route 126 near Brownwood, circa 1936.

LOC, FSA-OWI Collection

If Howard had been able to purchase a secluded fishing shack in the occasionally misty hills around Brownwood, it seems he would have had the opportunity to take more liberties which he previously only hinted toward. At the very least he might have brewed more beer, spent more time with friends, and had total writing privacy. As it was he was known to go on and off alcohol, at one point longing for the unrestricted access found both north and south of the border, at another going on a stretch of sobriety.

Of Howard's local friends the one who seems the biggest mystery is Lindsey Tyson, whom he met as a boy when his family moved to Cross Plains and who "was to remain Robert's closest and most steadfast pal for the rest of Robert's life." (*Dark Valley Destiny*) Lindsey, with a nickname of "Pink" amongst his friends, would together with Howard share interests in nature exploration and sporting events. Like Howard, Tyson was also the son of a country physician, but although the boys spent much time together, Howard would somehow separate Tyson from his other friends. The more literary inclined Brownwood locals Tevis Clyde Smith and Truett Vinson and Thurston Torbett in Marlin were "compartmentalized," as de Camp put it, and set apart from Lindsey Tyson. Torbett was several years older than Howard, and his uncle J.W. Torbett was the owner of a sanitarium which featured hot springs and which Howard's parents often visited. Howard and Torbett collaborated on one story, *A Thunder of Trumpets*, published in 1937.

However, de Camp's "compartmentalization" and separation hypothesis is at least partially disproved in one of Howard's letters to Lovecraft from December 1935. He relates of "hitting the bottle" with Pink Tyson and David Lee before going to see a football game which ended in "a lousy scoreless tie." Then the trio tries to look up Tevis Clyde Smith in Brownwood "because we wanted some more liquor which we knew he could be depended upon to produce." Howard speaks of Smith's second marriage and how it seemed to be agreeing with him, based on Smith's weight gain. Then Howard recounts, "I well remember the last riot we went on before he got married; he, Tyson, Vinson and I started to go somewhere to a movie, or some other innocent pastime, but we started drinking whiskey, and that called for beer, and along about midnight we found ourselves in a den of iniquity in a county-seat town about fifty miles east of here. [likely Fort Worth]"

To give de Camp the benefit of the doubt, he may have meant that Howard in general held Tyson apart from the more bookish "city dwellers" Smith and Vinson, and apart from the not-so-local Torbett, who was inclined toward the occult and not boxing. Howard could relate to Tyson without having to "talk shop," for Tyson wasn't all that interested in hearing it. Lindsey was apart from the members of *The Junto*, which it is said were held together by Howard, and apart from the other Cross Plains locals as well.

It was Tyson who, when Howard was fourteen, suggested he attend the Methodist church near the newspaper office (where Jack Scott, earlier quoted, worked,) even though Howard would later call himself an agnostic. And though while the average Cross Plains resident of the time commonly took "shortcuts" through land which somebody owned while walking to get somewhere, Howard would avoid this trespassing except in the case of cutting through Lindsey Tyson's property.

Lindsey Tyson is a bit of a contradiction. He boxed with Howard and was far stronger. Howard admired this strength and it has been said of Tyson that he was "so physically powerful that he could tear a pack of cards in two." (*Dark Valley Destiny*) Yet Tyson's manner was gentle, congenial, and he didn't try to demonstrate intellectual superiority with Howard the way certain literary types might. Instead the boys were content to take a couple of empty brass bullet casings, tape them over the ends of two dueling foils Howard owned, and fence in the backyard without the benefit of masks or other gear.

Lindsey Tyson was with Howard when he purchased his Chevy, from a dealership in Arlington, between Dallas and Fort Worth. He roomed with Tyson at 417 Austin Avenue while the two were attending Howard Payne College, and it was Tyson who sparked Howard's love of football. One game which he attended with Lindsey was between Howard Payne and Southwestern University, and Howard spent three single-spaced pages in describing the game in a letter to Lovecraft, who was completely uninterested in sports. The opening scene in *Post Oaks and Sand Roughs* features Howard (Costigan) at a college football game, and Tyson is given the name Spike Lafferty in the book. Spike is also the alternate name for the faithful bulldog of Sailor Steve Costigan, a.k.a. Dennis Dorgan.

When Howard got his first story accepted, *Spear and Fang*, Tyson was there to witness how he knelt down beside his bed and remained there in a moment of solemn silence. Biographer Mark Finn likes to say that when he arose, the literary Robert E.

Howard was born. Tyson reported him saying, "I'm so grateful, not just for this story, but because now it won't be so hard for me to sell. Now that I've finally broken in, it'll be easier."

In the same way that Howard often had to care for his ailing mother, Lindsey Tyson's father became ill and Tyson dropped out of college to care for him. All in all his father's protracted illness would require a decade of Lindsey's home health care, and this was something with which Howard could keenly relate. And although the two were no longer rooming together, Howard kept up the body building routine and the boxing which he and Lindsey did together. It is Tyson (as Spike) he lampoons in his early college-days story *Cupid vs. Pollux*:

> "You're looking for Spike, I take it?" said he, and upon me admittin' the fact, he gives me a curious look and remarks that Spike is in his room.
>
> I go up, and all the way up the stairs, I hear somebody chanting a love song in a voice that is incitement to justifiable homicide. Strange as it seems, this atrocity is emanating from Spike's room, and as I enter, I see Spike himself, seated on a divan, and singing somethin' about lovers' moons and soft, red lips. His eyes are turned soulfully toward the ceiling and he is putting great feeling in the outrageous bellow which he imagines is the height of melody. To say I am surprised is putting it mildly and as Spike turns and says, "Steve, ain't love wonderful?" you could have knocked me over with a pile-driver. Besides standing six feet and seven inches and scaling upwards of 270 pounds, Spike has a map that makes Firpo look like an ad for the fashionable man, and is neitherto about as sentimental as a rhinoceros.
>
> "Yeh? And who is she?" I ask sarcastically, but he only sighs amorously and quotes poetry.
>
> [...] But afterwards Spike says to me, sitting on the ring floor, still in his ring togs, he says, "Steve, girls is a lotta hokum. I'm offa 'em," he says.

Says I, "Then if you've found that out, it's worth the soakin' you got," I says.

The story itself concerns preparation (or lack thereof) for a boxing match, and its early date may indicate Lindsey Tyson was a prototypical inspiration for Howard's various boxing stories. After all, a man who could supposedly tear a deck of cards in half would fit right into Howard's tough-talking, hard-punching boxing yarns.

Lindsey Tyson was in the car when Howard had his driving accident. The obstacle which Howard ran into on that wet and foggy night of December 29, 1933, was an ill-placed steel flag pole set in concrete in the middle of the street in the town of Rising Star. When another motorist ran into the pole soon after, it was taken down and the town paid the cost of repairing the car.

Finally, it was Lindsey Tyson's gun that Howard used to kill himself, and Lindsey Tyson he named to receive everything in his will—a will which would reportedly be destroyed upon its perusal by Howard's father. Family friend Kate Merryman was the one who found the will among Howard's papers and brought it to the attention of Isaac, who told her, "Don't tell anything to anyone about this." (from de Camp's notes at the Harry Ransom Center, covered more completely in Chapter 12; also related by Howard scholar Patrice Louinet in his essay *Grief & Greed*.) One can only wonder how Howard might have phrased his final intentions for the disposition of his belongings and works.

Chapter Eleven:
Preparing the Way

"The spring of 1936 was so full of stress that Bob was overcome. With his pessimistic view of life, his lack of self-confidence, his many problems, his lack of sleep…stress did not permit him to look beyond these crises to hope they would pass and that life would be worth living. He could not hope. He could not believe."

--Novalyne Price Ellis, *Day of the Stranger*

On June 10, 1936, the day before his death, Robert E. Howard had a discussion with his father's friend Dr. Dill of nearby Rising Star (whose name in *Dark Valley Destiny* is given as both J.D. Dill on page 7 and J.R. Dill on page 347.) Dr. Dill had come to the Howard home to provide support for the family after Hester had slipped into a coma from which she would not awaken, and also because Isaac may have had concerns about what his son might do if they were alone.

With Dr. Dill came two of his in-laws, Vera McDonough and Leah Bowden. Additionally, Isaac requested that a local Cross Plains couple, teacher Clarence Martin and his wife Birdie, come to the home to sit-out Hester's final hours with him. Neighbor

Kate Merryman was already a regular, helping whenever she could.

During this time of excess company and somber activity, it would have been easy to have a quiet, private conversation with someone. It seems likely that in such a moment, perhaps while Dr. Dill was in Howard's small room looking at the young writer's collection of books and magazines, Howard asked him about the survival rate of gunshots to the head. Maybe Dill had mentioned, intending it to be a comfort, that he had seen some people who never got a chance to say goodbye to their loved one, due to the sudden infliction of fatal injuries. Or perhaps Howard gently opened the door to the subject by prefacing his question with the guise of research for one of his hardboiled detective stories featuring Steve Harrison. At any rate, Dr. Dill gave him the answer.

There were many cases on record where people had survived gunshots to the frontal lobe of the brain. Certainly it was even possible that a healthy person might survive a gunshot to certain other isolated sections of the brain. But Dr. Dill knew of no known instances were a person had survived a gunshot which penetrated both the front and back of the brain.

Was Howard unable to obtain this information from the libraries in Brownwood or at Howard Payne, or was this one of his last thinly-veiled warnings as to his state of mind and impending actions?

> "The old Texas is gone or going fast. All the plains are fenced in, where in my childhood I've ridden for a hundred miles without seeing a foot of barbed wire. I can't remember when I've heard a coyote. And one of my earliest memories is being lulled to sleep in a covered wagon camped on the Nueces River, by the howling of wolves." –REH

To say that there was any one reason for Howard's suicide—even one as great as his mother's imminent demise—is likely incorrect. The fact that he could not seem to escape the endless pressures which he keenly perceived were building all around him encompasses more than just the decline in Hester's health. And it was escape which flitted before his eyes as he bragged to Lovecraft in December of 1935 about the aforementioned "den of iniquity" he visited with Tyson, Smith and Vinson: "The beer was punk and the girls were worse—well, there was one I remember with pleasure, a blond with a figure like—well, no matter." Even in this rather escapist fanciful tale in which Howard tries to lead Lovecraft to believe he debauched mightily with a woman of ill repute (apparently the only good-looking woman in the joint, seemingly reserved as if by appointment just for Howard) we are instead led to picture, at the most, a scene where a modestly drunk Howard (his friends said his idea of getting drunk was none too extreme) caught sight of a woman with a pleasing figure. And even in this he aborts his escape by cutting short additional details.

Consider the feelings behind the sentiments in the poem *Surrender*:

> *I will rise some day when the day is done*
> *And the stars begin to quiver;*
> *I will follow the road of the setting sun*
> *Till I come to a dreaming river.*
>
> *I am weary now of the word and vow*
> *Of the winds and the winter weather;*
> *I'll reel through a few more years somehow,*
> *Then I'll quit them altogether.*
>
> *I'll go to a girl that I once knew*
> *And I will not swerve or err,*
> *And I care not if she be false or true*
> *For I am not true to her.*
>
> *Her eyes are fierce and her skin is brown*
> *And her wild blood hotly races,*
> *But it's little I care if she does not frown*

At any man's embraces.

Should I ask for a love none may invade?
Is she more or less than human?
Do I ask for more, who have betrayed
Man, devil, god and woman?

Enough for me if she has for me
A bamboo hut she'll share,
And enough tequila to set me free
From the ghosts that leer and stare.

I'll lie all day in a sodden sleep
Through days without name or number,
With only the wind in the sky's blue deep
To haunt my unshaken slumber.

And I'll lie by night in the star-roofed hut
Forgetful and quiet hearted,
Till she comes with her burning eyes half shut
And her red lips hot and parted.

The past is flown when the cup is full,
And there is no chain for linking
And any woman is beautiful
When a man is blind with drinking.

Life is a lie that cuts like a knife
With its sorrows and fading blisses;
I'll go to a girl who asks naught of life
Save wine and a drunkard's kisses.

No man shall know my race or name,
Or my past sun-ripe or rotten,
Till I travel the road by which I came,
Forgetting and soon forgotten.

When he first speaks of the girl and not caring whether she is false or true, one cannot help but think of Novalyne, and how she informed Howard that she intended to date Truett Vinson after dating Howard (and how she had dated Tevis Clyde Smith before dating Howard.) Note the term "dating" is used in the old-fashioned sense here, and it is not meant as a euphemism for something else. Novalyne is also described by authors such as Mark Finn (*Blood & Thunder*) as being "dark-skinned" with intent eyes, which is in keeping with the line "Her eyes are fierce and her skin is brown." By citing the implication that the girl in the poem is being "false," we do not mean to convey any disparagement to NPE. It is the author's potential viewpoint we are trying to explore.

The bamboo hut in the poem being "enough" is much akin to Howard's stated wish that he would like to have been born "in a hut among the hills of western Ireland, the forests of Germany or the steppes of Southern Russia." And the end of the poem implies that Howard felt he would not become known in the world until after his death. He chooses to say "till" for "until" in the next to last line, meaning that until he traveled the road by which he came (the circle of life) and until his earthly presence was forgotten, his work would not shine to its fullest.

This, of course, is merely an interpretation, just as would be any speculation as to the line "For I am not true to her." It would be easy to brush it aside as being nothing more than a suitable rhyme, but since Howard consistently put so much of himself into everything he wrote, there would be scant reason for him to avoid doing so. Many things are veiled by degrees which vary. Howard not being true in the poem may indicate his perennial split between his mother and the rest of his life. It may even be indicative of Howard's almost equal weighing of life and death. Also, with a fierce pride in his family history, it is somewhat incongruous of Howard to draw up a will in which he left everything to Tyson. Whether or not he expected his father to outlive him, there were still many other distributions and proportions Howard could have included in his will, such as his cousin and fellow *Junto* member Maxine Ervin.

Howard writes of spending a great deal of time with a cousin. From his short piece *The Beast from the Abyss* (the title refers to cats by the way, not his cousin,) Howard mentions being with his cousin during his childhood on a farm and their exploits with cats and rats. We know that he cared for a great many cats throughout his life, and there is little reason to think what Howard writes in this article is entirely fictitious. In fact, we see in this story a reflection of Howard's relationship with Novalyne, in the cats "The Persian" and "Barn-Cat." From the article:

> *The Persian was an exception. He was the biggest, most powerful, mixed-breed I ever saw, and the fiercest. He was always ravenous, and his powerful jaws crushed chicken bones in a startling manner. He ate, indeed, more like a dog than a cat. He was not indolent or fastidious. He was a lusty soldier of fortune, without morals or scruples, but possessed of an enviable vitality.*
>
> *He was enamored of Barn-cat, and no woman could have acted the coquette with greater perfection. She treated him like a dog. He wooed her in his most ingratiating manner, to be rewarded by spitting abuse and scratches. A lion in dealing with members of his own sex, he was a lamb with Barn-cat.*
>
> *Let him approach her in the most respectable manner, and she was transformed into a spitting, clawing fury. Then when he retired discouraged, she invariably followed him, picking at him, teasing him, and giving him no peace of mind. Yet if he took hope and attempted any advances on the ground of her actions, she instantly assumed the part of an insulted virgin and greeted him with bared teeth and claws.*

This description is rather in keeping with one of Howard's last letters to Novalyne. In a February 21, 1980 interview with Kate Merryman, she described finding a letter from Howard to Novalyne in which "he chided her for ragging him about his black sombrero, adding that, considering the ordeal he was facing, it seemed small-minded to make a fuss about a hat." (*Dark Valley Destiny*)

Could it be that of Smith, Vinson and Tyson, Lindsey was the only one who did not date Novalyne? The name of Spike which Howard gives him in the *Cupid vs. Pollux* story and later in *Post Oaks and Sand Roughs* is also the name he gives to Steve Costigan's (aka Dennis Dorgan's) faithful bulldog, who accompanies him to exotic ports and remains true to him always. It is a fine line to go on with this, and say that Sailor Steve bunked with his dog and Howard bunked with Tyson in their college days, and ultimately the characters seem to prefer bunking with each other rather than the oft unstably portrayed female elements in their lives. Certainly the main reason was the chemistry of comradery.

From almost the very beginning Howard's writing has been accused by various persons of having homosexual undertones, such as in the way he describes the male body in far more detail than the female, and how his story characters are consistently highly aware of the shape and state of the male bodies around them. He describes himself in *Post Oaks*: "As for Steve, fire for his work burned his soul clean of any lurking desire for vice. He never thought of drinking or carousing—simply because he never thought of it. He found pleasure enough in writing and his occasional reading....As for women, Steve was strictly, almost fanatically, moral." When he learns that his friend Spike, whom he thought adhered to the same code as he, was "polluted" with liquor one day after "running with a gang, a bunch of wild-living, hard-drinking and hard-gambling young roughnecks who were sowing their wild oats in the dives of Frontier," Steve in appall confronts his friend. "He sought Spike and told him what he thought of him in no uncertain terms; then was ashamed afterward, for Spike, instead of being angry, seemed merely hurt.

They drifted further apart, and Steve practically forgot about him, following his usual custom of setting aside lost friends"

Yet we know that Howard did anything but set Tyson aside in the long run. One begins to wonder just who was Pollux and who was Cupid in his college tale, but wonder is where it must end, for it is the latter interpretations of Howard's work and not the original contents or the man himself which have contributed and fueled alternate implications.

In Ed Waterman's 2001 review of Wandering Star and Cross Plains Comics' graphic adaptation of Howard's *Worms of the Earth*, he calls attention to the way hero Bran Mak Morn is visually depicted. He is troubled by various panels of artwork, saying, "Not only does the artist draw Bran Mak Morn nude to convey a needlessly sensual mood, but he has the hero don an outfit that only a young woman would wear—a chain mail tank-top and what looks like a bikini loin cloth with an odd string of silver balls hanging in front of his crotch." It is implied that the sexual symbolism at work here is not at all flattering. Artists Tim Conrad did mention that he took some liberties with his portrayal, but Waterman clearly felt the overall visual impact was doing a disservice to Howard, not to mention the fact that the scanty apparel would have been foolhardy in the cold climate. Waterman states that if he were new to Howard's writings and this piece was his first introduction, he would conclude that Bran Mak Morn was "a flaming homosexual."

This and similar perceptions of some of Howard's characters has partially influenced and fueled some of the more negative portrayals of Howard's work. Mr. Waterman continues with regard to the official corporate image of Conan Properties, Inc. In it he sees a bare-chested man in a fur loin cloth, and Waterman states, "First of all, Conan never, ever wore a fur loin cloth." Although he does sometimes appear in a loin cloth in the stories, to make it a fur one simply to stress the "barbarian" aspect comes off as more of a cave man thing. Waterman asks why the image of a muscled man in a fur diaper has become so popular, for it is not a very accurate reflection of Howard's Conan.

Wasn't it Thundarr the Barbarian (a tv cartoon of the early 1980s) that made use of fur diapers anyway? Yes, Thundarr had a whole fur outfit, even though the story roughly takes place in the new earth of 3094, with story themes influenced both by Conan as well as Star Wars. Bob Ridgely was Thundarr's voice actor for the 21-show run of the series (first on ABC then on NBC as reruns,) frequently uttering such pronouncements as "Demon dogs!" and "Lords of Light!" while Thundarr's fur boots, fur diaper and fur suspenders (or thereabouts—presumably to ensure fur diaper fastidiousness) contrasted sharply with his futuristic Sun Sword. Sadly the cover for the non-Howard Conan series *The Chronicles of Conan: Volume 12* (2007) depicts our hero donning the fur diaper and suspenders of Thundarr the Barbarian (it sort of looks like a really wide V-neck toddler onsie.) Fortunately, the 2009 release of a new Conan feature film does not quite so wholly embrace the fur diaper legacy (also of interest is the Solomon Kane film starring James Purefoy.) Conversely, to support the fur diaper depiction, there is Dale Rippke's study of Conan chronology, *The Dark Storm Conan Chronology*, in which he states, "Conan the Cimmerian is born on a battlefield, during a fight between his tribe and Vanir raiders. Clad in a pantherskin loin-cloth, he spends his youth amid the continual warfare that takes place on the mountainous northern frontiers of Cimmeria." (Howard had the proclivity of inserting panther references here and there in his writing.) So it would seem the official Conan logo, if parties unknown were to insist on the fur loincloth, would have to be of a barbarian *child* in a fur loin cloth.

The success of the Funcom computer game *Age of Conan*, released to a sea of waiting pre-orders on May 17, 2008 with a first installment entitled *Hyborian Adventures*, is further proof of the ever-present allure of Howard's writing. Notably written-up in *The New York Times*, the game is a massively multiplayer online role-playing game (MMORPG) which takes place a year after the event's described in Howard's *The Hour of the Dragon*. Funcom plans tremendous expansion for *Age of Conan*.

Social scholars such as Joseph Campbell might have pointed out that one of the surest signs that an advancing culture has adopted and carried forward stories or characters which they enjoy and admire is the adaptations which they add to that story or character, or the alterations which creep into these things over time. And it still holds true that the more times a complex image is photocopied, the less true to the original each copy of a copy becomes. As the very gene sequences of Howard's many writings are recollected and rearranged by the editors of various anthologies and the publishers of comic books, the more we may continue to expect a distortion to be present. It need not be taken as confirmation of anything, and to the non-purist it oftentimes comprises more of a compliment than an affront. If sampling the bubble gum image of Conan gets new readers to taste the chewing tobacco of the real thing, it's not such a bad compromise when compared with the alternative of touching fewer hearts and minds.

A precursor to Howard's ultimate views on death was how he treated not only the much-mentioned death of his dog Patch, but more humanly so the death of his German friend Herbert Klatt (known as Hubert Grotz in *Post Oaks*.) Glenn Lord was quite right to mention some errors de Camp had made on this man in *Dark Valley Destiny*, such as not originally intending to include Klatt in the book at all. De Camp was under the assumption (aided by newspaperman Jack Scott) that it was local boy Winifred Brigner who accompanied Howard, Smith and Vinson to a woodsy cabin for the wild night of drinking and sudden, barmy werewolfery mentioned in *Post Oaks* (*Herbert Klatt: The 4th Musketeer* by Glenn Lord.) Klatt recounted the event: "We arrived in the night of a new day under a leering moon with a new norther and Truett drunk on three bottles of beer. We found well-under-porch-roof nondescript house, stove, table, chairs. Bed and a cot, lamp and chaps, and a bottle of blackleg medicine sitting on a two cent stamp. Talking, laughing, roaring. Clyde and Bob sick on Jake. Truett and Clyde slept and I and Bob sat at the stove and talked till the vague cutting cold sunless dawn."

In *Post Oaks* Howard neglects to mention that he too got sick from drinking, putting it all on Smith ("I noticed you didn't kick when he [Klatt] brought in a tub for you to vomit in, neither.") After his first and only get-together with Howard, Klatt would return to his family's farm and write of doing chores such as digging ditches in rocky soil and "picking scrappy cotton under a broiling sun." Howard mentioned to Clyde Smith in October of 1927, "Yes, I heard from Klatt the other day and he hints of coming to see me; I've invited him so much that maybe he wants to get a rest, but I'll bet he disappoints me." Klatt managed to secure a teaching position at a German school in Aleman, but his health deteriorated and in early 1928 Klatt was admitted to a sanitarium, where he died that May. To Howard the cause of death was especially poignant, for it was said to be tuberculosis.

That month Howard wrote to Clyde Smith:

Salaam:

So Klatt has gone West. I don't know; it seems hard lines. Struck down in the very beginning of his manhood—without a chance to fight.

Maybe this is right:

Flower of the Morning
Bill Adams

Tell them when I'm gone. Then.
Say, "He was glad to go."
Say, "He heard a ringing voice, a great wind blow."
Say, "He'd always wandered in sort of a maze."
Say, "He knew this would bring
An end to wonder:
Flames of light and sons a-wing,

And doubting trampled under."

Tell them
"Death is but a birth
A burst of flowers
Fairer than the blooms of earth
Its beauty ours."

Yet what do such things signify? A mere tangle of words. Empty sounds. Bare vocal noises. Where are the sunrises and the sunsets, the lights and the shadows, the sting of winds, the vivid shiftings of radiances and colors, when a man is dead? Yet the body of him will go back to the elements again; he will throb with life in the sap of the tree, in the haze of the heat. Flowers and hot grain will spring up and wave and live and the essence of their being will be the essence of him.

Yet the pity of it, that his manhood and his great dreams should perish before he had a chance to make them live—that all his killing toil and struggles should go for nothing. He was a fighter but the odds were far too many. Yet I know he went out smiling.

What shall I say when a friend has vanished behind the doors of Death? A mere tangle of barren words, only words.

Still, I feel that there is such a thing as a Hereafter that he will find a place among his fearless ancestors in the high hall of Valhalla and I like to think of him sitting at the right hand of Thor amid the glory of everlasting revel. Yes, if there is a Hereafter, as Longfellow says:

There from the flowing bowl

Deep drinks the Viking's soul!

Skoal! To the Northland! Skoal!

Thus the tale ended.

Chapter Twelve:
June 11, 1936

"I am prepared to meet my Maker. Whether my Maker is prepared for the great ordeal of meeting me is another matter."
—*Sir Winston Churchill*

True to the very most weird of his tales, once he was buried, Robert E. Howard's remains did not stay in the ground. They saw the light of day again, and not due to any coroner's investigation or rabid fan turned tomb robber. They arose not because of any construction mishap, not because of any sudden oil gusher, not because of any cemetery relocation, and not, almost regrettably so, due to any supernatural agency. They rose for a reason that some could not believe and many found hard to fathom.

And his mother rose with him.

But of course we are getting a little ahead of ourselves.

It is the morning of June 11, 1936, and Howard has been drinking coffee nonstop. He had spent a night's vigil sitting beside his mother, and his brain, unused to the effects of coffee as he had rarely if ever drunk the stuff before, must have been zazzing and popping in the rarified air of a caffeine buzz coupled with sleep depravation.

By now he knows that his mother cannot recover. His father

had done little to discourage Howard's surging spells of hope in prior months when Hester seemed to slightly rebound. But Isaac knew his wife was taking the long road away from them, and what he as a doctor might have freely imparted to the loved ones of a patient, he could not as a father wholly impart to Robert: recovery did not happen once this far gone.

What had Howard thought of that boy, all those years ago when he went to Howard Payne, who was said to have committed suicide upon the death of his own mother? He didn't really know him, and little is mentioned of him at all, but it certainly must have stuck in Howard's mind. He wrote of it to Tevis Clyde Smith in October 1923: "I see in the papers where Roy Guthrie committed suicide. Why, I wonder? Do you have any idea?" Just as with the fall of Herbert Klatt in early 1928, that same time saw the Howard family briefly rent out two rooms of their home to the Oliver family, and what a funny circle of life it must have appeared to Howard to have a friend depart as new people arrived.

Nathan Oliver was an oilfield worker and his wife Opal was a patient of Isaac's. They rented the living room and the dining room of the Howard home, for although the peak of the oil boom in Cross Plains was already in the rearview mirror, housing was still not easily available. The two families shared one bathroom and one kitchen, but little is known of the Olivers (Howard mentions an Oscar Oliver, an oilfield worker who died, earlier in this book in Chapter Two) and their stay did not much exceed a year at the most. Still, the tighter quarters and less privacy certainly placed an unwelcome strain on Howard, and that summer he needed to escape, and he took a train to Galveston accompanied by Lindsey Tyson.

Howard had visited Galveston the previous year with Truett Vinson. This time he and Tyson rented a small cabin near the water. One of their activities while there was taking a boat tour out into the Gulf of Mexico, and Howard was again inspired by the sea...so much so that Tyson later reported being told by

Howard that, when he died, he wanted to have his ashes cast into the sea.

Was Lindsey Tyson expected to oblige him? If Howard were not cremated and were buried on land, was Lindsey Tyson meant to use his muscles to single-handedly exhume his friend in the murky dark of night, transport the great fallen writer to some covert place of incineration, and then make the doleful trip alone to Galveston and then the waves, perhaps taking the care to rebury a now-empty coffin, or, in true *Weird Tales* fashion, replace the body with some unlucky drifter's remains?

No. It was a fancy which would not come to pass. To the best of anyone's knowledge what brought Howard out of the ground again was not Lindsey Tyson and it had nothing to do with the sea.

But we're getting ahead of ourselves once more.

What memories may have been flashing through Howard's mind at this time? Perhaps with a melancholy grin he was thinking back to that time in late 1927 when Tevis Clyde Smith took a job working to advertise Camay soap and he (Howard) suggested, "Here is a speech you can use in your business: 'My dear lady, it is to your interest to listen to me; if your husband is a drunkard, your brother a sex pervert, your sister and all your aunts morons—all of which is more than likely the case—then you should give heed to my spiel.' Then you can go on with the rest of your remarks."

Maybe he briefly thought of that conversation he had with Novalyne about himself, his education, his writing, and who might get credit for it. From *One Who Walked Alone:*

"Someday, some biographer will come along, and when he reads that story [*Beyond the Black River*,] he'll say, 'Who was this Robert E. Howard? He couldn't have written these stories. Why he was not college bred!

Remember, when he went to Howard Payne, all he did was sit around writing yarns, trying to break into Weird Tales. He didn't even try to get a college degree! But isn't it written somewhere that he dated a school teacher who dreamed of being a writer?"' Bob was listening with a broad grin on his face. "He'll say: 'That school teacher wrote those yarns, every single one of them. Wrote 'em and didn't have nightmares at all.'" "By God, you may have it right." Bob ran his fingers through his hair. "I wouldn't be a damn bit surprised. Trouble is they won't know that the school teacher only wanted to write things that are all sweetness and light. Nobody has any trouble. Nobody has a hard time. Everything works out. "

After pacing back and forth in front of his father, after talking with Dr. Dill, after staying awake all night and the previous day, could Howard still have clearly held in his mind the oft-expressed philosophy that, in essence, death did not really exist because life did not really exist; it was all just a reaction between two insubstantial points. After putting on a brave face and telling his father, "Buck up! You are equal to it; you will go through it all right. Everything has to come to an end." did Howard then step back into his small room to write his final poem? We hearken back to a letter from Howard to Smith, circa January 1928:

"Let us talk of life; I am damnably weary tonight. What are you? What am I? Listen, I'll tell you; Life is Power, Life is Electricity. You and I are atoms of power, cogs in the wheels of the Universal system. Life is not predestinated, that is, the trivial affairs of our lives are not, but we have certain paths to follow and we cannot escape them. Do you think we can? Then let me see you raise yourself even seven inches off the earth and remain there unsupported save by your own efforts; let me see you look at a star and tell me if grass grows there, with your naked eye; let me see you swim to the bottom of the ocean and back or walk on water; let me see you live a thousand years.

"Listen, I'll tell you; we are sparks of star-dust, atoms of unknown power, powerless in ourselves but making up the whole of some great power that uses us as ruthlessly as fire uses fuel. We are parts of an entity, futile in ourselves. We are merely phases of electricity; electrons endlessly vibrating between the magnetic poles of birth and death. We cannot escape these trails in which our paths lie. We do not, as individual entities, really exist, we do not live. There is no life, there is no existence; there is simply vibration. What is a life but an uncomplicated gesture, beginning in oblivion and ending in oblivion? What man of history ever really accomplished what he desired to accomplish? No, what men name life is simply the sparkle of an electron as it flashes from the pole of birth to the pole of death. There is no beginning, nor will there ever be an end to the thing."

Of this and similar expressed attitudes Frank Coffman wrote in 2001 that they, "suggest a belief in a universal Life Force or essence, and, elsewhere, clear evidences of a belief in reincarnation and what might be termed a 'conservation of soul' much like the conclusions of many physicists (certainly in Howard's day) of a conservation of matter..." And it is certainly true that Howard's belief in things like the occult and reincarnation was not only reinforced by his occultist friend Thurston Torbett, but also by his father Isaac, who for a time held an open mind regarding reincarnation and also attended several "faith healings" where after he would claim to be relieved of his discomfort, only to have it promptly return. To Howard, it seemed, life was like a kind of woman who fixes you in her eye, and there you are to remain spellbound until she looks away. From his poem *Love* (*Shadows of Dreams*):

> I have felt your lips on mine
> Your hair has veiled my eyes
> When my blood was wild as singing wine
> And star-gold flecked the skies.
>
> We have watched the moonlight dance
> On the breast of the still lagoon

> But now I am tired of your changeless glance
> In the eye of the wrinkled moon.
>
> What have you given me
> To name as an ultimate bliss?
> Am I more strong, more free?
> What slavery is this?
> For a single star on a dusky sea
> I would barter your hottest kiss.

Though it is tempting to take this poem at face value and assume it is about a woman, it seems equally compelling to put forth the suggestion that Howard is really talking about life here. In the first verse he is saying that he has lived gustily (or at least courted life to the best of his ability,) in the second he is echoing one of his favorite sentiments that all things loose their luster, and finally he is questioning the worth of it all, and looking beyond to a place he now values more. The whole thing has a dream-like quality.

As he sat down in the kitchen to halfheartedly notice Kate Merryman tidying dishes by the window, maybe Howard thought of dreams. Hardly any of his dreams are documented, but he did recount one he had in a September, 1928 letter to Harold Preece: "I had such a damnably peculiar dream last night while sleeping off my drunk that I am moved to inflict it on you, in part at least. I had sunk low in the world, so low that I was scrubbing floors for my living. My companions were a woman of young middle age, a huge female; and a rather pretty girl. All of us were scrubbing floors and it seemed that the girl was of a high and wealthy family, but had been kicked out because of something which I forget. Now, I was a slum rat if ever there was one—a hard, gnarled fellow, who talked out of the side of my mouth in the patois of the Bowery. I was myself and yet not myself.

"I concocted the scheme of kidnapping the girl—all the success depended on whether her family still cared enough for her to save her life. She had grown hard, too, and she, the woman and I formulated the plan. She wished to bring into it her lover who had remained faithful to her throughout all her vicissitudes of fortune and he came with two friends. And, oh hell, he was the most stupid looking scut I ever saw. He was tall, six-three or four I should say, with an abnormally large mouth and a sappy stare. I sat and shot my instructions at him until his face got on my nerves and I snarled: 'Get that damn face outa my way before I bust it! You got the crummiest lookin' front of any bastard I ever saw. Here, you look like some *sabe*, listen close to me.' This last to one of the friends as the lover stepped back abashed. The idea was to take the girl off in a motorboat to some island—we must have been in a sea-coast town—and then send word for her family to come across with the cash: a thousand dollars, which we'd all split between us. But the girl and I had planned to cross the rest and beat it with the swag, only she wanted to work her stupid lover in on the deal.

"Then, the next thing the scene has changed incredibly. We were the same gang, but it was the latter part of the Middle Ages or later. There were three of us out on some wild and barren rocks just off a rugged coast. The girl, bound hand and foot, the lover and myself. The man and I were dressed in close breeches and deerskin, feathered hats and other apparel of that time, the girl in long flowing garments. A boat floated by the rocks and some disagreement had come up between us—he had bound the girl and was about to beat it with the money or something. I came leaping down across the rocks toward him and we fired simultaneously with flintlock pistols and my ball knocked his gun from his hand. Then we closed with cutlasses and the sparks flew until both blades broke short at the same time and I knocked him cold with a left swing to the chin. Then the dream faded, but how strange—I had regained my lost youth in the second scene and was no longer a slum rat."

Note that the dream seems to hold five people aside from Howard: a woman of young middle age who is rotund, a young girl, and three men; also note the dream involves a boat and an island. The first thing that might pop out about this dream is, in the kidnapping of Charles Lindbergh's son in 1932, a gang of three men and two women were represented as the kidnappers (in a meeting at Woodlawn Cemetery in New Jersey between John F. Condon as liaison and a purportedly Scandinavian sailor calling himself John on behalf of the kidnappers.) As proof the group of five kidnappers was the real thing, John said the toddler's sleeping suit would be sent, and upon arrival Lindbergh identified it as his son's. Moreover, boats and islands were involved in both the dream and in the Lindbergh kidnapping, where after payment Condon was told the boy would be found at the island of Martha's Vineyard in a boat called The Nelly. (Sadly, the boy's body was found less than five miles from Lindbergh's home.) The details of Howard's dream bear a notably prophetic similarity to what H.L. Mencken called "the biggest story since the Resurrection." Even the lowly occupation, the "patois of the Bowery," and "slum rat" status which Howard mentions was echoed in the numerous spelling errors and grammatical irregularities found in the ransom notes.

Did Howard really catch a distorted glimpse of the future that night, or were the numerous identical factors still just far-flung pinpoints still covered by the umbrella of coincidence? It's worth some thought at least, as research has failed to reveal the noticing of these strong similarities by any other Howard scholar. Also of unusual note is the date on which Lindbergh received the first Distinguished Flying Cross ever awarded: June 11, 1927. Considering the interest and perhaps occasional belief in the mystic and the occult which Howard had, this dream could potentially have been bolstered by others if their details had been recorded. It is intriguing to imagine Howard as having many dreams which bore just as many parallels to things which would later come to pass.

He did tell Novalyne that he was haunted by the memory of a recurring dream, which he thought may have been a window into one of his past lives. The dream involved him falling in love with a woman, only to have his best friend betray him. It became a sort of self-fulfilling prophecy when Howard's actions caused

Novalyne to seek the company of Truett Vinson. He confronted her one day after her class ended and told her how he just wanted to love and be loved in return, flatly asking her if she loved Truett instead. Novalyne replied that she was not in love with anyone at the present time, and that she had been accepted to Louisiana State University. She had promised herself that she would write to him, but she never did

Maybe none of these things were on Howard's mind that morning. As he took his last cup of coffee and looked at his home for the last time, did he realize that the flesh he was about to harm was the only legacy his mother would have? Did he assume his father would follow him beyond the borders of life? It seems so, as Howard during his final preparations had purchased a plot for three in the Greenleaf Memorial Cemetery in Brownwood, including the coffins and perpetual maintenance of the grave site. His mother always liked Brownwood, and she was friendly with Lena Vinson who lived there, Truett's mother. The day before his death Howard spoke with secretary of the Cemetery Association Mr. Bass, reserving Lot 13, Block 5 in Greenleaf for a triple burial.

It is believed that Howard had pondered taking his Dad's life with him, as if by silent understanding. Isaac himself reported that, during his son's pacing, he would often stop in front of his father and look at him in a certain pensive way. It may have been the reason so many guests were summoned to the Howard home in Hester's final hours, but Isaac later recanted his belief that such a thing might have been done to him by his son.

In Howard's writing the clearest case of a killing out of love and mercy occurs in *The People of the Black Circle.* Yasmina watches in terror as her brother Bunda Chand, the king of Vendhya, lay dying due to foul sorcery which sought to draw his soul from his body. "Aid me!" cries her brother. I am far from my mortal house! Wizards have drawn my soul through the wind-blown darkness. They seek to snap the silver cord that binds me to my dying body. They cluster around me; their hands are taloned, their eyes are red like flame burning in darkness…"

As she sees her brother continue to writhe in agony, he tells her, "…My soul clings to my body, but its hold weakens. Quick—kill me, before they can trap my soul for ever!" Yasmina replies that she cannot kill him, but he is her king as well as her brother, and he commands her to do so. "You have never disobeyed me—obey my last command! Send my soul clean to Asura! Haste, lest you damn me to spend eternity as a filthy gaunt of darkness. Strike, I command you! *Strike!*"

And so with a heavy and panicked heart Yasmina removes a jeweled dagger from her girdle and plunges it to the hilt in her brother's chest: "He stiffened and then went limp, a grim smile curving his dead lips. Yasmina hurled herself face-down on the rush-covered floor, beating the reeds with her clenched hands. Outside, the gongs and conchs brayed and thundered and the priests gashed themselves with copper knives."

This theme of providing someone with salvation by bringing them death may have crossed Howard's thoughts those many times he regarded his father during his last day. He may have foreseen or at least imagined the lonely life which lay ahead for his father, and likened it, in a way, to being ensorcelled by forces beyond his control. On that final day in the sad eyes of his father he may have seen a touch of the dying king Bunda Chand, and he may have sensed a conspiracy within the darker elements of his world. In the story the two-faced wizard Khemsa says, "Even the arts you call sorcery are governed by cosmic laws. The stars direct these actions, as in other affairs. Not even my masters can alter the stars.…The slant of the moon presaged evil for the king of Vendyha; the stars are in turmoil, the Serpent is in the house of the Elephant. During such juxtaposition, the invisible guardians are removed from the spirit of Bunda Chand. A path is opened in the unseen realms, and once a point of contact was established, mighty powers were put in play along that path."

But Howard did not act upon whatever perception of mercy he may have wished to bestow upon his father. It could be because this would entail Howard leaving the world himself with the image of his father's death face on his mind, and no thanks emanating from those ice blue eyes which he shared with Conan. Perhaps, while pacing, all those times he stopped in front of his father, Howard was waiting for the old man, like Bunda Chand, to ask for relief from the burden and conflict which assailed him. As it was the closest answer he got was the day before, when Howard asked his father, "Where will you go, Dad?" and Isaac replied, "Why, wherever you do." To Howard, that may have been enough.

So after not sleeping for a day and only sleeping in snatches the previous two, after eating little but drinking vast quantities of black coffee, after spending most of his time in his mother's bedroom beside her comatose form, Robert E. Howard was ready. For one final confirmation he asked the nurse Mrs. Green on the morning of June 11 whether she thought there was any possible chance his mother would awaken again, and she said gently, "No."

Howard is said to have paused then, to take a long last look at his mother, the illness in complete power over her. How different she looked then from the animated, attentive, determined woman of his youth; different, and yet of course to him the same. He had cared for her at the end of her life like a servant, though his every effort could not reverse her disease. Her fine dresses, which she wore while on the town doing errands or serving a dinner for friends, hung in the closet never to be worn again. And that beautiful picture of her, taken outdoors in 1905, where she is wearing ruffles and a bonnet, holding a planter next to a metal basin on a table—even on that gardening table there was linen, and her face is unbroken by age and sickness, her eyes intense but loving. That was the mother he wished returned to him—that was the mother he wished to somehow find again, though he knew for all the world and the stars that it was impossible. Her husband sat on the couch in the living room, being consoled by friends.

There were no friends present for Howard, nor could he be consoled.

With heavy feet he went from his mother's room to his own small bedroom office. He saw his work desk for the last time, touched the keys of his Underwood typewriter, and thought perhaps of that piece of paper he had put into his wallet. It was a couplet he had typed:

All fled, all done, so lift me on the pyre;
The feast is over and the lamps expire.

Then he walked outside that morning of June 11, into the yard where he had played with Patch in younger days. His mind was likely drawn to that solemn place long-covered, under the mesquite tree in the corner of the lot on the east side. But his steps carried him to the west side of the lot, beside the white fence where his Chevy sedan was parked. He got inside the car.

A newly-hired cook saw him from the kitchen window and assumed he was fixing to run an errand, likely his usual run to the post office. She paid it little mind and continued with her work.

Howard sat in his car, tensely still as the sun was rising. He rolled up his window, probably not wanting anyone else to be hurt by the act he had so long contemplated. Then after a deep breath he reached into his glove compartment and withdrew the Colt .380 automatic which he had borrowed from Lindsey Tyson. He flicked off the safety.

You have built a world of paper and wood,
Culture and cult and lies;
Has the cobra altered beneath his hood,
Or the fire in the tiger's eyes?

You have turned from valley and hill and flood,

You have set yourselves apart,
Forgetting the earth that feeds the blood
And the talon that finds the heart.

You boast you have stilled the lustful call
Of the wild ancestral ape,
But life, the tigress that bore you all,
Has never changed her shape.

And a strange shape comes to your faery mead,
With a fixed black simian frown,
But you will not know and you will not heed
Till your towers come tumbling down.

—REH, in a letter to August Derleth, May 9, 1936

He could not linger. Too much time spent in further contemplation would be far more likely to catch the attention of someone. His father had anticipated the possibility of such an act and hidden Howard's own guns, but he would later confess that he never thought Robert might actually kill himself before his mother had passed.

But how could he watch her die? That final moment, envisioned in his mind, must have loomed far larger than any dread of his own termination. When she took her last breath and was no longer counted among the living, there was no Brownwood, there was no location on earth that could put Howard far enough away from that awful realization. He loved her too much to watch her die.

Taking the best aim that he could, Howard pulled the trigger.

Everything that had weighed upon him was released the only way he knew how to release it. He had taken the path of the warrior—taken his future into his own hands to grimly compare it to what he desired it to be, and he made no concessions.

In a letter from Isaac Howard to H.P. Lovecraft a little more than two weeks after the suicide, the doctor describes what happened that morning: "…after three weeks of vigilant watching at his mother's bedside, on the morning of June 11, 1936, at eight o'clock, he slipped out of the house, entered his car which was standing in front of the garage, raised the windows and fired a shot through his brain. The cook standing at the window at the back part of the house, saw him go get in his car. She thought he was fixing to drive to town as he usually did. When she heard the muffled sound of the gun, she saw him fall over the steering wheel. She ran in the house and called the physician who was in the house. The doctor was taking a cup of coffee in the dining room and I was talking with him. We rushed to the car and found him. We thought at first that it was a death shot but the bullet had passed through the brain. He shot himself just above the temple. It came out on the opposite side, just above and behind the left ear. He lived eight hours and never regained consciousness."

His final haunting couplet was long reported by L. Sprague de Camp to be taken from the last stanza of Ernest Dowson's *Non sum qualis eram bonae sub regno Cynarae*:

> I cried for madder music and for stronger wine,
> But when the feast is finished and the lamps expire,
> Then falls thy shadow, Cynara! the night is thine;
> And I am desolate and sick of an old passion,
> Yea, hungry for the lips of my desire:
> I have been faithful to thee, Cynara! in my fashion.

De Camp was so sure he had found the source poem that he went so far as to name a chapter of *Dark Valley Destiny* "Faithful in His Fashion." And of course Cynara and Cimmeria are similar-sounding names.

We owe it to the diligent research of Howard scholar Rusty Burke that the true source of Howard's final grim goodbye to the world was discovered. In his article *All Fled, All Done* Rusty Burke explains, "Engaged in literary detective work, I have been scanning a number of poetry collections for scraps that Howard had quoted. In a little book called Songs of Adventure, edited by Robert Frothingham (Houghton Mifflin, 1926), I stumbled by chance upon a poem by Benjamin De Casseres ('The Closed Room') which Howard used some lines from in 'The Door to the World' (published in Fantasy Crosswinds as 'The Door to the Garden'). Then, scanning over the contents, I found that the collection included Bill Adams' 'Flower of the Morning,' which Howard had used in memorializing his friend Herbert Klatt, although this anthology presented it under the title 'Light of the Morning.' So I'm paging through the book wondering if maybe I might stumble upon the sources of a couple of other little scraps of poetry which Howard had quoted but not identified. And I ran across this..."

THE HOUSE OF CÆSAR

Yea—we have thought of royal robes and red.
Had purple dreams of words we utterèd;
Have lived once more the moment in the brain
That stirred the multitude to shout again.
All done, all fled, and now we faint and tire—
The Feast is over and the lamps expire!

Yea—we have launched a ship on sapphire seas,
And felt the steed between the gripping knees;
Have breathed the evening when the huntsman brought
The stiffening trophy of the fevered sport—
Have crouched by rivers in the grassy meads
To watch for fish that dart amongst the weeds.
All well, all good—so hale from sun and mire—
The Feast is over and the lamps expire!

Yet—we have thought of Love as men may think,
Who drain a cup because they needs must drink;
Have brought a jewel from beyond the seas
To star a crown of blue anemones.
All fled, all done—a Cæsar's brief desire—
The Feast is over and the lamps expire!

>Yea— and what is there that we have not done,
>The Gods provided us 'twixt sun and sun?
>Have we not watched an hundred legions thinned,
>And crushed and conquered, succorèd and sinned?
>Lo— we who moved the lofty gods to ire—
>The Feast is over and the lamps expire!
>
>Yea— and what voice shall reach us and shall give
>Our earthly self a moment more to live?
>What arm shall fold us and shall come between
>Our failing body and the grasses green?
>And the last heart that beats beneath this head—
>Shall it be heard or unrememberèd?
>All dim, all pale— so lift me on the pyre—
>The Feast is over and the lamps expire!
>
>—Viola Garvin

"And when I come to the end of the trail, if I have lost, I can say that at least I never whimpered for sympathy in my work....But God, the utter futility of it descends on the soul of me like a thick fog through which I can see no light. Surely, for by the time I have gained the heights of success I will be old and hardened so by life that the taste of success will be as dust and ashes in my soul—a man without hope, without joy and without friends. The finished article—and what care the accursed throng for the labor that went to make it? There always remains, Sin's mockery be thanked, the longings of the flesh and if a man can never satisfy the mind and the soul, he can at least satiate the belly and its brothers. They promise nothing and though they desert a man in the end, they do not betray because, blind and torture-hunger, they promise nothing. Nothing beyond the moment—but a man can live in a sort of manner, in that moment.

"The emptiness of success I know—though I have never tasted it—is a reality for always through the cheers of the mob will come like a writhing serpent the memory of the jeers of the mob when I worked and sweated pure red blood. And I will always think: you uplift me now, but you scorned me then, and where is the difference? For I am now and I was then, and then I built the cornerstones and the foundations, and now I stand on the spire and where is the difference? Damn you all. That's what I will think in the days to come; but now I must bend my back to the cornerstones and the foundations and make them firm so that my spires may rend apart the stars and all the world may see the glimmer of my skeleton against them when I stand on my spires at the end."

—Robert E. Howard to Tevis Clyde Smith, October 1928

Chapter Thirteen:
The Afterlife of Robert E. Howard

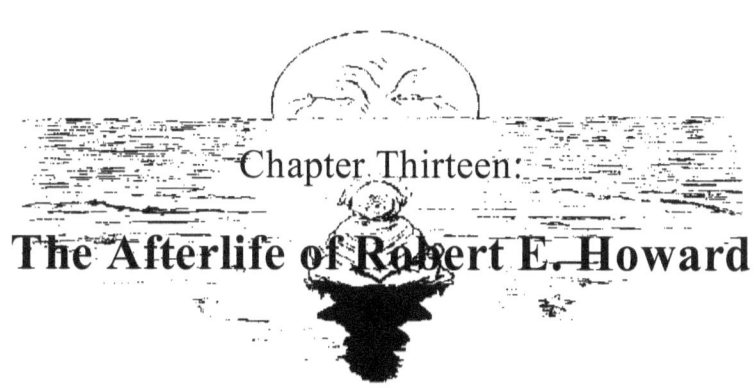

The future is not a result of choices among alternative paths offered by the present, but a place that is created—created first in the mind and will, created next in activity. The future is not some place we are going to, but one we are creating. The paths are not to be found, but made, and the activity of making them, changes both the maker and the destination.
--John Scharr

"The more people know about you, the more advantage they have over you. A man weakens himself just that much with every secret nook in his soul that he lays bare. I care not if my real life be made public property when the time comes because the first thing a writer learns is to sacrifice himself on the altar of his art, but I wish someone to profit materially by it, when it is done, and I do not wish my soul to be exposed to the gaze of a lot of immature and amateur gropers, which after all, is what most of them are..."
--REH to Tevis Clyde Smith, late 1928

It is with a heavy heart and no small amount of perplexity that we begin to recount the actions of Isaac Howard in the weeks and months following the deaths of his son and wife. Hester had clung to life a mere thirty hours longer than Robert, who, despite his fatal wound, lingered eight hours after its infliction. Neither mother nor son ever regained consciousness.

Isaac took to visiting the grave site and he was distressed when he noticed the way water would puddle around the area after a rain. His medical experience could paint all the more vivid a picture within his mind of just what was happening below his feet. For weeks he fought this off, unbidden as it was, but when he went home to look through his son's vast papers and figure out which remaining stories would be best to have published, the themes of death and blood would leap off the page to even the glancing eye.

None of Howard's stories specifically focused on bodily decay, but enough of them mentioned it or hinted at it, and it was something which Dr. Howard could not expel from his thoughts. He well remembered the sermons and ceremonies of the double funeral, wherein he was concerned one Baptist minister was "trying to preach my boy to hell" by using a quote from the Bible about falling on one's sword. And increasingly Isaac's mind was drawn toward the coffins, and how they were only made of unfinished pine.

As the weeks passed and spring turned into summer, morbidly Isaac must have been tormented by the mental image of what was happening to the remains of his wife and son. Much of this may have been from a certain guilt, the source of which we will soon discuss, but for now, after months under the earth in the full Texas weather, with autumn closing in like a bloodless hand in the dark, Isaac Howard had reached his mental breaking point and he would have the bodies exhumed.

Five cemetery workers were paid $25 each for a day's labor, which was a goodly sum in the Depression. But the work would be some of the most unpleasant they would ever experience. Note that Howard scholar Patrice Louinet attributes the time before exhumation as only "a few weeks." From his essay *Grief & Greed*: "Thus, a few weeks after his son's and wife's deaths, he bought a granite stone for the burial lot and had their coffins replaced. At the same time he had no problems with the gruesome act of driving the car in which his son had literally blown his brains out." In a February, 1979 letter from Gomer Thomas, one of the workers hired that day, L. Sprague de Camp learned how "both the pine coffins and their contents were badly decomposed."

Dr. Howard had the gore cleaned out of his son's car by a garage worker who years later could still recall "the indescribable stench of the blood and human remains after the car had stood untended for days." He began driving Robert's Chevy, and likely used it to transport himself to the newly-altered burial site. To put his mind at ease he had paid for his wife and sun to be reburied in steel vaults.

Perhaps Isaac was familiar with the Edgar Allen Poe work *The Premature Burial*. Certainly his son was a fan of Poe and would have had material on hand. In an early scene Poe relates of a young French girl from an illustrious family, and the poor journalist that falls in love with her, "but the pride of her birth decided her, finally, to reject him." She marries a banker who is suspected of mistreating her, and after some wretched years of marriage she dies…

> "…at least her condition so closely resembled death as to deceive every one who saw her. She was buried—not in a vault, but in an ordinary grave in the village of her nativity. Filled with despair, and still inflamed by the memory of a profound attachment, the lover journeys from the capital to the remote province in which the village lies, with the romantic purpose of disinterring the corpse, and possessing himself of its luxuriant tresses. He reaches the grave. At midnight he unearths the coffin, opens it, and is in the act of detaching the hair, when he is arrested by the unclosing of the beloved

eyes. In fact, the lady had been buried alive. Vitality had not altogether departed, and she was aroused by the caresses of her lover from the lethargy which had been mistaken for death..."

Poe goes on to relate the story of Edward Stapleton, a young London attorney who was presumed dead and buried for two days before being exhumed by practitioners of dissection and revived by the charge from a battery: "A rough gash was made, and a wire hastily brought in contact; when the patient, with a hurried but quite unconvulsive movement, arose from the table, stepped into the middle of the floor, gazed about him uneasily for a few seconds, and then—spoke. What he said was unintelligible; but words were uttered; the syllabification was distinct. Having spoken, he fell heavily to the floor."

Finally, the teller of the story, who has now recounted other people's misfortunes of being buried alive, himself "sank, little by little, into a condition of semi-syncope, or half swoon; and, in this condition, without pain, without ability to stir....I remained." Finally he awakens in blackness, tries to yell, but cannot:

> "The movement of the jaws, in this effort to cry aloud, showed me that they were bound up, as is usual with the dead. I felt, too, that I lay upon some hard substance; and by something similar my sides were, also, closely compressed. So far, I had not ventured to stir any of my limbs—but now I violently threw up my arms, which had been lying at length, with the wrists crossed. They struck a solid wooden substance, which extended above my person at an elevation of not more than six inches from my face. I could no longer doubt that I reposed within a coffin at last."

Poe concludes, "There are moments when, even to the sober eye of Reason, the world of our sad Humanity may assume the semblance of a Hell..."

Images such as this may have troubled Isaac's sleep, but the doctor in him was able to reject any thought that his loved ones were buried alive. Rather, it was his ability to know exactly what was really happening to them that proved to be the more chilling torture. Even after the transfer to steel vaults, Isaac could not let go of the grave site, and began to scour the countryside's greenhouses and nurseries for what he felt would be more appropriate landscaping. Norris Chambers, the son of a medical colleague and friend, reporting driving with Isaac and witnessing his obsession with plant prices and growth patterns. Maybe in his mind Isaac thought that if something could be nurtured to bloom by the soil surrounding his family's remains, each year of its marked growth would serve as a more positive reminder of the circle of life.

In the end, however, it is said he planted "practically nothing."

Next would come a rather inexplicable urge within Isaac to teach an informal Sunday school class. Although not particularly church-going, Doc Howard marched himself into the offices of *The Cross Plains Review* and declared his intentions in no uncertain terms. However, when a group of over a dozen young men met Isaac at the Liberty Theater for their first class, the doctor kicked things off by asking everyone who had been in a whorehouse to stand up. A few did, understandably embarrassed. If this kind of humiliation awaited them in future classes, they would just as soon have it officially sanctioned by the church and doled out by a vetted minister. Class size instantly dwindled and Isaac soon lost interest.

Again Isaac enlisted Norris Chambers, the son of his doctor friend, this time to travel with him around the state looking for good farm land so that Isaac could "live close to nature." But not just any farm land would do. In addition to having the right setting and the right feel (normal requirements for any potential buyer,) Isaac had developed the particular stipulation that the land be free of nematode worms. "We'd carry a post-hole digger with us, and we'd go to an old farm," related Norris Chambers in

July of 1977. "He'd first go to real estate agents, and they'd point out the ones that were available…and I'd dig holes for him there, and he'd take that soil there, and he'd put it in little bottles, and he'd send it to College Station to have it analyzed. He was afraid he'd get some land that had nematodes in it." The doctor's actions would make it seem as if he were unaware that nematodes are plentiful in normal soil. If he was aware of this, it lends all the more foundation to his misdirected and abortive energies in the wake of personal tragedy.

"I was watching Robert as this was premeditated, and I knew it," Isaac wrote to Lovecraft that fateful June, "but I did not think that he would kill himself before his mother went. His mother was in coma and had been for many hours when this occurred. There were two trained nurses in the house and doctors there all the time. He did not ask a doctor, neither did he ask me, but he asked a nurse if she thought his mother would ever regain consciousness enough to know him, and the nurse told him she feared not. This was unknown to me. Had I known, I might have prevented this, because I know now that he fully made up his mind not to see his mother die.

"Last March a year ago, again when his mother was very low in the King's Daughters Hospital in Temple, Texas, Dr. McCelvey expressed a fear that she would not recover; he began to talk with me about his business, and I at once understood what it meant. I began to talk to him, trying to dissuade him from such a course, but his mother began to improve. Immediately [when] she began to improve, he became cheerful and no more was said. Again this year, in February, while his mother was very sick and not expected to live but a few days, at that time she was in the Shannon Hospital in San Angelo, Texas. San Angelo is something like one hundred miles from here. He was driving back and forth daily from San Angelo to home. One evening he told me I would find his business, what little there was to it, all carefully written up and in a large envelope in his desk. Again I begged him not to do it, but he positively did not intend to live after his mother was gone."

The idea of bee-keeping entered Dr. Howard's mind. Here were patients whose individual deaths meant little and whose very living meant sweetness and riches. It was a fanciful, unrealistic concept that never got off the ground. Perhaps the guarded inner clique of the bee hives would remind him of the relationship between Robert and Hester, within which his presence was so often shooed. At any rate he went from fancies of bee-keeping to the idea that he would write a biography of his son. One can only imagine what this might have been like. The ice delivery man could have taken a stab at it and not made a single deliberate changing of whatever facts he had, but Isaac would be compelled to embellish and distort, such as when he wrote to E. Hoffmann Price in June of 1944 and declared, "...Robert was always hearty and cheerful in his home, never saw him morose, crabbed, or cross in all his life." And earlier in the letter Isaac had declared that Robert was happy just to have his parents and be at home. These claims may have been true a portion of the time, but Isaac clearly would have had plenty of opportunities to witness the inherent falseness of his statements if applied to his son in whole. Isaac would next invite E. Hoffman Price and his wife to come and live with him, suggesting that his wife could do all the household chores. The Prices expressed their level of interest by not responding to the invitation. Nonetheless, Isaac sent Price the famous trunk, which contained a vast quantity of Howard's lesser-known material. Price would prove to be a mediocre steward, lending papers out and not keeping much track, and letting what remained become damaged by mildew due to where he stored it. Glenn Lord would later step in to rescue and preserve the work, and even track down the various pieces Price had indefinitely lent out over the years.

Next Dr. Howard approached his friend and colleague Dr. Chambers with the proposition that a one-room addition be built on the back of the Chambers home in which to house Isaac. One cannot help but get the feeling that he was almost asking for a doghouse in which to retire. One room was such a humble request that Dr. Chambers was giving it some thought...until he discovered Isaac was becoming obsessed with the title to the home and wanted to do a title search of the Chambers' land. Needless to say it was off-putting, and the arrangement fell through. A more local family, the Bakers, next received the same proposition from Dr. Howard. They declined.

What Isaac *did* accomplish was to dispose of a handwritten will Robert had left in which he bequeathed all his property to Lindsey Tyson. French Howard scholar Patrice Louinet wrote in his article *Grief or Greed?* "Thus, Robert Howard, who had been preparing to commit suicide three times in less than a year, who had, each time, 'set his house in order', had left his insurance to his mother, knowing of course that she would not need it very long, since she was dying. It is difficult to tell if Robert Howard expected his father to commit suicide or die from the shock: he had instructed the Otis Kline agency to send all checks to his father in a letter dated June 9, 1936, two days before the suicide, but, at the same time, had asked the sexton of the cemetery to prepare the lot for three burials. At any rate, it would be hard not to notice that Robert Howard, who had planned his suicide so carefully, who had even bought the burial lot, had not left a will, causing his father to be left in a very difficult situation."

Among L. Sprague de Camp's notes at the Harry Ransom Center were the notes taken from a March 7, 1978 interview with Howard neighbor and friend Kate Merryman, who was present with Isaac to help him go through his son's papers. The notes are as follows:

> She volunteered about finding [Robert's] while she + Dr. H. [Howard] were sorting through piles of papers that he had scattered all over the floor that night. The doctor had purchased a new leather cover trunk (large) to put the papers in + they were trying to put together the scattered sheets for the various stories + pack them neatly in the new trunk.
>
> She came upon a handwritten sheet which she read and saw that it was a will leaving all his property to

[Lindsey] Tyson. She said, "Look at this Doctor." He took it, read it, and said "Don't tell anything to anyone about this." And this was the last she or anyone else ever saw of it. Then later IMH swore solemnly that R. had died intestate.

This is independent confirmation of what L. Tyson himself told us the same day. He (L.T.) said a few days after the suicide, a lawyer in town stopped him on the street and told him R had willed everything to him, But that the doctor had destroyed the will. L. Tyson was disturbed + upset + didn't even ask for details Didn't want to profit from his friend's loss anyway, but he now resents it - feeling everybody's making money on Robert but him.

Obviously it seems Kate Merryman confided the incident to at least one other person at the time, and news travels fast in a small town, which might explain the reluctance of the court to grant Isaac's wishes and close the estate of his son.

Isaac was already dealing with Howard's literary agent Otis A. Kline, trying to sell more material and extract from *Weird Tales* the large quantity of money which it owed his son. Isaac wrote to Kline on August 29, 1936, "I had asked the court to permit me to close the estate. It became an estate because Robert left his mother his Insurance and he died before she did; therefore we had to settle this as an estate and in so doing, the court ordered Robert's business to be settled as an estate. It seems that they will not allow me to close the estate until business pertaining to Robert's writing and etc. have been definitely settled. They seem not to be satisfied for me to deal with you outside of written contract and have so informed me that it must be acceptable to the court before we can proceed farther.... All that Robert had was mine and all that his mother had at her death was mine but the court has refused to declare my heirship until I have things settled satisfactorily to them. I assure you that it is quite a handicap because they demand settlement from me and every penny of money that comes into this estate. They also refuse to let me close the estate or release the bonds until such time as they see fit... In the meantime; however, try to get a check from Weird Tales. I need money to carry on under this administratorship. I am compelled to use money from it."

Two days later Dr. Howard told Kline, "I am hot, tired and mad. I drove thirty miles to the County Seat and back today. Twice I have appeared before the county court and asked that they close the estate of Robert E. Howard and release me as Administrator, and also my Bondsmen. Twice they have refused... I have succeeded in closing the estate of his mother, but the court obstinately refuses to close Robert's estate."

But when more time passed and Lindsey Tyson did nothing to contest it, Isaac was finally granted what he had sought, with full rights to handle his son's properties in any way he saw fit. The estate was declared closed by Judge Carpenter in early November. Of the judge Isaac wrote to Farnsworth Wright shortly after, "Judge Carpenter was a hard boiled old skate, very jealous of Robert's rights, like yourself; once you said Robert was your discovery; Judge Carpenter seemed to consider Robert as his Ward and was very jealous of Robert's rights; so much so at times he interfered with the business we were trying to settle." As French Howard scholar Patrice Louinet wrote in *Grief & Greed,* "Isaac Howard's decisions would often oscillate between those of a bereaved man and those of a man who was interested in what he could get from his son's properties."

The guilt Isaac may have felt could have stemmed from a kind of regret with regards to his marketing efforts of his son's work, and how it seemed he just couldn't help himself from trying to generate income from it. The reason he had moved his young family around from town to town, from east Texas to west, all those formative years of Robert's childhood, was because Isaac perceived greater opportunity at each new stop. His own father had started west dreaming of striking gold, and Isaac had over the years dreamt of schemes of his own, always with his medical background to fall back upon for income, such as it was. When patients couldn't pay him, he accepted food and goods for his services, and when he paid calls to their homes, whether for social reasons or to check on health, he expected a little something to eat. A debt was perceived, just as Isaac perceived the *Weird Tales* debt. Trouble was, with him so far away and unable to collect alternate liberties, something in Isaac had to keep pushing.

Isaac wrote to agent Otis Kline in July 1926, "Since Robert's death, I have had letters from certain writers who have intimated to me that sometime the game was not played exactly square. I do not wish in any way to question any agreement Robert may have had with his publishers, but I certainly want to know exactly the terms under which he sold his stuff."

Writing to Farnsworth Wright on September 4, Isaac pushed hard to collect payment, and furthermore implied that *Weird Tales* was keeping for itself the money it owed Robert. Promptly replying as soon as he received the letter, Wright said: "My sympathy is not feigned, but entirely sincere. It was a great shock to me to learn of your son's death; all the more shocking to me because of my own sickness (encephalitis letargica), which, though its further progress was stopped five years ago by electrical fevers, had already progressed so far that it is physically impossible for me to even sign my name in ink [Wright contracted sleeping sickness during World War I and ultimately suffered from Parkinson's disease].... I must correct the impression that I or anyone else connected with Weird Tales 'put in our pockets' the money that was due your son during the period when Weird Tales was in the throes of the depression. Fact is, I often did not know from one month to the other whether I could receive any money at all from the magazine; and I often received nothing (a serious condition, with my wife and son Robert to take care of); and it has been years since I received more than a fraction of the salary I used to get. My wife and I borrowed on our life insurance up to the limit of the policy's capacity; and when I got my veteran's bonus this year it all had to be applied on repayment of the loan from my life insurance."

In what was a bit of a characteristic pseudo-placation, Isaac responded by telling Wright he was sorry to hear of his physical condition and "I think I shall be more patient about things in the future." Several days later Isaac wrote to Kline and explained, "I wrote Mr. Wright perhaps while in the state of mind that I should not have written anyone…" But in the same letter he instructs, "…keep a continued pressure on Weird Tales for collection." It seems Isaac was contemplating taking *Weird Tales* to court. All the while he pushed Kline for sales and made suggestions as to suitable material. Knowing of Wright's illness made Isaac even more jumpy about keeping his son's unsettled material at *Weird Tales* for too long, and Isaac told Kline about Wright being a sick man, emphasizing the need to settle things.

Eventually August Derleth would work with Otis Kline to publish *Skull-Face and Others*. Although Isaac felt the Conan tales would make a finer collection, Derleth was not a big fan of Conan, saying that "Such a collection would almost have to be printed on blood-colored paper and be introduced to readers with appropriate thunderclaps." (*Psycho* author Robert Bloch was also not a fan of Conan, as he wrote in *The Eyrie* section of *Weird Tales*.) However Dr. Howard was still in a position to make things difficult for those he perceived to have ulterior motives. Derleth wrote, "…we had the devil of a time with old Dr. Howard, then still alive; he had fixed ideas paralleling Bob's—while Bob had delusions of persecution, the old man was convinced that everybody was out to 'do' him. OK finally got around him and the deal was on."

Isaac eventually had less of an impetus to pursue such aggressive marketing as he had earlier attempted, and with the advancing years came diabetes and cataracts. In 1942 he approached a colleague, Dr. Pere Moran Kuykendall, who was the director of a small clinic in Ranger Texas called the West Texas Hospital. Isaac offered to bequeath everything to

Kuykendall in exchange for letting him work the remainder of his days at the clinic. Offer accepted, he sold his house and furnishings and in November of 1942 moved into a boardinghouse near the clinic. He found the work to be a good way to spend his time and direct his remaining energy, and he reported having a dream about his wife and son, both busily working on typewriters.

"Since the day they left me," Isaac wrote shortly before his death, "life has been loneliness indescribable....I am the last of my father's family, not one left."

On November 12, 1944, Isaac died due to coronary thrombosis.

Robert, Hester and Isaac Howard

There came to me a Shape one summer night
When all the world lay silent in the stars
And moonlight crossed my room with ghostly bars.
It whispered hints of weird unhallowed sight;
I followed, then in waves of spectral light
Mounted the shimmering ladders of my soul,
Where moon-pale spiders, huge as dragons, stole –
Great forms like moths with wings of wispy white.

Then round the world the sighing of the loon
Shook misty lakes beneath the false dawn's gleams.
Rose-tinted shone the skyline's minaret.
I rose in fear and then with blood and sweat
Beat out the iron fabrics of my dreams
And shaped of them a web to snare the moon.

—REH, "Forbidden Magic"
Weird Tales, July 1929

Afterword

Originally, this project was going to be a collection of some of my favorite Howard works that are in the public domain but which are still hard to find, and what became the biography was originally just the introduction. It grew rapidly, and I knew that the perspectives I wanted to share about REH would best be presented in context to a larger picture of the man. After more than ten years of digesting the Necronomicon Press double edition of his selected letters—there really is a lot to think about in there, plus in my defense I am a slow and deliberate reader—and having first read through *The Last Celt* more than 25 years ago, I found connection points which were enhanced by each new piece of additional material I encountered.

I've owned *Dark Valley Destiny* for many years, but after initial attempts at reading it, I had to put it aside for almost ten years. With the exception of the initial framing device (a flash-forward to Howard's death,) the book proceeds in a very straightforward manner, and the much-discussed style of its (de Camp's) pseudo-scientific conclusions about Howard left me feeling a little off. Although I could easily appreciate the copious information *DVD* contained, it was hard to expel the image from my mind of de Camp doing a rather impersonal public dissection of Howard's character and psyche, and seeming to get key things wrong.

De Camp, however, should be remembered for the information he did preserve while creating *DVD*—information which might otherwise have been lost. And of course, as a writer, my fondness for de Camp works such as *Lest Darkness Fall* remains quite thoroughly intact.

The decidedly "non-Yankee" biography of Howard is the newer Mark Finn book, *Blood & Thunder*. I read this as I was wrapping-up *The Supreme Moment*, initially as a way to be sure I didn't miss anything or get something wrong. I was relieved to see Finn took a very different approach to the way he told Howard's story. I will put it on his publisher, Monkeybrain Books, that the back cover matter claims Howard "lived all of his thirty years in the small town of Cross Plains, Texas," when he only lived half that time there. Finn to his great credit employs a fluid storytelling style that relies less on quotes and more on exposition. Compared to this book, it places a greater emphasis on quoting Howard's fiction—quite a different animal from this book, for I have endeavored to focus on quotes from Howard's letters as a way of best telling (and preserving) the story.

Regarding the issue of photograph inclusion, or lack thereof, I felt that since so many of the known Howard photos are readily available on the internet, displaying all of them here was not necessary. Since the Howard family photos I do include are all over seventy years old, rather than cite many sources of use, under the copyright law of their time I use them as the public domain photos which they are. I have elected to go with a print-on-demand (POD) publisher for two main reasons: Firstly, I despise marketing and have published most of my other books this way, and secondly, POD publishing helps to insure that the book stays in print and is readily available, keeping the price from increasing due to limited press runs. Anyone familiar with collecting some of the rarer Howard materials will quickly appreciate this.

What I hope has been one of the benefits of this book is that it draws upon multiple sources and offers a spectrum of fair-use glimpses into works which are now very expensive and very hard to find. I have also tried to broaden the lens of analysis by offsetting some of these passages so that they reflect off one another, ultimately providing more than one facet for the reader to consider. However, as mentioned in the introduction, I am a writer of fiction and not a biographer. Of all my twentysomething other published books, only one comes close to a biography, and that is the compilation of my father's World War II letters in *Veteran of the Ardennes* and *Soldier of the Ardennes* (the latter including artwork and scans of the actual letters.) So in this matter I must ask for your forgiveness if any (or much) of what I have presented has not been in keeping with your expectations. I, like many, started reading Howard when I was 13 or so, and my views on him are forever containing that fresh glimpse of wonder and admiration, made all the more clear when I learned he felt the same way as I about such things as school and "society."

In what can be nothing other than a confession I must tell you that, for the most part, I am not well-liked by editors. It is even more fair to say that I do not like them. A clear case in point, which I had forgotten about but of which my wife recently reminded me at the dinner table, is the instance of my caulk causing a stir at *Writer's Digest* magazine. This was many years ago, and as one of their "Your Assignment" contest entry guidelines, they asked you to submit a paragraph of praise about an everyday household item that you use. Being the owner of a sometimes rickety 1910 colonial home, I chose to extol the virtues of my caulk. From what I recall the entry went pretty much like this:

My Glorious Caulk

Bathroom have a leak? I grab my caulk. Cold air coming through the window frame? Sounds like a job for my caulk. Truth be told, my caulk can handle anything. I use it so much, it's quite a Red Devil.

I may have added something like "I just give it a squeeze and my problems are solved," but you've pretty much got the full of it. You can imagine my disappointment when they selected the winners and, of the entries, someone who praised his toilet (oh darling how gauche) was selected as a runner-up but my caulk gained no favor with them—in fact my caulk was thoroughly ill regarded. I then wrote what came to be known in-house as "The Cowardly Piglet Letter," wherein I called their Your Assignment editor just that, ranted a bit about their total loss of edge, their outdated Art Linkletter sense of humor, and how they seemed to cater these days to the housewife dabbling in glitzy schmaltz writing, and dared them to print it (which they did.) Next thing you know I'm not getting issues. I waited a few years and tried subscribing again through Publisher's Clearinghouse, but the issues never came. So in all the years between then and now I have been hard-pressed to forgive Writer's Digest for so begrudging my well-intentioned caulk. (I still think it was the most entertaining entry.)

This is just one example in a rather long and jaundiced stream of how I have rubbed certain mainstream editors the wrong way, not to mention certain mainstream people. Thank Crom the salvation for so many of us is Genre! If you should dare to read my novels, not only will you be among the first, but I think you will quickly see that my humor is somewhere between Burroughs and oblivion. It took Howard as a subject to get me to produce something that didn't absolutely reek of forlorn cynicism and deep blue humor. You have been fairly warned not to expect in my other books the sort of love which underlies these pages about Howard.

Come, spit on my shoes. The latter chapters which address things such as Howard's hashish references in one of his stories and the significance of his destroyed will to Lindsey Tyson contain speculative angles which, if left unsaid, would have nagged at me something fierce. Fans who see Howard as nothing but perfect could once count me in their ranks, and because of this I hope they and others will pardon the liberties I have taken while attempting to address what I perceive to be little-explored angles to this complicated story. Whether people agree with them or not, it would be a mistake to simplify the diverse and remarkable elements of Robert E. Howard.

Bibliography

I have endeavored to provide bibliographic information in steps throughout the book as quotes were used, in the form of citations for quotes and their authors, and the title of the work in which those quotes appeared. REH quotes from his extensive letters are identified by date of letter, as are the quotes from other cited authors and their letters concerning REH. Brief excerpts from essays of Howard scholars are named and attributed to their authors within the body of this work. However, many sources in this bibliography will overlap with their previous citations in the body of the text. This is indicative of the extent to which they were useful in providing sources of information upon which to draw. I have tried to minimize the extent to which a reader might have to flip back and forth to identify the source of any given passage.

De Camp, L. Sprague, Catherine Crook de Camp, Jane Whittington Griffin. *Dark Valley Destiny: The Life of Robert E. Howard*. New York, NY. Bluejay Books. 1983.

De Camp, L. Sprague. *The Best of L. Sprague de Camp*. Garden City, NY. Doubleday. 1978.

De Camp, ed. *The Fantastic Swordsmen*. New York, NY. Pyramid Books. 1967.

Ellis, Novalyne Price and Rusty Burke. *Day of the Stranger: Further Memories of Robert E. Howard*. West Warwick, RI. Necronomicon Press. 1989.

Ellis, Novalyne Price. *One Who Walked Alone: Robert E. Howard, The Final Years*. Hampton Falls, NH. Donald M. Grant. 1986.

Finn, Mark. *Blood & Thunder: The Life & Art of Robert E. Howard.* Austin, TX. Monkeybrain Books. 2006

Gordon, Lyndall. *Eliot's Early Years.* Oxford University Press. 1977

Grun, Bernard. *The Timetables of History.* New York, NY. Simon and Schuster. 1982.

Herron, Don, ed. *The Dark Barbarian, The Writings of Robert E. Howard: A Critical Anthology.* Gillette, NJ. Wildside Press. 2000.

---. *The Barbaric Triumph: A Critical Anthology on the Writings of Robert E. Howard.* Gillette, NJ. Wildside Press. 2004.

Howard, Robert E. *Post Oaks and Sand Roughs.* Hampton Falls, NH. Donald M. Grant, Publisher. 1990.

---. *The Black Stranger and Other American Tales.* Lincoln, NE. University of Nebraska Press. 2005.

---. *The Bloody Crown of Conan (Conan of Cimmeria Book 2).* New York, NY. Del Rey. 2004.

---. *Boxing Stories.* Lincoln, NE. University of Nebraska Press. 2005.

---. *Bran Mak Morn: The Last King.* New York, NY. Del Rey. 2005.

---. *The Coming of Conan the Cimmerian (Conan of Cimmeria Book 1).* New York, NY. Del Rey. 2003.

---. *The Conquering Sword of Conan (Conan of Cimmeria Book 3).* New York, NY. Del Rey. 2005.

---. *The End of the Trail.* Lincoln, NE. University of Nebraska Press. 2005.

---. *The Essential Conan.* Bedford Hills, NY. SFBC. 1998.

---. *Kull: Exile of Atlantis.* New York, NY. Del Rey. 2006.

---. *Lord of Samarcand and Other Adventure Tales of the Old Orient.* Lincoln, NE. University of Nebraska Press. 2005.

---. *The Riot at Bucksnort and Other Western Tales.* Lincoln, NE. University of Nebraska Press. 2005.

---. *The Savage Tales of Solomon Kane.* New York, NY. Del Rey. 2004.

---. *Selected Letters: 1923-1930.* West Warwick, RI. Necronomicon Press. 1989.

---. *Selected Letters: 1931-1936.* West Warwick, RI. Necronomicon Press. 1991.

---. *Shadow Kingdoms, The Weird Works of Robert E. Howard, Volume 1.* Holicong, PA. Wildside Press. 2004.

---. *Sword Woman.* New York, NY. Berkley. 1979.

Kaye, Marvin, ed. *Weird Tales: The Magazine That Never Dies.* Garden City, NY. Doubleday. 1988.

Lord, Glenn. *The Last Celt: A Bio-Bibliography of Robert Erin Howard.* West Kingston, RI. Donald M. Grant, Publisher 1976.

Lord, Glenn, ed. *The Howard Collector.* New York, NY. Ace. 1979.

---. *The Book of Robert E. Howard.* New York, NY. Zebra. 1976.

---. *The Second Book of Robert E. Howard.* New York, NY. Berkley. 1980.

Poe, Edgar Allan. *Complete Stories and Poems of Edgar Allan Poe.* Garden City, NY. Doubleday. 1966.

Robertson, Lexie Dean. *Red Heels*. Dallas, TX. Southwest Press. 1928.

Rudman, Mark. *Realm of Unknowing: Meditations on Art, Suicide, and Other Transformations*. Hanover, NH. University Press of New England. 1995.

Silverman, Harold M., ed. *The Pill Book, 6th Edition*. New York, NY. Bantam. 1994

Smith, Tevis Clyde. *Report on a Writing Man and Other Reminiscences of Robert E. Howard*. West Warwick, RI. Necronomicon Press. 1991.

Stevens, Serita Deborah, Anne Klarner. *Deadly Doses: A Writer's Guide to Poisons*. Cincinnati, OH. F&W Publications. 1990.

Van de Castle, Robert L. *Our Dreaming Mind*. New York, NY. Ballantine. 1994.

Additional Howard Photos

Boxing

Looking like Rube from "Dead Like Me"

Ready for a showdown?

With Patch.

Standing over his opponent.

"One way or the other…"

High school photo

Last known photo

Period Photos of Interest

Brownwood sign in 1939
Library of Congress, Prints & Photographs Division, FSA-OWI Collection

Unloading at the Brownwood Poultry Cooperative, 1939
Library of Congress, Prints & Photographs Division, FSA-OWI Collection

Weigher at the Brownwood Poultry Cooperative, 1939
Library of Congress, Prints & Photographs Division, FSA-OWI Collection

Brownwood Poultry Cooperative House showing turkey pickers removing feathers after birds have been scalded. 1939.
Library of Congress, Prints & Photographs Division, FSA-OWI Collection.

Activity at oil well showing one length of pipe resting on the kelly joint into the rat hole with operations for removing other lengths of pipe from the hole. Oil well, Kilgore, Texas. 1939.
Library of Congress, Prints & Photographs Division

Fort Worth, 1910

Fort Worth, 1920

Ranger in 1919 (where I.M. Howard moved)

San Antonio in 1910

all panoramic photos courtesy LOC

An old abandoned mansion in Comanche, less than 40 miles from Cross Plains, as it appeared in 1939. One can only wonder if this may have lent some inspiration to Howard as he wrote *Pigeons from Hell*. (Comanche had a large peanut processing plant, which would have attracted birds.)
Library of Congress, Prints & Photographs Division, FSA-OWI Collection

another view of the abandoned mansion
Library of Congress, Prints & Photographs Division, FSA-OWI Collection

Bob Lemmons in 1936, born a slave about 1850, south of San Antonio. Came to Carrizo Springs during the Civil War with white cattlemen seeking new range. In 1865, with his master was one of the first settlers. Knew Billy the Kid, King Fisher, and other noted bad men of the border. This is the type of Old Timer that Howard often sought to speak with about the Old West and its legends.
Library of Congress, Prints & Photographs Division

Farmers' Market in Weatherford in 1939, less than ten miles from where Howard was born.
Library of Congress, Prints & Photographs Division, FSA-OWI Collection

Signs at a wholesale grocery store in San Angelo in 1939. This town is where Howard stayed while Hester had treatment at Shannon Hospital. Staying a boarding house, it's quite probable he ate food from this store.
Library of Congress, Prints & Photographs Division, FSA-OWI Collection

Burk-Burnett District, 1919.
Library of Congress, Prints & Photographs Division, FSA-OWI Collection

Sign in storefront of agricultural supply store in Brownwood, 1939.
Library of Congress, Prints & Photographs Division, FSA-OWI Collection

A farmer's beat-up car stops beside an Indian Gas pump in Brownwood, 1939. It seems likely Howard himself refueled here.
Library of Congress, Prints & Photographs Division, FSA-OWI Collection

Divided panorama of the 1927 International Pageant of Pulchritude and Annual Bathing Girl Review, held in Galveston May 21-23. Howard and Truett Vinson took advantage of a bargain rate on the Sante Fe expressly to come and see the legs of the bathing beauties. From *Dark Valley Destiny*: "That afternoon was devoted to the Pageant of Pulchritude. The young men [Howard and Vinson] sat like gulls along the sea wall." From Howard's "The Galveston Affair," which appeared in the Galveston Daily News on May 29, 1927: "But we were there to see legs, and legs we were going to see if we sat there till Hell froze over and the Devil took sleigh rides on the ice." So it would seem likely that this photo, taken before a winner was crowned, could very well capture Howard and Vinson by the sea wall in the background. There is a second photo of the event, taken from the same position but cutting out slightly more of the upper portion of the people on the sea wall. On the following page I will attempt to isolate the leading Howard & Vinson location. At any rate, we know for a fact that these are the same women which Howard came to see.
Courtesy LOC

Although the top of the panorama ends too soon here, note the way the man is folding his arms. It is the same right-over-left fold that Howard does in an existing photo in front of a white fence. The more common arm fold is left-over-right, as struck by the fifth person over from the potential REH. The attire also fits, and the man to the right could be Vinson, who was not as muscular as Howard. Their location is roughly center in the full panorama.

The Brownwood feed store in 1939.
Library of Congress, Prints & Photographs Division, FSA-OWI Collection

An additional panorama of Ranger in 1919, where I.M. Howard retired. From left to right building signs read Ranger (main building), Frick-Reid Supply Company, The Continental Supply Co. (Oil and gas wells).

Cattle roundup near Marfa. 1939.
Library of Congress, Prints & Photographs Division, FSA-OWI Collection

Passing the time in Raymondville. 1939.
Library of Congress, Prints & Photographs Division, FSA-OWI Collection

Migrant farm workers living out of their car in Edinburg. 1939.
Library of Congress, Prints & Photographs Division, FSA-OWI Collection

Remnants of the Goose Creek oilfield after a 1919 cyclone.

An abandoned café in Carey. 1937.

Library of Congress, Prints & Photographs Division, FSA-OWI Collection

Sign in front of Brownwood laundromat in 1939. It seems likely Howard may have had his clothes done here while living in Brownwood during his senior year in high school as well as college. West Texas commonly had hard gypsum water.

Library of Congress, Prints & Photographs Division, FSA-OWI Collection

Workers in Brownwood wait to start their shift.
Library of Congress, Prints & Photographs Division, FSA-OWI Collection

Crowd in a circle at the San Angelo Fat Stock Show, 1939.
Library of Congress, Prints & Photographs Division, FSA-OWI Collection

Period sedans in front of the Weatherford courthouse in 1939. Weatherford is less than ten miles southeast of Howard's birthplace of Peaster.
Library of Congress, Prints & Photographs Division, FSA-OWI Collection

Children using a well pump in Wichita Falls, where Howard lived briefly as a child. 1936.
Library of Congress, Prints & Photographs Division, FSA-OWI Collection

Andrews County. Drillers and roughnecks on night tour. Circa 1939.
Library of Congress, Prints & Photographs Division, FSA-OWI Collection

Sizing things up at a horse auction in El Dorado, 1939.
Library of Congress, Prints & Photographs Division, FSA-OWI Collection

Brownwood, 1939:
One man. One chicken.
One knowing grin.

Library of Congress,
 Prints & Photographs
 Division, FSA-OWI
 Collection

West Texas family farm on the very edge of the Dust Bowl. 1937.
Library of Congress, Prints & Photographs Division, FSA-OWI Collection

Storm cellar at West Texas farm. 1937.
Library of Congress, Prints & Photographs Division, FSA-OWI Collection

Moore County. Oil company production camp with smoke from carbon black plant. 1942.
Library of Congress, Prints & Photographs Division, FSA-OWI Collection

A dust cloud approaches the Texas panhandle. Circa 1936
Library of Congress, Prints & Photographs Division, FSA-OWI Collection

Addendum

Discussion regarding *Robert E. Howard, The Supreme Moment: A Biography* in message boards such as the REH Inner Circle, the REH Comics Group, and Conan.com has caught me a bit by surprise, considering that I have not yet approved the final ISBN version of the book for publication and availability at B&N, Amazon, etc. I hope that any board members reading this will accept my apologies for not responding directly in each forum. I have a bit of a disorder when it comes to things like that. For example, recent Howard biographer Mark Finn said in the acknowledgments section of his bio Blood & Thunder "Many people had to endure endless readings, rants, late-night theories, musings, and explosions of frustration and euphoria [...] I sent barrages of email..." Well, I have never been able to feel comfortable doing anything like that, and that is just my personality. I highly respect the excellent work of all the Howard scholars, and to them I offer my deepest thanks for and appreciation of their research, findings and essays. I am simply not social enough to consider sending "barrages of email" or asking people to "endure" anything related to my writing. I detest marketing and will gladly allow anyone to fill in the marketing crap that publishers ask of me. Even my own family doesn't read my writing, as far as I know, and that is just fine. I was thrilled when I read that members of the REH Inner Circle suspected a fellow member with a name similar to mine as having written this book, and if any of you are reading this then let me go so far as to say that I will not deny it was him. Go ahead and direct all attention in this matter to that individual if you wish, and I will be here in my little nest writing like a lugubriously demented hermit. As I said, it is a disorder, and if I have to apologize for it again I just don't think I'll have the self-respect to properly fondle myself anymore. (I realize that some of you are rooting for this outcome.) You had me pegged as a lurker, which sounds a little sinister, but I can live with it.

Please realize that a strong part of me would not charge anything for any of my books, and it is primarily the faces of my wife and daughter which cause me to approve this selling nonsense. So far I've produced over twenty books with pretty much no income to show from it, but when I offered free stories on the old Rocket eBook site before the birth of our daughter, I had over twenty thousand downloads in a few months. Ultimately I find it harder and harder to care about sales; all that matters is that I've done the best I can with writing.

For as brief a bio as I can manage, considering some folks have asked, I went to Harvard when I was 16 as part of my high school's Gifted & Talented program to study one-on-one with Professor Alan Lightman, mostly because a teacher or two had mistaken papers I had done on astrophysics and black holes as a love of that subject and not a love of writing. I edited a newspaper called the Mustang News when I was 17, spent a month in China when I was 18 as part of the People to People student ambassador program founded by Dwight Eisenhower (I was talking with students in Tiananmen Square in the summer of 1988--a year before the protests--and I passed my wallet around to use as a writing surface so that they could give me their names and addresses, and I watched my wallet make the large circuit and return to me, brimming with addresses and missing nothing.) When I got back I killed a man named Michael Ryan who had escaped from a halfway house, gotten drunk and walked in front of my pickup truck at night from the middle of I-93 just after the Assembly Square on-ramp in Somerville. It was the single worst experience of my life and I hope that it is never surpassed. Feeling low, I took an absolutely horrible desk job doing (drum roll) marketing. It sickened me, literally. That was twenty years ago and I haven't answered to a boss since. I started writing full-time and was published in various small pulp magazines that still existed in the early and mid 1990s. I got married in 1998 and moved from eastern Massachusetts to central New York, where I was able to purchase a good home for eleven thousand dollars.

Did I mention that I am an excellent bargain hunter? Well, you're pretty much filled-in now. When I started I used to think that a writer had to list every damn piddly little publication on their resume, and it has been my salvation to realize that stuff like that doesn't matter to me, and I just don't care about that anymore. All I want to do is a good job, and be able to entertain people, and be satisfied with my work.

--Francis DiPietro
May 23, 2008

To those who may have purchased previous editions of this book while it was still being updated on lulu.com: the way lulu works, to the best of my knowledge (unless you simply want to store your file in a folder somewhere like an amorphous blob and not do a front or back cover or book description or get an isbn or anything) is you have to set a price, even if the project is incomplete in your eyes. I'm making only about twelve percent with each printed purchase. The rest goes to lulu, the printer, and the distributor/retail outlet. Absolutely no one has noticed my other stuff at lulu so I didn't try to restrict access to this like it was some A2M pygmy porn manual or plaster a "under construction" line in my description like I was waiting for some crew to come in and tighten my nuts for me. I was just a happy numbskull figuring I could keep updating what I had and then, when ready, approve it for distribution at Amazon, B&N, etc. Anyone who has one of the 22 previous printed editions, for what it is worth, has an item that will not be printed again and may therefore be considered "collectible."

I am pleased to report that, as of June 20, 2008, the aforementioned War of Vituperation between Mark Finn and myself has successfully run its course. As Mark posted at the REH Comics Group, "As of 9:55 PM, Mr. DiPietro and I have exchanged a couple of civil emails that explained our situations more fully and without resorting to the flinging of poo." We, as the two most recent Howard biographers as of this writing, have gained a greater respect for each other. In fact we're thinking of starting a Registry at Macy's, but please no toasters.

But Why Was the Moment Supreme?

Since Mark Finn and I have put away our long-collected arsenal of excrement-flinging implements, the air between our respective biographies has become unseasonably clear. His June 9th review, stemming from my own mistake of making the incomplete draft accessible, had me a hair's breadth away from challenging him to an REH-style boxing match at the next Howard Days, preferably in a setting as close to the old icehouse as possible. To add to the spectacle I was going to suggest that we duct tape our respective bios to our fists in lieu of boxing gloves.

One of the questions which has been floating just below the surface of this matter is why I would elect to put more than just casual emphasis on the circumstances surrounding REH's suicide. Indy Cavalier and other Howard scholars easily saw that there was a deeper connection I was trying to make, and although one of the more interesting facets to the term "The Supreme Moment" is in reference to Howard's short and brilliant *life*, it's perennially difficult to escape the mindset of personal destruction. Even when such concepts as future re-edification are thrown into the mix (i.e. the path being necessary as a bridge to where we are today), the polarity of suicide as a topic is one which rings in the mind with a shrill primal tone of warning. Why pay special attention to something like that?

Perhaps because it is something which has never fully left my own mind. Just as de Camp likely transferred many of his own admitted childhood experiences of being bullied onto his subject of REH because a slight opening was there and de Camp was able to feel that much closer to REH as his biographer, I have inevitably been influenced by many of the darker moments I have had, both as a writer and a biological entity in this world of ours.

What do I mean by that? Well, here's an example I often dwell upon because of how serious I was about doing it: In 1994 I had completed a 500+ page novel which I had focused much time and energy in writing, and although I had been published in many small press pulp magazines, a major book publisher eluded me. Several assistant editors wrote to me saying that they really liked the book but they could not convince enough of the others in the editorial meeting to go for it. It became a pattern of great disappointment, and I contemplated the drastic: I would make the trip to New York City, chain a bulky copy of the manuscript around my neck, and jump off the tallest building whose roof I could access (preferably a publishing house). Then, maybe, as my various corpuscles graced the loosely binded pages of my unpublished book, whatever soul I had could be at peace knowing that I gave the effort everything I had, literally.

It was, I feel, a mindset I may have shared with Howard, in the poor lesser extent of the maundering fleck of an artist that I am. In a recent email to Mark Finn I tried to explain my REH connection (and general outlook) a bit more completely. Here is an excerpt:

"The subject of REH is one that pretty much got me through high school. It was early 1984 when I read *The Last Celt*, and that stuff that Glenn Lord put together which let Howard speak in his own words really connected with so many of the ways I felt about school and society. Of course at this time I had already read the Conan paperbacks (mostly the Ace series but when I could get my hands on the older stuff I did,) and that darkness and brooding which ran like a rich black vein beneath the surface—so much so that you could practically touch it hanging in the air as Conan traveled through the remnants of some long-accursed place—seemed to ring so true with untold majorities of what lurks beneath the skin in the world of the here and now, in our time as well as Howard's. Like witnessing the first moment those seemingly pleasant-from-a-distance REH fans bare their fangs at the new guy, like looking into that innocent stroller to behold Rosemary's Baby, it all has a snarling, vituperative core beneath a veneer of distracting marquetry. Back then I and perhaps you saw that life was that soft and tempting landing pad laid out by the Venus flytrap, and once you let yourself forget that it was bound by its uncaring nature, that's when the jaws closed. A few shots of VO before leaving for first period, paragraphs of REH snatched in study halls and between bells, hanging out with a girl who seemed willing to blow everything with a nub to it but me (did she think we wouldn't be friends afterwards? Man chicks are strange...she would have suddenly become my surrogate REH in terms of allegiance, but I digress) and of course dreaming that there existed some way to click out of this boresome regimented mess, out to that open and free land of which REH himself dreamed but knew he could not have. And of course the ultimate sense of irony in the oft-pondered question, 'What could I really do if Scotty beamed me back to that morning in 1936, and I waited for him under that tree where Patch was buried. Could I have said any possible combination of words to get him to change his mind?' Could any of us have?

"The ultimate proof of the teeth which wait below the conveyor belt which takes us through life is often found within the irony of little moments—small things which still prove to be beyond our control, and thereby highlight with increasingly translucent tones how thin the layer is between us and the teeth of the machine we are placed upon. Being around people gets me depressed. It gets me replaying all those silly little moments which could have been more meaningful, all those perfunctory transactions and ministrations which might have been dispensed with had the participants been privy to some greater Accord."

In terms of classifying a condition, the "supreme moment" constitutes more than just an internal monologue or a random pondering of what truly comprises, contributes to, and emulsifies the development of a personality. It's more than just an enumeration of enthetic factors, such as a given society's effect on the individual whose life path is outside of conventional parameters. Each of us has our own series of "supreme moments" which are played out all along the twisting courses of our lives. They mark the turning points, put bullet points next to our major decisions, bob like buoys in both the deep and shallow ends of our psyches. Sometimes they're plaques of honor and other times badges of shame. But above all, they are highly individualistic. That is their nature. And to those of us who often feel like the pinballs between the paddles of the machine, there is, always locked somewhere, the awareness that the next "supreme moment" may be the last.

I do think there is one scenario which might have gotten REH not to do it. And that is, purely hypothetically, if at some point near the end you could have introduced yourself to Howard and offered him the proposition that, based upon a modern drug you could administer, Hester would have longer to live than even Howard would have rightfully acknowledged (say, at the end he thinks she only has days, and you offer him six months of acceptable life for Hester based on this new medication of which you possess the only doses...and here comes the but) BUT you ask for his solemn word, sworn on the memory of Patch and Klatt and his ancestors and the soul of his mom, etc., that he shoot YOU (and of course you'd make it clear that you don't want to die) before he harm himself, I'm not sure he could destroy the person who gave his mother more time than he had reason to expect. Add the stipulation that he would first have to beat you and kick you, look you long and hard in the eye, hear about your family and children, and then shoot you. Would he dishonor everything and break the deal, go off and shoot himself anyway after the six months was up? Does a reasonable doubt exist here?

A Galveston Affair?

While conducting further research at the Library of Congress, having known REH to travel to Galveston more than once, I asked myself whether it might be possible that, in addition to attending the 1927 Pageant of Pulchritude, he might also have attended the 1928 pageant.

I was hard-pressed to pin down Howard's location during the time of this pageant, June 3-5, 1928. I consulted *Dark Valley Destiny* and *Blood & Thunder*, which both tend to go from early to late 1928 pretty quickly. Howard's 1928 letters as published in volume one of *Selected Letters* skip from May to September, 1928. I next wondered if perhaps the Santa Fe railroad was offering another special at that time from Brownwood to Galveston, for Howard had taken advantage of such a special for his 1927 trip. This I could not determine.

Howard's "Galveston Affair" article appearing in The Galveston Daily News the previous year might have prompted him to attend the 1928 event, with an eye toward possibly writing another while at the very least getting to see the contestants, indulge in some fresh seafood, and possibly take a boat tour around Galveston Bay, as he had done with Vinson the previous year.

Upon examining the archival panoramas of the event at the LOC (again there were two of them, as with the 1927 event, and both of the 1928 photos show the complete crowd along the sea wall without cutting off any heads) sure enough, I saw a man fitting Howard's description, wearing what Howard would wear, and striking the exact same right-over-left folded arm pose. Of course, if Howard's location during June 3-5, 1928 is known to be elsewhere, then I am clearly hoping in vain. However, barring such information, it seems possible Howard could have made the trip without a companion that year, simply to revisit a place he enjoyed and to see the sights. This time we have two uncut photographs of what could be Howard in the background, presented here for those who want to have a look for themselves.

First photo of the 1928 pageant (divided panorama above.) Note the people to the left and right. They change from the first photo to the second, but the potential REH remains stoic. This could lend some substance to the possibility that, if it is indeed Howard, he may have traveled alone.

Courtesy LOC

Located to the left of center in the panorama (divided above), the posture, clothing, arm fold are all there. Different people to his sides this time, which could mean he traveled alone. This would have been on the heels of Herbert Klatt's (and possibly Patch's) death. Perhaps Howard sought a reflective retreat which also included an activity. At any rate, the figure at least bears a strong resemblance to REH.

Courtesy LOC

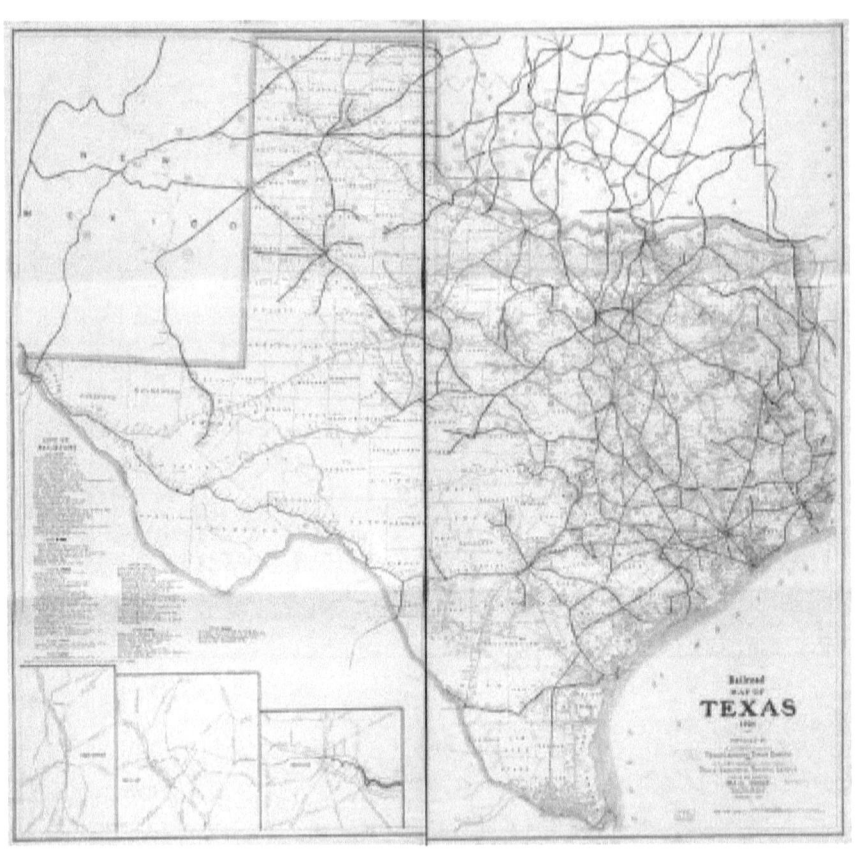

1926 map of the Texas railway system.
Library of Congress, Geography and Map Division

AND NOW...

Nocan Du the Grammarian and the Grabass Wizard of Skelos

a special preview

by Francis DiPietro

His thick muscled shoulders rippled with a thoroughly non-gay suppleness. They spoke of vast reserves of manliness beneath his sun-baked skin. An absolute shock of pitch black hair held remnants of the twigs and leaves of the fields, while his eyes spoke of icebergs and untold power within azure depths. His hulking arms terminated in vast thick fingers which worked at a very small wooden puzzle he had purchased at a Zingaran bazaar. It vexed him.

To think that he, Nocan Du of Cimmonia, the most manly and least gay of all the northern barbarians, could not solve a child's puzzle bought at the market for little more than three pieces of lint and half a fart (in Turth they would have settled for three pieces of lint, but these bedamned Zingarans always wanted a little extra for their wares.) The little metal ball within the wooden box was faced with too many pitfalls, he concluded, to make its way safely through the maze. It reminded him of the time he was in the lair of the dread Grabass Wizard.

He was wearing nothing more than a loincloth and sandals in those days, but on him it was the most heterosexual of attire. Women who saw him in full would suddenly go nude and swoon, but he paid them no more attention than their place in society deserved.

"Come and spend some time with me and my brother!" one called. "Who will not mind if we are wanton? We'll have your sword sharpened!"

"No," corrected Nocan. "It should be, *Come and spend some time with me; and my brother, who will not mind if we are wanton, will have your sword sharpened.*

The woman gave him a perplexed look and stopped soliciting him. And her brother's pout was a sight to behold.

Why did they just assume that every barbarian had a sword? These city folks seemed to think that northern barbarians always had a sword somewhere on their personage, but that was not the case with Nocan. Although proficient in all combat weapons, capable of dealing grim death with either a Claymore or a corn cob holder, a sword was worth money, and whenever he had one he would trade it for food, drink and lodging. Instead he preferred to keep a slender curved dagger, and since he was only wearing a loincloth, he found that his buttocks made the perfect sheath for such a weapon, so that whenever he wanted he could reach behind himself and pull out some death, and often strike before his victim could get over the shock of seeing a dagger come out of a barbarian's ass. Withdrawing it quickly, however, had the tendency to slice his loincloth asunder. So the last thing many of his victims saw was a nude barbarian who had produced a dagger from his fundament. Nocan imagined it was not a calming way to pass from this world.

He had plundered and raped and pillaged aplenty in his teenage years back in Cimmonia, so much so that the whole process became perfunctory. Sometimes he had to be reminded to rape after plundering. At these times, which began to increase exponentially, he would trudge back into the burning cottage and bend the startled housewife over a table. He would stand behind her with his back to the door and he would tell her to moan and scream and shout out names of strange gods, while he did a little reading. Sometimes the woman's privates smelled so awful that the ruse of lifting the skirt over her back would be abandoned. A comrade once remarked to him that he seemed to have a preference for "dry humping." Nocan only nodded and suggested gruffly that if all the men tried it, they might live a little longer. Spurred and intrigued by this notion, news quickly spread of the strange band of northern barbarians who pillaged and then dry humped.

Sometimes Nocan found the genitalia of certain unwashed bucolic females so odiferous and generally displeasing that he took to the habit of carrying bunches of fragrant hillside wildflowers in his pants, and when he was obliged to stage a lusty raping, he would simply smatter the offending area with sweet flowers and stand there for a few minutes reading. Soon word began to spread that one of the northern barbarians was magical and could somehow ejaculate flowers. This claim was bolstered by several local women who scurried into the small towns and villages in outlying areas with petals still clinging to their privates and wondrous tall tales on their lips of the dry humping northman who ejaculated flowers.

Nobles in the cities heard of this and, having nothing better to do, tried it on their slaves and serving wenches. They even organized theme parties where guests were encouraged to dress scantily as barbarians and reenact tales of looting and dry humping. One bored socialite ponce was heard to remark, upon completion of the deed with a fellow popinjay, "Sweetness, the only thing *dry* about this is its creator's sense of humor."

Such was how Nocan established a name for himself even before he mingled with the civilized world. The raiding parties of Cimmonia begged him to stay and be their leader, but they were content to perform the same sort of aimless plundering for the rest of their days. Nocan dreamed of finding more to the world than wattle and daub huts to burn and reeking genitalia to stuff with flowers. He often thought it was the genitalia that should be burned and the little houses that should be filled with flowers, but when he expressed this to a comrade the man acted as if he had been told the most hilarious and impossible of japes.

And was it so wrong for Nocan to dream of a little cottage brimming with daisies that he could call his own?

After that instance in the city, upon refusing the offer from the girl and her brother, Nocan wished to mull things over at a tavern. These subjects of the southern king could certainly drive a country barbarian to drink.

"What you have?" the hairy barkeep inquired.

"What I *have*," replied Nocan, "is my dignity and my innate sense of justice. What I *want*, however, is ale."

He was getting tired of the looks these people gave him simply because he was uncivilized and didn't talk in the manner of the city folk.

"Three coppers apiece or two for five," said the barkeep.

"Two for five," said Nocan and he put down two coppers and laid a beefy arm upon the bar to indicate he would brook no dispute with his expectation of five ales appearing.

The barkeep almost said something...almost. There was a vague warning about the look of this man that made him uneasy, as if he were hiding something deadly. He took a loss on the transaction and paid special attention to how he phrased future conversations with the northern giant.

Nocan found a quiet corner and sat mulling. It was all so common and tawdry, the way people lived and died, and what was left of them after they died. A thin merchant hangs himself from a balsa and later his wife finds unsent love letters to the blacksmith amongst the smallclothes in his office trunk, along with an inexplicably bloody horseshoe. A caravan rider is found murdered in a garderobe and later it is discovered that one of the promiscuous farm girls on the trade route is pregnant, soon ready to pop out a tanned hook-nosed baby ("What did she *think* would happen?" an old crone would gossip. "Did she think it might look like one of us? Ha! Ah ha ha! The little scoundrel is all ready to lead one of our milk cows into the desert! Ooh-hoo ha ha ha! Let's stone her."). All so terribly petty and mortal. The reasons for death so rarely equaled the meaning of death.

Outside they were bickering and bartering and screwing and dying, and none of it was very magical or important. Nocan started his fourth ale with trepidation. The brew of these city folk was cut with something strange, like perhaps the juice of certain local berries with disreputable properties. He had seen women take these berries to help ease the desire to murder their husbands during certain times of the moon, and the priests sometimes gathered them to help ease the protestations of their sacrifices as well as their apprentices.

All the while he was drinking, a keen pair of gray wizened eyes watched him from across the room. Finally, when Nocan was halfway through his fifth ale, he noticed someone was sitting next to him.

"How long have you been here?" asked Nocan.

"Time is relative," said the stranger.

The barbarian nodded. "Indeed it is." He finished the fifth ale with four big gulps, and the stranger eyed him appreciatively.

"Are you in need of lodging?" inquired the stranger, a lean older man with leathery skin and a sharp nose. "My name is Graman. I have a cottage to the west." Skillfully while speaking Graman managed to place one of his hands over one of the barbarian's massive fists.

Nocan frowned distastefully. "I've run into your kind before, Graman. I am not some trollop girl to be taken abed. Curse you I'm not even inclined to see men as attractive!"

Graman put on a moue. "You misunderstand me, my friend. It is obvious you are an adventurer. Tonight by my hearth in privacy I would have told you the tale of the golden caverns of Skelos, which are less then four days journey on foot from here. But since you are clearly so unreceptive to my presence…"

Graman rose, and damn the man if he did not actually keep walking without pause when Nocan tried to test his veracity and intentions by not calling for him to return. Another moment, and Nocan also rose.

Tracking an old man on his way home from a tavern was about as difficult for the northman as tracking the flight of an eagle bearing a salmon across a clear daylight sky. Nocan often wondered how otherworldly those final minutes of airborne life might seem to the salmon. One instant you're swimming with your fellows upstream to spawn and the next you're soaring above the treeline and there's not another fish in sight. Did you take a wrong turn somewhere, and why can't your tailfin steer you anymore?

He had spent longer in the tavern than he surmised, for the sun burned low and the ridges of the distant clouds were tinged with deep hues of vermilion. As usual women who saw him ripped their clothes asunder and swooned, but they were getting harder to see as the moon waited to rise. Nocan was often tracked this way by enemies. After all, one nude woman by the side of the road might be taken for incredible luck, but a whole string of them harkens something auspicious. Nocan had tried smearing himself with offal and detritus in order to prevent the swooning, but it made little difference, as women of the time generally expected men to smell like that.

And when Nocan thought back to how some of those women smelled, he had to concede that any olfactory assault on the peoples of this area would be met with indifference. Perhaps an invading army that actually smelled clean would strike more fear into the hearts of these folk than the foulest of foreign troops. Filthy locals scampering away from soapy smelling soldiers, full of the primal fear of the unknown.

The old thin man wound his way to the west, a mere black shadow in front of the top sinking fifth of the sun, walking slowly and deliberately down the rutted dirt road. If this was the old git's idea of living "close" to town then Nocan had to wonder how skewed the coot's perceptions might be in other departments. Yet still he followed, a shadow which skirted the border of the road, traveling half within the meadows yet always aware of the position of the old man.

He did not seem to tire, and miles stretched into dark evening by the time Nocan saw his shadow slink away from the road and head toward a stand of trees. The moon was a mere distant crescent in the vastness of the deep black sky. And somewhere beyond the heavens the old gods and vanished titans waited in abysmal exile for the end of days.

The Cimmonian's eyesight was considerably better than that of the average civilized man, and Nocan could see a fair deal under such dim conditions. He waited until the old man was inside his small dwelling and had started a fire and lit a candle, then he knocked gently upon the door.

"It's unlocked!" called the cheery voice of Graman.

This Nocan liked little. An old man who lived so far from the city would have great need to lock his door at night. Brigands often prowled the roadways and they were not above slinking into wayside cottages and slitting a throat or two in the hopes of finding a mere few silvers.

"How do you know I'm not a thief?" grumbled Nocan.

"Well," came Graman's voice, "if you're a thief who's polite enough to knock and identify himself before he's even opened the door, perhaps you'd be so kind as to depart? I'm just an old man without anything good to steal, and I won't even be much fun to take advantage of, I'm afraid, due to virulent anal fissures. Once you break the crust you had better pray to Mitra."

Nocan made an awful face at the thought of this, yet he entered.

The room was clean and modest, with a rich wood table at its center, a small, divoted bed on the periphery, and a modest fire in the hearth against the far wall. Iron cooking implements were hung on hooks near the fire, and half a loaf of bread was on the table.

"I pray to Crunk," declared Nocan. "Strong in his tower, he doesn't care about anyone who needs help, but if you are strong and fearless he will laugh at you as you die and drink and pleasure himself in your name."

"I see," said the old man. "Well, let us have a drink of our own to this Crunk of yours." And from underneath the table he produced a large jug that was half wrapped in wicker. "Good port from the trading docks of Zaproska," he announced, and pointed to two tin cups which hung near the fire.

Graman admired Nocan's backside as he fetched the cups, but he was *not* the Grabass Wizard, and would make no such forward attempt on his guest. He had learned that lesson long ago when he absentmindedly stroked the hair of an adventurer who almost hung him for the offense. He selected a tree by the bedside window and had the rope around Graman's neck, but the tale of the Grabass Wizard and the allure of his treasure were enough to buy pardon.

"It was three centuries ago," began the old man, adding, "Please, help yourself to the bread; it's fresh from the market this morning. And drink some more wine, and be comfortable." Seeing Nocan take him up on the offers made Graman smile warmly. He continued, "The Grabass Wizard was known as Obra in those days, and he had recently joined the ranks of the masters in the tower of Hurich. There the best gathered to cast spells, learn forgotten lore, protect the realm against evil magic, for a price, and generally enjoy each other's company."

Nocan nodded gruffly as he tore off a chunk of bread. "Aye, the tower of Hurich was destroyed by a dragon they say."

"Yes," said Graman. "The dragon Jegohu, but that was over a century and a half later. In the time when Obra was in the tower, the influence of the masters was at its apex. In general their conduct was impeccable, and many were the kings who sought favors and audience with them. But the years of reading dusty volumes and crafting spells always for the good made Obra restless. His tension and dissatisfaction with his situation was building, for a master was expected to remain at the tower for life, always on call. And although the spires of Hurich were both beautiful and spacious, Obra felt them grow small and drab as he paced them. He searched for an outlet that would allow him to escape his dull confines and repetitive regiment." Graman leaned forward and whispered, "He began abusing his power."

Nocan grunted. "Much like a town guard captain might go corrupt?"

"I suppose," said Graman after a moment of thought. "But Obra began abusing his power with greater and greater frequency. The masters began finding him in the midst of abusing his power. At first they let him off with warnings about how unseemly it was for a wizard master of Hurich to do something a common vagabond might do by the side of the road, but once Obra began abusing his power, he could not stop. Here was escape, however fleeting, from the drudgery of his day. One old master nearly had a heart attack when he opened a storage closet and found Obra there, crouched in the shadows, furiously abusing his power. Another time the cook noted with disdain that someone had abused their power all over the scallions. Soon Obra began abusing his power throughout the many chambers of the tower. An apprentice found that key pages in the learning volume of Tanech could not be separated due to a flagrant abuse of power. A visiting king was befouled from above as Obra abused his power in the rafters of the main audience chamber. Sometimes he would abuse his power on the handrails of the many winding steps which led to various garderobes, and woe be to sleepy wizards who had to tinkle in the night and did not bring adequate illumination and a studious eye. At first it was thought that there were several who were abusing their power, for the sheer volume of the evidence, but behind every case the trail led only to Obra.

"An expulsion council was convened, and on the very night of his trial Obra snuck into the room of the wizard magistrate and abused his power not only on the man's soft downy bedpillow, but also on his fluffy cat. This latter offense was not discovered until the magistrate went to pet the little creature."

Nocan had stopped chewing, his eyes fixed on the teller of the tale. He switched exclusively to drink and said, "Go on."

Graman smiled. "The expulsion council was prompted to take punitive action, and on this they discussed at length, finally agreeing that the punishment should match the offense."

Nocan was somewhat nonplused. "Did they...*abuse their power* all over Obra and his personal belongings?"

Graman chuckled. "Nothing so temporary," he said. "No, the council ultimately concluded that Obra's, *ahem*, 'power' should be made, for the most part, nonfunctional."

"Crunk," muttered the barbarian. To him it was a fate worse than death.

"Yes," said the old man, "it drove Obra that much madder. Coupled with his expulsion, he was now an outcast, bent on revenge. He took refuge in the cave of which I spoke, and there he plotted. He spoke with things which dwelt in black wells and sacrificed some of the local villagers to an old and nameless god. And within two years of his exile, the magistrate who pronounced his sentence was found dead in his office, his ass grabbed to a bloody pulp. And that was just the start. One by one the wizards of Hurich would find one of their brethren dead in his chambers; always were their faces contorted in the most agonized of death masks, and always were their asses ravished and gnashed and masticated and distended, as if pressed against a blacksmith's anvil and ruthlessly hammered. It was the beginning of the downfall of the wizards of Hurich. Their strength was weakened faster than it could be replenished, and when Jegohu the dragon attacked them much later, what should have been a successful thwarting turned into a ghastly casualty.

"By this time Obra was known as the Grabass Wizard, and he retreated into his cave after being the first to loot the riches of the tower of Hurich directly after its downfall. All the choicest volumes of arcane lore were his, not to mention the priceless artifacts, precious metals, jewels, and trunks of gold payments from kings who had called upon the wizards for assistance. All these things he paid a wandering caravan to carry into the cave for him—yet once they had their gold and were again traveling on the desert sands, one by one they were killed, their asses left defiled and unrecognizable to even the most learned of their colleagues. Several attacks and sieges were tried on the lair of the Grabass Wizard, but all of them failed and all of them died the same horrible way. One man, though… One man, brave and crafty, may have a chance where masses of others have failed. Seek not to find the wizard, who may yet sleep for years, seek only to find his treasure and carry away as much as your arms can bear. In this, if you are lucky, you may succeed."

Nocan thought on this and asked, "In your younger days, why did you not seek to capture some of the wizard's treasure?"

Graman smiled, and slowly stood. He put his back to the barbarian and slowly lowered his pants.

What Nocan saw almost made the wine come back up. Graman's posterior was missing vast and vital pieces, and the bottom of his spine was clearly discernable, like a tail protruding from a sunken hollow.

"I did try, long ago, in my youth," said Graman. "I went there like a fool, with a cheap breastplate and a nicked sword. The Grabass Wizard was awake and he toyed with me to his great amusement, but when he thought I had passed out I managed to make a dash and escape. He was laughing so hard at the way I was running that he bothered not to follow, and called after me, 'I shall let you live, for that will give me more amusement!' And I settled here and nursed my grievous wounds, and eventually settled for the life of a poor farmer. But," said Graman, his eyes intense, "I have never forgotten the location of the cave entrance. It is well hidden, but I can tell you how to find it."

"And in return?" asked Nocan.

Graman shrugged. "Merely a few spare trinkets. A gold cup, a sack of silver, it matters not. Such things will go a long way for me. I daresay they will be more than I need, considering the few years I have left, but they will allow me to indulge in some comforts, and that is all I really want."

It seemed a more than fair offer to the northman. Such a thing was representative, to Nocan, of the disparity in value between things here and things in his homeland. In these markets a string of sparkling trinkets could be had for almost a smile, yet in the frozen wastes of the north such costume jewelry was rare and worth a high price. Hence, although even the oldest of northmen would not settle for such a small cut of treasure to which they alone had access, the priorities of these civilized folk were arranged just so that it was plausible and practically made sense. Yet another great bargain to be found, prompted by a life of which Nocan only partly understood. An old war chief would need as much gold as he could get, just to be safe and hire good bodyguards, but an old farmer on the fringes of the city could live just as comfortably on a mere fraction of such wealth.

"You shall have a healthy fraction of my plunderings," Nocan declared. "Now tell me how to find the way into the cave."

"Oh it's more than just a cave," said the old man. The candle beside him flickered as he said this. "The golden caverns of Skelos are a vast underground network, rumored to be the finding place of the Book of Skelos, an ancient text written in our prehistory which speaks of arcane doom. The book itself is long lost, though some say the bald-headed mountain priests of Khitai guard a copy with their lives and very souls. But the caverns are still golden, caused by a rare phosphorescent sulfur which clings to the walls and permeates the area with a foul stench. Somewhere in the many chambers and antechambers you will find the treasure room of the Grabass wizard."

"And what will I find in others?" asked Nocan.

At this Graman shrugged. "Most would be empty, I suspect, but who can say what lurks in the depths, eh? It has been many years since I ventured there, and what I saw was but a smattering."

Nocan heard the tale of Graman's unsuccessful foray and his near deadly encounter with the wizard. He paid close attention to the details of direction, committing them to memory, as well as how the small cave opening was concealed, which Nocan thought was both clever and sadistic. He listened patiently until the candles burned low, and then he spent the night on a thick wool blanket on Graman's floor. The old man made no further advances.

When morning came Nocan had a breakfast of quail eggs and salted mutton, and he washed it down with water which Graman had painstakingly sweetened with flower nectar. After this he said his thanks, accepted a small leathern pouch with a wrapped flint, a vial of oil and strips of rags for a torch, and some dried apple slices, and went briskly down the road.

"Wait!" called Graman. "You appear to be going on this treacherous voyage unarmed!"

Nocan halted and smiled. He pointed to his buttocks and said, "My weapon is in here."

This puzzled Graman profusely, but he did not delay his guest any longer.

Nor could Nocan have been delayed, for with a firm grasp of the location of the cave entrance in his mind, his long strides carried him quickly down the road to the west, with the unobscured sun at his back. Nocan was as healthy a walker as he was an eater, and when noontime passed and he made his first stop to relieve himself by the side of the road, anyone who might notice what he left would surmise a horse had passed, or perhaps a mule. Occassionaly Nocan's droppings were mistaken as those of an ox or a bear, but that was only after the barbarian was lucky enough to bag a few pheasants or the like for his supper the night before. As it was, considering the modest meal he had at Graman's, what he left behind actually approached the borders of possibly being of human origin.

Nocan always felt a twinge of shame whenever he left behind a less than behemoth dropping. Despite his occasional veneer of civility, the barbarian within him could not rationalize the cause as being anything less than a temporary decline in manpower and vitality. Some Cimmonian children could leave behind a more impressive testament than his latest effort, and that gnawed at him to the point of great vexation. Finally, after walking a mile doing nothing but brooding, Nocan stopped. He turned around and marched right back to where he had relieved himself, squatted yet again, and forced, through a sheer and unreasoning act of will, his face tense and flushed red and his veins and muscles bulging every bit as much as they did when he hefted great boulders, a reasonable addition to his work which safely propelled the body of evidence as a whole into the realm of the elk.

Such was the indomitable spirit of the man.

The first day of Nocan's journey passed with little incident. He stopped walking long after the sun had set, his keen eyes able to navigate by moon and starlight. He camped at the edge of a clearing, pounced on and strangled four rabbits for dinner, and used one of their finer bones to pick his teeth. He slept restfully, but at the slightest untoward sound was able to summon full alertness. Some thought this ability was linked to his wild barbaric heritage, and although such a factor certainly doesn't detract, the real reason Nocan could spring to wakefulness stemmed from an episode in his late teens. He had fallen asleep in the parlor of a brothel, and when he awoke his money was gone and his face was made up in rouge and lipstick and gaudy accents. He had killed three snickering fools before he realized he had not only been robbed but also deeply humiliated. Most perturbing perhaps was the odd thrill he felt when he fully realized his appearance. Ever since then, he got better and better at waking quickly. But on this night there was no threat.

Once he had dreamed that he was a prostitute. In the dream he guaranteed to beat any competitor's price. And for those who paid to keep him for the whole night he offered to make their beds and wash their sheets in the morning. The dream left his soul raging, and it was one of the only times he consulted a cleric, who seemed more interested in getting unexpurgated details about the dream than offering any practical help. At one point Nocan imaged that he was panting, plus the wide brimming robes of such clerics allowed easy and surreptitious access to themselves.

One day he would emerge from the briar thickets of obscurity and stride the marble steps of a capital covered in gore and holding a crown which still had the former owner's scalp attached.

Through the Limrik Hills and over the Vale of Thwaite he walked, his loins as bronzed as his back due to the penetrating rays of the sun and his flimsy though entirely ungay loincloth. So ungay was his loincloth that Nocan could actually become tumescent at the thought of it. He, the most macho and least gay of all the men in the kingdom, striding along in garb not unlike a diaper, with a keen wedge of steel planted in his buttocks like some dangerous and yet to bloom bulb. No other man could pull-off such a look without being considered irretrievably queer. In all the fabled fourteen hells of Zametto, surely not one soul twinkled who would dare challenge the grim northman.

He had fought in the stone pits of distant ports, and he had crushed startled heads between his powerful thighs. Sometimes they would utter a last muffled phrase into the pit of his crotch. Sometimes they would try to bite, but even Nocan's private skin was as thick and tough as a hammer. After a fight it was not uncommon for him to find a brittle tooth dangling from his jewel basket. These he would place in a small wooden box which he would bury ritualistically beside the decedent's grave. Nocan did not want to encounter any zombies who wished to retrieve their bicuspids. Magic to him was something which diminished his brute strength, and therefore he disliked it. A wizard could fight without wielding a sword, and in Nocan's eyes that made him less of a warrior and more of some kind of enchanted animal.

Nocan had foreknowledge that the secret entrance to the caves would be devious and abominable in nature, but this was enough to unsettle even the great warrior's nerves.

Disguised as a way station for travelers, the niche along the winding path up the cliffs was barely large enough for a small camp. It had bramble and boulders partially obscuring it, so if one were on horseback traveling at anything faster than an easy trot, it would likely be missed.

As it was the camp had not been used for some time. No tracks were discernable, and whatever remnants of a cookfire there may have been were poorly represented by a partial ring of stones. Perhaps it had been years since someone camped here.

Yet somehow, as if by supernatural agency, the lingering odor of a chamber pot came clearly to Nocan's nose. He soon discovered the source was a small crack in the rock face of the mountain, at just the right height and shape to suit the need for relief in travelers. For untold centuries that convenient gap had been the receptacle for the waste of Nocan's ancestors.

It was also the devious entrance which Graman had described.

For long minutes Nocan's mind presented the argument that it was beneath his stature and self respect to defile himself by attempting to enter such an orifice. But the lure of treasure ran strong in his veins.

Times like this he wished he wore more to cover his skin than a bedammned loincloth. Just stretching an exploratory arm into the hole yielded him with satanic sludge. He wished he had never touched it, for it was like a kind of living wet clay. He wondered what arcane spell could be keeping it so awfully moist and sickeningly spongy? Had the dread Grabass Wizard trained the animals in this area to use the hole as humans would?

He did not wish to envision the gross and unnatural scene of an antelope, spellbound, squatting on the hole to do its beastly business.

If his health had been foul, that unspeakably filthy entrance alone might have killed him. But Nocan possessed the heart of a musk ox, the grit of a battling bear, the stamina of a mating lion, and the will of a hungry ape.

Even so, it was close.

Cover all those animals with the excreta of eons and they become far less vicious and far more viscous. Nocan knew it took a special kind of breed to still be cantankerous and focused whilst plastered with offal. Just look at the way babies were born, covered in slop and wanting to do nothing but cry.

At that moment Nocan had great empathy for babies.

In many ways going through that hole was like being born, except in reverse. As he squirmed and struggled through that blackened muck, Nocan could not help but feel as though he were wedging himself up the fundament of the mountain. He, a muscular worm trying to invade a vile organic cavity.

The few items which Graman had given him had been the first things down into the depths. He had to let them lead otherwise he would be tempted to spend the rest of the day looking for another, cleaner, nonexistent way in. Now he followed, like a ship struggling against the sea to retrieve a small buoy in the middle of the night.

Scum and ooze engulfed him and he could not see; dared not open his eyes lest the foul mixture blind him. The smell of it was akin to a great many corpses, were it customary to bury corpses in dung heaps. He wished he had thought of finding something to use as a pomander—flowers to tie around his face or even some pieces of fruit wedged up his nostrils. He would have gladly sniffed the backsides of a dozen unwashed nomads than suffer that muck a moment longer.

Suddenly he became worried that the slop was too deep; would go on forever before he had a chance to escape. Which way was up? He grabbed for the rock walls but the gap had widened and he could feel only spongy atrocities. He wanted to scream but when he imagined what would enter his mouth the urge quickly passed.

Finally he felt a slimy bottom which had a curve to it like a giant hook. There on the sticky bottom he felt for and retrieved the few implements he had earlier dropped inside. He followed that wide curve upward, using his legs to give him a push off the bottom and slowly ascending the face of a slick wall. He had traversed a large half oval pattern in the rock which kept the muck in place like a drain trap, and now, for what seemed like the first time in a year, his head broke the surface and air could once again be his.

Anyone observing what emerged from that well of excrement would not say it was a man, but rather some mythical monster which some cultures might believe was the progenitor of all diseases. Nocan dearly wished to vomit but he knew that once he started he may not be able to stop, so with a titanic effort he held back the bile which boiled within him. How could any wizard be as awful as what he just endured?

He shook off what he could and carefully unwrapped the small pack from Graman. He soaked the strips of cloth with the oil from the small vial his benefactor had provided. Within minutes he had adequate light.

He was in a small chamber with only one exit. The walls were rough and unadorned, the ceiling maybe ten feet high. Faintly he could see the touches of golden phosphor of which Graman had alluded.

Oddly enough, the prolonged contact with waste matter had given Nocan the urge to relieve himself, and he certainly was in the appropriate place for it. Plus those two otters he had eaten the night before were ready to try to swim again.

Just then a young boy who was passing by the opening stopped and stared at the giant who had his back to the portal and was squatting beside the pit. To him it appeared as if Nocan were some mythical Atlas-type figure who had always been in that chamber, constantly defecating since time immemorial.

"What purpose does this serve?" the boy asked.

Nocan, startled that he had not heard the approach, wheeled around to face the speaker. His hands were ready to strangle.

"What?"

The boy asked, "Were you given some penance long ago? Did you lose a wager with some devil?"

Nocan was just about to grab the whelp when, just as suddenly as he had appeared, the boy vanished.

"A damned ghost!" said Nocan, his neck hairs wanting to

prickle but being unable to due to matted sludge. "What manner of foul deviltry do these cursed catacombs hold?"

As if in response a haughty laugh shot to his ears from some distant chamber. It was closely followed by a raucous bit of what seemed to be otherworldly flatulence.

Between the muck in the present cavern and the noise his ears just witnessed, Nocan's primitive brain was able to dimly grasp the thread of a scatological theme to this accursed lair. And it took considerable concentration considering his present condition to remind himself he had not morphed into some large and belligerent dropping himself.

In his mind Nocan knew he had to keep a crude chart of the interior of the caverns. The small entry point was but one chamber, and using a torch supplied by Graman, he left the small chamber and walked into a branching hall. He chose the path to the left, which made a slight curve and opened into a wide pool whose opposite shore was smothered in darkness. Lifting the torch, he noted the roof over the water was an intricate tapestry of stalactites. A music of dripping, slow, unchanged for centuries, filled his ears as water from above crept down the cones of the stalactites and plunked into the mineral-rich pool. The visible portion of this cavern was easily four times as large as the entry room, and how far beyond the range of his torch that water stretched Nocan did not care to guess.

He retraced his steps past the small entry cavern and took what would have been his right-hand path. The corridor was narrower here, and longer. Nocan began to feel that another large chamber might be behind the rock walls to his left, but with no apparent way to access it, he followed the narrow hall.

It opened into a rectangular cavern whose ceiling was very high. There seemed to be an alabaster statue at the far end of the room.

"I am the guardian," said the statue. It resembled a eunuch from times of old, and the curved tulwar at its hip was most certainly not made of alabaster. "You shall not gain entrance to the chamber behind me."

"Tell me," said Nocan, "what is it that you guard?"

"I guard the treasure room," said the eunuch. "Forever shall it remain guarded."

Nocan considered this an open invitation, and he was slowly reaching for the curved blade he kept.

"Go ahead," said the eunuch. "That weapon you chose to keep in your rectum will not harm my skin." As if to demonstrate the guardian slashed at his own arm with his tulwar. It left only the ghost of a scratch. Then he tossed a rock up and struck it in midair with the tulwar, which split the rock in three. "Many have tried to get past me," said the eunuch. "I suggest you save yourself."

Although Nocan did not fully realize his plan at the time, he knew he could not turn around when faced with a cavern full of treasure and only one guardian, no matter how strong or enchanted.

"You look terribly slow," said Nocan. "You must weigh more than the wives of five olive merchants put together."

"I am fast as a gazelle," the guardian declared.

Nocan snorted. "You probably haven't had a bowel movement in centuries. I doubt you could outrun a gazelle giving labor."

And with that the guardian sprang upon him.

So fast was the former statue that it sent a strong tinge of distress up Nocan's spine. Had his loose words finally cost him the ultimate price? It was all he could do to dodge the incredibly speedy attacks, and Nocan was the fastest of all non-gay men.

He found that the guardian pressed the attack, backing him to the entrance of the chamber, and then beyond into the corridor.

"Another fool!" said the guardian. "No one heeds the warning! Why do I even bother!"

Nocan ran, and the mighty eunuch was bare footsteps behind him, the echoing thuds of his weighty steps filling Nocan's ears like the beatings of a frantic, fraudulent heart. Straight past the small entry chamber he ran. Quickly Nocan thought of trying an unexplored hall, but then he worried that it would put him at even more of a disadvantage. No, Nocan did not need any further disadvantages at this point. He led the guardian straight to the pool chamber and dropped his torch at the shore.

The water was frigid upon his skin, but Nocan waded deep. The floor was slimy and dropped at a precipitous angle. But this did not stop the guardian.

Into the water the two figures trudged. With water up to his waist, the eunuch's movements seemed ever so slightly slower. With water up to his chest that suspicion was confirmed.

"Is this where you wish to die?" inquired the guardian. He raised his tulwar. "It will be a bloodbath...ha!"

Thinking quickly, Nocan dove under the water. He advanced on the guardian with speed and stealth, closing the short distance between them in a sparrow's heartbeat, and latched onto those mighty legs and tugged with all his might.

Initially, the guardian did not budge.

"Hey!" he bellowed. "What are you doing down there?" When Nocan did not answer but continued to struggle with the guardian's legs the guardian cried, "You shall not appease me thusly! Give-up your awkward attempt at placation and stand so that I may carve your head!"

And with air running shorter and his efforts seemingly in vain, Nocan was delighted beyond words to find the tip of a large buried boulder on the bed of the water. Using this to give him leverage, he pulled upon the guardian's legs with much greater strength. One heave and the guardian was wobbly. Another and he had fallen under the water.

Nocan raced to the shore. He used several rocks to hit stalactites on the roof of the chamber which hung above the water, and he sent scores of them crashing downward into the depths like mighty ancient spears. The water became a rippling dark mass as, suddenly, a great cluster of the stalactites fell at once, directly over the spot the guardian had fallen. Nocan's curiosity compelled him to wait several moments at the water's edge, and he was rewarded with the slow calming of the surface, devoid of further stirrings.

Back along the cavern's paths he went, to the edge of the rectangular room of the guardian. In the spot behind where the ancient eunuch had stood, there was a portal. A sturdy oaken door with iron reinforcements was fitted to an opening in the rock. Nocan tried the handle but rust had weakened it and it broke away, leaving a gash along the barbarian's palm. Nocan swore lustily at the door and kicked it, and one of the iron horizontal braces fell to the floor with a clack.

One by one Nocan stripped away the door's metal, until only the oaken planks and their nails stood in his way. Then with a mighty charge he crashed through the door.

He found himself in no treasure room. The place reeked of sulfur, and with the light from his flagging torch soon revealed itself to be a sulfur repository. The foul substance was hoarded here as if it might someday replace the country's monetary system. And from somewhere deep within the particles of the distant stuffy air he seemed to hear the laugh of the eunuch guardian.

"I hope I am able to laugh as deeply," Nocan shouted, "if I ever lose my manhood and am forced to guard a roomful of fart dust for a thousand years!"

That seemed to silence the spook laughter.

Had his prize of treasure been transformed into sulfur because he had fought the guardian less than fairly? He had to think no, for the caverns were vast and this apparent early victory was surely just a grand diversion which had sent many seekers before him to their deaths.

Returning to the rectangular cavern, Nocan found an exitway along what he figured was its western wall. He took this new path carefully, with a guttering torch and a keen awareness that traps might abound.

A short distance further and a corridor opened to his left. Nocan almost took it, but he reasoned that if he allowed himself to be diverted by every passage, he would soon be exploring in the dark, not much further from where he had started.

He continued down the passage, and another, wider corridor opened to his left. A spider had built its web in a vast nook in the cave wall here, where once an idol may have been placed…an idol or a torch.

Nocan burned the webbing with his torch and allowed the spider to escape. He peered inside the nook and, to his great fortune, he found an ancient torch and a small, well-sealed jar of oil. There was a label on the jar which made him think it may once have served as some ancient queen's sexual lubricant.

If any cloth had once covered or been supplied with the old torch, it had long since disintegrated, but upon further inspection of the torch Nocan found that it was of clever design, with a top that unscrewed so that the oil could be poured within. All that was needed was a wick. Nocan used a small fragment of cloth which had not yet burned through at the base of his torch. His new light was not as bright, but it would be long lasting.

Now he, Nocan Du, the most macho and least gay of all men, chose to take the wide corridor path which diverged to the left. It seemed to be the way the spider ran.

The air was mustier here and ancient carvings were upon the walls. Some depicted what appeared to be a muskox eating supper upon a table. Others showed a stately queen of old, except she had the head of a frog. But still, she wasn't so bad. Nocan had seen uglier barmaids. And one time he had been drugged by a fat ugly barmaid who was in the process of removing her bodice when he awakened and jumped out her window like a startled Vendhyan bat. Compared to that, the frog queen was a real catch, and Nocan imagined her domicile to be quite free of annoying flies, although most likely a trifle damp.

He continued down the wide corridor, passing more strange etchings of symbols and moon phases, and found himself facing a cobweb-encrusted open portal which led into blackness. Again he burnt away webbing, watching as several startled spiders fled.

Entering the dark chamber, Nocan felt a softness beneath his feet. His new torch could not penetrate the depths or heights of the chamber, but from what it revealed below and around him, Nocan was taken aback. Everywhere and in thick profusion, intricate rugs were scattered, as if some over-friendly host were trying to make welcome a gaggle of diplomats. Around him were rugs of all colors and sizes, in shapes triangular, ovoid, circular, octagonal, and rectangular. They were musty, to be sure, and it smelled as if some were rotted. But they were devoid of the kind of sedimentary layer one would expect old unmoved objects to have gathered.

Nocan muttered, "First a roomful of shit and now a roomful of tapestries. Truly I do not understand this southern culture."

He advanced, and the room did not reveal its far wall. Briefly he wondered if taking any of the rugs back with him as plunder would be a worthwhile proposition, but he did not look forward to carrying hunks of cloth for the remainder of his adventure, plus getting them back through the way he entered would most likely have a deleterious effect upon their value. Nocan imagined that a crown, no matter how fancy, would ultimately be sold for less than face value if it seemed to bear remnants of the feces of ten generations.

Picking up one just to test its weight and quality, Nocan's primitive brain was given an earnest shock when the smaller-sized rug began to scream.

"Help me, oh help me my kin!" the rug screeched.

Nocan dropped the haunted rug immediately, and it fell with a whump and commenced sobbing. The barbarian couldn't help himself, and he gave it a kick.

"You are a blasted rug!" Nocan declared. "Stop acting thusly!"

"It kicks me! It *kicks* me!" the rug wailed.

Concluding that the fabric was both possessed and insane, Nocan chuckled and said, "I could do far worse than kick you. Now tell me where is the wizard's treasure?"

"Oh! Oh!" wailed the rug. "It interrogates me! It *threatens*!"

Nocan scoffed, tired of the foolishness. He carefully withdrew the curved blade he kept between his buttocks and laid its sharp side against the rug.

"You will tell me," said Nocan, "or you will be reduced to threads!"

"A knife!" yelled the rug, and with that, a deep rumbling came.

At first Nocan thought the very earth might be quaking, but he soon realized with even greater alarm that it was the rugs. Hundreds if not thousands of them were stirring to life, prompted by the screeching of their comrade. It made the few hairs which were not encrusted with offal on the back of Nocan's neck prickle. The rugs were rising up from the floor like dragons awakening.

Nocan backed his way to the entry but several large rugs darted past him and blocked his exit, piling one on top the other and stiffening over the portal. He gave them a few slashes with his blade but more of their comrades joined and the exit became a thick blockade. Then he felt a large rug smash into his shoulder blades and nearly knock him over.

His primal instincts taking over, Nocan snarled and slashed at the flying carpets. His blade inflicted what would have been grievous and mortal wounds upon human enemies, but the rugs could withstand long slashes with little adverse impact.

"Split us in two and you will have twice as many enemies!" one of them yelled.

The rugs continued to beat upon Nocan, making him stagger back and forth like a drunkard. He was furious that his beloved blade was working so poorly against this foe, and that is when he remembered that his new torch contained a reserve of oil.

As the rugs made their passes at him, Nocan partially unscrewed the lid of his torch. As they passed, he made a blessing motion with the torch which allowed small quantities of its oil to splatter through the air and gently douse the attacking carpets. He made his way back to the blocked portal and gave a healthier dousing to the rugs which barred his path. Then he secured his torch's top once again, hoping enough oil was left to complete his quest, and with a quick prayer to his god Crunk, he touched the flame to the blocking rugs.

A bluish haze spread over the carpets which blocked the exit and almost instantly they began to scream. Their comrades came to their aid with attempts to help stifle the flames, but luckily most of the responding comrades were also partially flecked with oil, and they also caught afire.

"The brute burns us!" one of the octagonals yelled.

"Rugs should remain underfoot!" chastised Nocan.

It took a short time for the blaze to catch among other rugs, and soon the chamber began to be filled with flying streaks of fire and smoke. It gave Nocan the opportunity to see the far walls, and the impressive height to the room. The absence of dust he had earlier observed upon the rugs was now clearly attributable to their propensity for flight, and this room would have been a good hangar of sorts for them. Individually and in good condition, each would have fetched a small fortune in exotic bazaars, but the small amount of intelligence which flying carpets possessed had eroded just as surely as their fringes. Without the company of masters of greater intellect, and with only the spiders to observe (and occasionally perhaps even transport on a whim), the rugs had rendered their effective service to man useless. Nocan almost felt sorry for them.

With the blockers of his freedom sufficiently engulfed, Nocan again drew his blade and this time was able to easily hack through their weakened forms. Once outside the chamber he turned to look back, and his eyes were met with the sight of mostly burnt rugs falling to the ground like dead soldiers, no more to be animated. The roar of the flames filled the chamber and the rugs flew crazily, bumping into one another and spreading the blaze completely. All of them were soon destined to fall to the floor in a smoky ruin, with the last of their craftsmen long dead and the secrets of their manufacture lost..

In days of old, perhaps the rugs had transported the frog queen and her armies to a great victory of the muskox people. Nocan could only wonder.

An inspection revealed that well more than half his oil had been depleted, and he could not surmise how far into the cave system he had traversed. He was thankful that the dread Grabass wizard had not yet made an appearance. Perhaps the wizard was now defunct, and his caverns a mere series of traps without a master. Perhaps Nocan would find an old set of bones dressed in a raggedy ermine cloak and conical hat somewhere deeper within the cave system. Would the wizard still hold some power, even in death?

Nocan reasoned that any wizard would be far less impressive once a rat had made off with their femur.

"Besides," Nocan uttered to the rough walls, "I cannot die in here. It would greatly displease my biographers." He imagined some line-faced scrivener putting down his quill when he learned that his hero had died in a cave of shit and flying rugs.

He followed a rounding path where the sediment was heavy upon the floor. Still in his mind was the spectacle of the burning carpets. He had not seen such a quantity of burning rugs since an invading Nymodium army had set afire the Guntleund Mens Club.

Upon turning a wide sweeping corridor Nocan came upon a causeway of sorts which branched in two directions, roughly southwest and southeast. His mind approximately knew the southeastern route would be headed back toward the murky pool where he had foiled the guardian. The southwestern way led off into wide and somber blackness.

The modest light from his torch barely reached outward to the far-spaced gold-colored walls on his left and right. As he walked, he could not help but get the impression that those side walls were growing dimmer and becoming further away. After another minute of looking ahead, Nocan was not entirely surprised to note that the side walls were now lost within the murk.

He felt something brush upon his face. It was merely a spider web. He took a few steps then he felt another. He ignored it.

The webs became thicker, and Nocan beheld a great interconnecting concourse of webs, which seemed to span the distance between the walls. And behind these webs were webs even denser and more impressive. Already their gummy strands were irking him.

"However long it took you blasted creatures to make this," Nocan uttered, "I am willing to wager my blade that you did not make it fireproof." And with that he brought forward his torch, but before the flame could kiss the interlocking gray strands, a great quantity of spiders came into view.

"You things again," said the barbarian. "In Cimmonia we have few spiders, and none that can withstand the open weather. You should all be grateful that I spared your comrade back there. I think that should at least buy me passage—"

Suddenly he noticed that the spiders were also amassed on the cave ceiling several feet above him. He took a step backward, but already they had begun to drop by the hundreds.

Faced with such startling numbers, Nocan turned and ran. It was all he could do not to scream like a castrated Jeballian sheep. And when he soon realized that dozens of the creatures had actually managed to land upon his personage, that final measure of restraint and dignity was reflexively abandoned.

Nocan screamed high, womanly screams as he ran northward along a blackened corridor he had not yet traversed. He must have missed it when his torch could not reach the far walls upon his approach. At any rate, it somehow felt more comforting to be running in a northerly direction, and his speed was forcing many of the spiders off...perhaps even his screaming was helping in that regard.

By the time he reached an immense triangular chamber, all of the spiders were gone save for a few, which Nocan disdainfully executed. "You blasted creatures have made yourselves a powerful enemy," he said to their crushed forms.

And he heard a boy's giggle.

What sort of room was he in? Its vastness made it hard to be sure. But the giggle. That was familiar. It sounded like the same blasted spook boy who questioned him in the offal room.

Nocan advanced cautiously into this, the largest chamber he had yet seen. From the point of his entry at one tip of the triangular cavern, the walls fled away at ever widening angles. And lined within the heart of these vast spaces Nocan soon observed rows of stone-carved figures. The statues were lined in ranks almost military, save for the variance in the dress and appearance of the statues themselves. Rather than having rows of guardian soldiers like Nocan heard existed in tombs far to the east, these sculptures were of mere villagers, it seemed to the northman's eye. The expressions on some of their frozen faces appeared to be downright apprehensive.

The Caves of Skelos were quite bedamned, Nocan thusly concluded.

"It's you again," said a small boy. "You've made it far."

Nocan wheeled and drew his blade so swiftly that it tore a gash in his loincloth, which presently dropped to the cave floor with a soft muffle. Nocan ignored his nudity and glared at the lad. "Who are you? How do you know me, or was your grammar merely a trick to relax me? Well, as you can see, I am not relaxed. At least not above the waist."

"I saw you at the entrance earlier," said the boy. "You went to the trouble of defeating the guardian, yet it seems you did not come here seeking sulfur."

There was a hint of insubordination in the lad's tone which ill pleased the grim northman. "Look here, whelp," said Nocan, "I don't know whether to ask you for information or just grind you between my buttocks like summer wheat!"

Instead of fearing the threat, as so many other children did, the boy actually chuckled. "I doubt even *your* buttocks could grind stone." And presently he turned into one of the statues—just for a moment—and turned back again. "You see, I am one of those trapped here by the wizard."

"Crunk!" swore Nocan. His buttocks would have difficulty even breaking off a finger, and presently he redonned his loincloth, never quite loosening his grip on the knife (it took him years to learn how to swiftly dress while holding a knife; he had seen other men castrate themselves while attempting the maneuver—it was the pulling up of the pants which was most treacherous.) "Can all of those blasted statues run around and startle each other?"

"Just me," said the boy. "I wish it were otherwise, but for some reason the wizard made me the lone animate. I cannot venture beyond the walls of these caves… Say, I used to play games with the guardian of the sulfur pit. You didn't destroy him, did you? He was the only one to talk to around here, save for the spiders."

Nocan shrugged. "He may be salvageable, if you can hold your breath. But about those spiders…you say you talk to them?"

"Yes. We have an agreement that they will not spin their webs around my fellow immobilized townsfolk. In return I leave the southwest corridor undisturbed for their use."

"And do you ever see the wizard?"

"Not so much, as of late, and sometimes not for long spells. He never talks to me, preferring to treat me as if I were like the other statues. But once he did look at me and say something."

"What was that?"

"Well," said the boy, "he came into this chamber panting one night. He had an odd look in his eye, as one who is greatly vexed. He looked straight at me and declared, 'It won't fit yet.' Then he stalked away. For months I feared that strange and arresting comment was connected to an act the wizard wished to torment me with, and I prayed for stunted growth, but slowly I came to the conclusion that the wizard had been vexed by some other perversion."

"Truly is my brain shocked and flummoxed," quoth Nocan. But the desire for treasure ran strong within his wild panther heart. "Is that a secret wall I see up there?"

The boy shrugged. "It's not much of a secret. But it is a wall."

Nocan looked around the rest of the chamber. "How the bloody hell am I supposed to come upon this wizard's bedamned treasure?"

"Stop!" yelled the boy. Unknowingly Nocan had begun to stroll down the center aisle of the room. "Just a few steps ahead of you lays a trap door. It leads to what the wizard calls the Cistern of Unmitigated Nonsense, from whose depths no soul returns in its rightful place."

"Crunk," softly swore the northman. "What am I to do now? I suppose I should give-up. It was a foolhardy dream to expect to find treasure easily."

The boy frowned. "But you came so far. More than half way."

"Is that all?" replied Nocan, in one of his gloomy moods. "I haven't had a decent thing to eat since I've been in this rathole. I wonder how much gold will be worth to me tomorrow compared to a big haunch of roasted mutton."

"But, sir, 'tis unmanly to just give-up!"

Nocan Du wheeled and his eyes flashed murder. "If it would be more manly to you I could find a hammer and start lopping the limbs off your stone kinsmen here."

The boy was taken aback for a moment, then asked, "Why would it be more manly to mutilate people who have been turned to stone?"

Nocan's lips pressed tight together. His cheeks trembled slightly. A single tear rolled down his muscular cheek. "Damn it! Damn it all to the fabled fourteen hells of Zametto!" He sat down with a heavy thud and a click (due to the knife in his buttocks) and buried his face in his hands. "If I don't eat a rat sandwich soon I fear that I shall go mad."

"I'm afraid that camel may have already left the tent," said the boy, "but for what it is worth, I know that behind the lair of the spiders is a compression wall. Press inward and it will yield. Beyond is an antechamber which holds the talisman you will need to get through this room and into the den of the wizard. If he is sleeping, his treasure may be yours."

Nocan's eyebrow raised thoughtfully but then he waved his hand at the boy. "I have no desire to negotiate with those blasted things again. I thank Mitra they didn't creep into my loincloth en masse. If I give them another chance they might discover a new home complete with carpeting. No. I do not wish to have my member mummified by their foul spinnings, to be slowly dined upon as if it were some helpless pupa."

Nocan had a friend who died that way. He fell asleep in the night and the spiders came and spun webs around his man parts.

They did not feed upon him, but he was so alarmed by the sight that when he awoke, groggy from a night of debauchery, his first thought was to remove the blasted thing. Thirty minutes after reaching for his sword he bled to death. So ashamed were his comrades that they did not say he died of spiders, but claimed he was the victim of a jagged-toothed hiccupping whore.

"I may be willing to help with the spiders," said the boy.

Nocan looked at him with new regard. "If you could ask those blasted things to take a walk to the opposite side of the cave I would gladly give you a share of the treasure."

The boy remained pensive. "I have little use for treasure," he said. "More important to me would be getting the wizard to break the spell which holds my kinsmen thusly."

Nocan frowned. "How in blazes am I supposed to do that? Just wake up the wizard and ask nicely, I suppose?"

"No," said the boy. "He used a large ruby amulet to cast this enchantment upon us. I think if you were to break that amulet, we might be freed."

"You want me to smash a giant ruby in the hopes your idea works?"

The lad shrugged. "You could always leave, or, of course, contend with the spiders on your own. It was quite a womanly scream they extracted from you. I could hear you coming from halfway down the hall. Perhaps you shall reach an even higher pitch with your nest—eh, next encounter."

Nocan did not wish to envision such a thing. Better to smash a priceless ruby than to have insects burrowing into your orifices.

"You have your deal," said the barbarian. "I shall wait here for your signal. But I warn you, if those blasted things don't budge, or if they take a detour through this room, I shall start toppling your friends and neighbors here with great indiscrimination." He put a meaty finger on a peasant woman's shoulder to indicate his seriousness.

The boy nodded sharply, and was gone.

Nocan sat and pondered. He liked doing that, and had practiced at striking a very thoughtful pose. Sometimes when he did this passers by would be impressed that a man with so many muscles could actually think. In truth, Nocan thought of little when he struck such positions. It was more a kind of meditation to him. He thought of a blank wall, then a side of beef, then, for some reason, a kitty.

The boy returned just as Nocan was running out of subjects to ponder.

"All gone," said the boy.

Nocan rose and adjusted his loincloth. "I'm not going to ask how you did it." But he really wanted to know.

The boy shrugged. "You'd be surprised how reasonable they are, once you know how to talk with them."

"I don't even know how to talk with my mother, much less spiders," volunteered the barbarian. "All she does when she sees me is yell and cook. Then she yells at me while I'm eating." He reflected that not once had he cared to actually *listen* to what she was yelling about. It could have been anything.

Thanking the boy, Nocan cautiously returned to that dreaded widening hallway...

West Texas dustbowl farmers gather at the local drug store to shoot the breeze. 1937.

LOC, Prints & Photographs Division, FSA-OWI Collection

"Thotful" sign near a San Juan funeral home. 1939.
Library of Congress, Prints & Photographs Division, FSA-OWI Collection

www.ingramcontent.com/pod-product-compliance
Lightning Source LLC
Chambersburg PA
CBHW022052160426
43198CB00008B/209